BASINGSTOKE
WORKHOUSE

AND POOR LAW UNION

To Tracey!
Best wishes,
Barbara A. Large
22/10/16

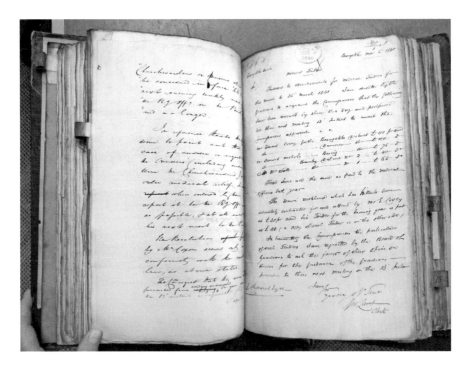

Folio image, MH 12, March 1840

BASINGSTOKE
WORKHOUSE

AND POOR LAW UNION

BARBARA A. LARGE

The
History
Press

In memory of Barbara Applin
1936–2015

First published 2016

The History Press
The Mill, Brimscombe Port
Stroud, Gloucestershire, GL5 2QG
www.thehistorypress.co.uk

British Library Cataloguing in Publication Data.
A catalogue record for this book is available from the British Library.

ISBN 978 0 7509 6240 7

Typesetting and origination by The History Press
Printed and bound by CPI Group (UK) Ltd

Contents

Foreword and Acknowledgements

The seeds of this book lie in the Victoria County History project for Hampshire, currently based in Basingstoke; its object is to rewrite and modernise the early twentieth-century county-based 'Red Books' beloved of all local historians. Members choose their personal subjects of passion in the history of the area, and are guided through rigorous and painstaking research by Dr Jean Morrin, formerly of Winchester University, with a huge amount of patience and help. And a great deal of fun is had by all, too! Thank you, Jean. I would recommend a visit to the VCH website and its associated *Explore* site: www.victoriacountyhistory.ac.uk.

The history of the poor and anonymous has always been an interest, and I found that no serious research had been done on the subject of this book. It was such an interesting tale, so relevant to the locality, that it asked to become a book.

The landscape of writing on the New Poor Law and the workhouse system in England is a truly vast one, and no attempt has been made here to produce a comprehensive history; the aim of this book is rather to deal with what happened in Basingstoke in the context of national implementation.

Most of the easily accessible documents found in many workhouse records are missing in Basingstoke. Those that remain tell a fascinating story, the details hidden away in unindexed folios where it is impossible to find anything unless the date is known. The only way to discover was to plough methodically through dozens of huge tomes, the Minute Books of the Board of Guardians in Hampshire Archives and Local Studies in Winchester, and the correspondence archives in The National Archives, Kew. About sixty volumes altogether and probably several yards of papers! Using the old-fashioned, conventional method of pad and pencil, this would have literally taken a lifetime, which is why nobody has ever done it. But we are in the twenty-first century, and my methods are technological: photograph the relevant pages and do the research at home. Following the 1914 restrictions on records I resorted to the reports in the local newspaper to take me to the end of the story. The work has taken about five years – I have certainly missed some things and misinterpreted others.

Both main archives have their own character. Minute books are formulaic, soulless and administrative. The correspondence archives at Kew are the opposite: they are dirty and finger-marked, dusty and sometimes smelly, scrawled upon, badly written, odd papers shoved unceremoniously into the gutters of massive old leather folders. Some of them are restricted because they are mouldy. Yet they are real – after the dry efficiency of the minute books, one can feel the people and characters rising up from the pages like ghosts.

Statistics and numbers are hard to come by; often several months of some random figure will appear and then disappear, and odd numbers turn up here and there throughout the record. Piecing them together often produced useful information, and some truly awesome spreadsheets. Details relating to particular events are messy and it is often difficult to establish exactly what happened or how it happened – we go with what we have. Secondary sources have been used in describing background history.

It was difficult to stay on track, having to ignore fascinating side-subjects like the provision of supplies and early traders in nineteenth-century Basingstoke, more detail on the powerful people who became guardians, and the Ladies Visiting Committee, sale of parish properties, the events surrounding the controversial town drainage systems, and so on. Only a small part of all the research has gone into these pages, and I intend to produce a website to share it with everyone.

Many people have given enormous support to this project. Top of the list have to be the late Barbara Applin and her husband Bob, both with an impressive and encyclopaedic knowledge of the history of Basingstoke, and for providing friendship, encouragement and generous help.

Then all the active members of the VCH Basingstoke Group. I won't list you all here – you know who you are. John Hollands at the Willis Museum, Basingstoke, the Jervoise family for supplying a lovely portrait of one of our board chairmen. The list goes on of others, too many to mention, who provided gems of information, interest and motivation when the work got difficult and tedious. My lovely sons and their families for just being there, and numerous friends. Sorry to anyone I've missed.

I am grateful to the staff at Hampshire Archives and Local Studies, with David Rymill deserving special mention; also to The National Archives at Kew, the British Library, and Basingstoke Discovery Centre. Finally, of course, members of the Basingstoke Archaeological & Historical Society and Friends of the Willis Museum, and staff at the Planning Department of Basingstoke & Deane Borough Council.

Last but not least, copyright. I believe I have obtained permissions wherever necessary, and acknowledged work and illustrations belonging to other people – apologies for omissions. Enjoy!

Barbara Large, 2016

Introduction

The Poor Law Amendment Act of 1834 was the single most important piece
of social legislation ever enacted … [it] touched almost every aspect of life and
labour in Victorian Britain. Employment and wages, housing and rents, migration
and settlement, medicine, marriage, charity and education.[1]

On quiet, wooded Basing Road, just east of Basingstoke town centre, closed off
by a raised bypass, is a modern private hospital, a small housing estate and an
electricity substation. To the south of the road is marshland, the flood plain of the
River Loddon, and up the slope to the north is the South West Trains main line
to London Waterloo.[2]

The legend is that, when the developers were working on the hospital site in
the 1980s, they came across tiny treasure troves of jewellery, lockets, small personal
items, buried in the ground for safekeeping by paupers before entering the forbidding Victorian edifice that was there for 130 years.

This book is about much more than life in the workhouse. We will look into the
organisation and administration of Basingstoke's Poor Law Union, a very typical
early rural union and an important social institution which influenced the town
and its surrounding area for a century. We will see that, in a system dependent
upon the empathy and interest of decent people, Basingstoke was among one of
the more humane and caring unions – it is certainly true that cruelty and neglect
gained much publicity and public attention nationally, whereas the more compassionate unions seemed to receive no recognition at all; they simply quietly got on
with the job. We will look at the difficult issue of cruelty and mistreatment later in
Part 3. We will also see the dawn of our modern local government administration.

To organise this huge and unwieldy topic, the enormous amount of data, we will
tackle it through the main historical landmarks of Poor Law history. In Part 1 we
will examine the Act of Parliament that started it all in 1834 and the setting up of
the union and workhouse under the first body, the Poor Law Commission (PLC);
in Part 2, we will witness the controversial downfall of the PLC and its replacement

by the Poor Law Board (PLB) from 1846 to 1871, the era which most people recognise as that of the 'Victorian Workhouse'. We will follow on in Part 3 with the
changes and challenges in the last quarter of the nineteenth century under the Local
Government Board (LGB). Finally, in Part 4, we will look at the twentieth century.

Very few of the books and accounts of Basingstoke Union survive. Some unions in
England have more: registers of births and deaths, admissions and discharges, books
of account and books relating to sickness, but none of these exist for Basingstoke.
We have the minute books, a couple of ledgers and one or two miscellaneous
documents in the Hampshire Record Office (Hampshire Archives and Local
Studies, HRO), providing a complete timeline to the end of the system in 1930.[3]
Unfortunately, these are restricted after 1914, and we revert to the fortnightly meeting reports in the local newspaper, the *Hants & Berks Gazette*. We also have folios of
correspondence between the government Poor Law authorities and various bodies,
officials, officers and individuals up to 1900 in The National Archives (TNA).[4]
These exist for every union in the country, totalling over 16,700 volumes.

Unfortunately for the historian, it appears that there was an early element of novelty: progress was initially carefully noted in detail while everyone was feeling their
way, but by 1845 it is noticeable that the minute books were becoming more routine,
with less detail, and this gets even worse after 1871. However the MH 12 series –
the correspondence collections – in The National Archives is a treasure-trove of detail
for anyone willing to trawl through. The papers in these archives are often difficult
to understand and practically illegible; much of the correspondence from London
is in messy draft form, and would later have been tidied and copied before sending.

Finally, it has to be acknowledged that this story is told from the point of view of
the authorities – there is no voice from the recipients of the system here. The only
fragments we have within the workhouse are in statements made to officers during
investigations; there is nothing from outside in the parishes. Paul Carter, in his
National Archives podcast,[5] describes his research into voluminous letters and
petitions by individuals struggling with the system, from a large petition in Basford
Union, Nottinghamshire, regarding the paucity of relief, to complaints from a
group of elderly people in Kidderminster about the quality of food provided. There
is nothing like this in Basingstoke, apart from occasional complaints about doctors
not turning up. But their presence threads through our story.

A note about the conventions used: the initials PLC, PLB and LGB are used
throughout for the London authorities, as are RSA and USA for the sanitary
authorities and RDC and UDC for the district councils in Parts 2 and 3 (all will
become clear!). Hampshire Record Office/Hampshire Archives and Local Studies
is referred to as HRO, The National Archives as TNA, the *Hants & Berks Gazette*
as HBG. All currency is, of course, pre-decimal. Where place names are quoted,
contemporary spelling has been maintained.

CURRENCY:

Until decimalisation of UK currency in 1971, the pound consisted of 20 shillings, and the shilling of 12 old pence or 'd' – £ s d. An old shilling is roughly equivalent, therefore, to 5 new pence. For simple shillings and pence 'ns', 'n/-' or 'n/nd' is used for ease of reading, e.g. *6s*, *6/-* or *2/6d*. This was the usual everyday method (a guinea was 21 shillings, or £1 *1s 0d*, and was a very common unit of payment for services throughout). The modern equivalent varies, depending on the reference, but it was approximately ×60 in the mid-nineteenth century, and decreasing to about ×30 by 1930.

A note on referencing: as most of this book is taken from the minute books or the MH 12 archive, it quickly becomes tedious and intrusive to reference every fact or quotation. These two sources will be indicated only where strictly necessary simply by HRO (the minute books) or TNA (the correspondence folios). The finding numbers for these are given in the Sources section and items can be found by date. Similarly, when the newspaper is referenced after 1915, HBG has been used and dated specifically only where necessary. Where dates are used for the MH 12 items these are usually those of the date stamp in the folios, since these are the dates on which they were filed – the date of the document itself is often not clear. It was found impossible to use the written folio numbers in TNA, since they are incomplete and inconsistent. Any departure from these two archives will be referenced in the usual way.

Part 1

Early Years, 1835 to 1845

The Background

A brief introduction to the 1834 Poor Law Amendment Act may be useful. Why were workhouses built?

In the early nineteenth century, and since the Elizabethan Poor Law in 1601, the existing system was that the poor, disabled and elderly were the responsibility of individual parishes, the vestries, supported by a land rate charged to those within each parish able to pay. The men responsible were called 'Overseers of the Poor'. A pauper was supported in his 'rightful place of settlement', and was to be returned back to his home parish for this purpose – there were thousands of cases within the legal system where this rule was enforced. The relief provided varied, but could be in the form of money, food, rent or work. Cottages and tenements were often provided, along with allotments for growing a little food. These were called 'poor houses' or 'workhouses', when the occupiers were required to perform work for the parish such as maintaining roads.

By the 1830s the population of England had increased dramatically – threefold in under a century. In a primarily agricultural country, new machinery was putting labourers out of work, and poor harvests in the late 1820s made matters worse. Thousands of unemployed men and damaged families were created by a series of European wars, and social unrest was inevitable. This led to the Swing Riots, firstly in Kent and then in Hampshire in 1830, resulting in hangings, imprisonments and transportations to Australia.

In 1832, £7 million was being spent nationally on poor relief, or 10s per head of population. There was resentment and resistance, and the government, which consisted at that time entirely of landowners and aristocracy, commissioned the 1832 'Royal Commission of Enquiry into the Operation of the Poor Laws'. The Commission pre-supposed that poverty was primarily a matter of personal choice for many, and that the current system of relief was open to abuse; the 200-year-old system had become obsolete. The chairman from East Ashford Union in Kent stated that the old Poor Law 'had become, from the rust of time, and a complication of other events, most shamefully abused; not only by the paupers themselves, but by the local authorities, such as Overseers and their assistants, tradesmen'.[1] Out relief (relief for paupers outside parish workhouses) was considered to demoralise the labouring classes and manipulate the costs of labour, and therefore it would eventually ruin the country – dealing with poverty could no longer be left to individual parishes.

A questionnaire, sent to each parish, was inadequate and poorly designed; the respondents could answer however they wanted or not at all. The result was an impressive bank of information but an impossible task for the historian to analyse. In spite of the fact that increased poor relief was often due to the lack of work in difficult local economies, the designers of the New Poor Law had already made up their minds.[2] There were many real errors in this judgement about the nature of poverty – that it arose from fecklessness and laziness, that it was a choice – and this is beyond the remit of this study, but the result was the 1834 Poor Law Amendment Act.

The main recommendation of the New Poor Law Act, as it was called, was that out relief and the system of small parish-based workhouses and cottages should be abolished, and that the able-bodied poor who were unable (or unwilling) to work would be consigned to a system of large, efficient, standardised workhouses, which should be deliberately designed to be of a forbidding and deterrent nature. Technically, if a pauper refused the 'offer of the House', the local guardians could refuse to take any responsibility for him.

The idea was that the totally destitute – the elderly, orphans, the chronically sick and disabled, and the mentally and emotionally struggling, people unable to work – would accept being consigned to the workhouse, and the able-bodied would withdraw their applications and make more effort to find work or other support. Eventually, in theory, out relief, uncontrolled and expensive assistance to people in the community and not in the workhouse, could be abolished altogether. As Crowther puts it, 'anyone who accepted relief in the repellent workhouse must be lacking the moral determination to survive outside it'.[3]

The prototype and model for the new system was Southwell Workhouse in Nottinghamshire, where an incorporation of forty-nine parishes had pooled their resources to build an Incorporated Workhouse in 1824, to reduce the poor rates and 'improve the moral demeanour' of the poor by housing them in a deterrent building. The local poor rate was reduced by 75 per cent in three years.[4]

There is a difference between destitution and poverty – the two words are not strictly interchangeable. People can survive in the most dire and extreme poverty, but destitution means they have absolutely nothing. This is, very roughly, the difference between 'deserving' and 'non-deserving' poor. Poverty as a way of life was to be discouraged. In a letter to Edwin Chadwick, the first secretary of the PLC, Revd H.H. Milman wrote: 'The workhouse should be a place of hardship, of coarse fare, of degradation and humility; it should be administered with strictness, with severity, it should be as repulsive as is consistent with humanity.'[5]

The new system was aimed at the destitute, whether temporary or permanent, and arguments were frequently made that it was not designed to support wages, or make lives more comfortable. That was the theory, but real life, complicated and chaotic as it is, was inevitably different – the new rules did not always work in practice.

Briefly, the 1834 Act created the Poor Law Commission (PLC), based in Somerset House in London. There were three commissioners (one of them George Nicholls of Southwell Workhouse), and a secretary, Edwin Chadwick, who remained permanently bitter about his subservient role and undoubtedly contributed towards the endemic infighting that took place. There was a team of clerks and initially nine assistant commissioners, who were tasked with visiting areas of England and ensuring that the new Poor Law Unions were set up correctly and expeditiously, and who 'met with everything from hostility to generous hospitality'.[6] From this small suite of rooms and offices, over the next hundred years, grew the twentieth-century Department of Health and Social Security and its successors, and we will see how this came about.

A group of parishes would be assigned to each union; the preferred design for a rural union was a central market town surrounded by its parishes, a configuration which is still seen today in many non-urban district councils. A Board of Guardians was elected by the ratepayers of each parish, and in each union,

A VERY BRIEF HISTORY OF BASINGSTOKE

The origins of the town are vague. A crossing of track ways, a nearby Roman road, a group of early Saxon settlements and, before the Norman conquest, an outlying settlement, or 'stoke', near the ancient larger settlement of Basing. It was well connected, situated on the main road from London to the south through Winchester, trading in agricultural produce and cloth making. It became a major hub on the turnpike routes north to Reading and Oxford, east to London, south-west via Salisbury to Exeter, and south to the port cities through Winchester, at one time servicing over thirty-seven coaches a day. Basingstoke was the first agricultural town in England to build a canal (1792) to take produce to London; this was unfortunately a failure. The London–Southampton railway opened in 1839 with later links to the north. Heavy industry followed, along with clothing manufacture and all the associated trades, most of which have now disappeared. During the mid-twentieth century there was a huge expansion of the town to accommodate the planned resettling of London population overflow, with large road and town development schemes including the routing of the M3 motorway immediately to the south. Its proximity to London enabled many national and international companies to move their headquarters out of the capital.

if a suitable single building was not available, a workhouse was to be built to accommodate the local poor. The Union Board would then take over all aspects of poor relief in their area.

Building plans were offered, off-the-peg designs created by a small group of architects commissioned by the PLC. The authorities knew that erecting a large public building was going to be completely beyond the capacity or experience of many new guardians, and it needed to be done properly. One of the leading architects was Sampson Kempthorne, who produced a set of three model plans, depending on the potential inmate numbers. It is thought that his designs were taken directly from those of American prisons, where observation could take place from a central core.[7] Needless to say, he did very well from this work, along with other government-inspired projects, and emigrated to New Zealand in 1841. Others became involved in the lucrative business of workhouse building, most famously Gilbert Scott and his partner, William Moffatt, and many of them established something of a regional design – this is why they all look similar. The proposed lifespan of these buildings was about forty years, and very few plans exist; most of them, like the example from Basingstoke which was badly drawn sixty years later, are inaccurate.[8]

Everything would be controlled, in detail, by the Poor Law commissioners in a series of regular General and Special Orders, and through the supervision of the local assistant commissioner.

By 1836 there were 351 unions in England, accounting for nearly three quarters of all poor law rates paid[9] and the process continued. According to the PLC, 'nearly the whole of Hants has been re-organised into 21 unions, comprising 275 parishes'.[10] A year later, great progress had been made across England in the 'easier' rural counties, and the PLC was starting work on the industrial areas – its first attempt, in Stoke-on-Trent, was met with problems, rebellion and strikes. The PLC was also beginning to tackle the complicated London parishes.[11] The whole of England had been 'unionised' by 1868. The New Poor Law and the infamous Victorian Workhouse had arrived.

This is what happened in Basingstoke …
By the start of Queen Victoria's reign in 1837, more than half the population of England was still dependent upon agriculture and associated trades. Basingstoke was a small north Hampshire market town, surrounded by rural parishes and tiny villages. Urbanisation and growth had not yet arrived here, and would not do so until the 1870s, and the local population was subject to seasonal fluctuations in poverty and prosperity.

Basingstoke Poor Law Union, the First Days

The assistant commissioner appointed for the Hampshire area, Colonel Charles Ashe A'Court, spent some time in the area around Basingstoke and sent a written report to the PLC on 25 March 1835. He had already decided on the basic geographical dimensions of the new union and complained that some of the parishes and their villages were so small that it would be difficult to find guardians – the job would have to be done by the existing warden or overseers, if elected. He included a detailed analysis of the situation with the poor, concluding 'that the district is at present completely pauperised'.[TNA]

He had established that the annual total poor rate for the area was £13,334 and at the time of his survey nearly 300 able-bodied paupers were claiming relief, many of them being employed on parish roads at between 6s and 8s a week, graded according to the number of their dependent children. He does not mention the number of non-able-bodied. The average rate of pay for those in work was 9s a week. No relief was given out in food or kind, only in money, but most parishes were paying rent for paupers, with the exception of Basingstoke and Basing. We know from vestry records that in Basing extra bavins (bundles of kindling wood) where provided in the worst winters and paupers were employed 'digging gravel, grubbing wood and picking stones' in return for a little money.[12]

A'Court went on to describe the existing provision:

> In almost every parish the scale system obtained: in some of them a casual distinction is made between the wages of single and married men: in one Parish (Pamber) the poor are financed by an individual at 13/3d in the pound on the poor rate assessed amount, so that here the farmers never hesitate to discharge even their best labourers in the winter season, in order to throw the expense of their maintenance on the Contractor, a system which must ultimately degrade & pauperise every man in the parish.

In a separate document, included with the above, are descriptions of paupers' accommodation in Basingstoke (the 'Pest House') and Basing. The provision in Basing is disturbing: 'the Parish rents a tenement from Lord Bolton at £20 a year, there are about a dozen rooms in it – great & small & in each room a family or more! Nothing can be imagined more filthy or disgraceful than the state of these buildings.'[TNA]

The actual placement of the new workhouse was careful. It should avoid conflicts of jurisdiction and possible interference within the town of Basingstoke, but be in a central area, accessible by foot. A'Court obviously came to an informal arrangement with Lord Bolton (who owned most of the land in the Basingstoke area at that time) about an appropriate plot of land 'where I have reason to believe that Lord Bolton will be disposed to cede as much land as may be required for the Union purposes.'

He also identified William Lutley Sclater, 'a very intelligent Magistrate', Edward Walter Blunt, from a prominent local family, and George Lamb, a leading solicitor, as the principal officers. He had already worked it all out, and the actual establishment seems to have been almost a formality. He called a meeting of proposed guardians in April 1835 to discuss final arrangements, and reported that, of the thirty-seven initial parishes, twenty-seven 'fully consented' to the union, nine 'decidedly objected', and one approved 'but objected to the great expense of erecting a Union Workhouse'. Later, one of the local gentry, Christopher Edward Lefroy, went so far as to write formally to the new guardians objecting to the whole thing.[13]

One of the objecting parishes was Upton Grey, the parish of William Lutley Sclater, the chairman of the board for the next twenty-five years, who, we will see, had serious problems with the new system.

On 27 May 1835, the first meeting of the Basingstoke Poor Law Union was held in the brand new, very stylish Basingstoke Town Hall.[HRO] Attending were the guardians of the thirty-seven parishes of the new union. We do not know who these locally elected men were beyond their names, but it was usual throughout England for them to be the ratepayers, landowners, professional men and farmers, and established tradesmen – in other words, people who were unlikely to be the recipients of relief, but contributors. All the local influential families and aristocracy, 'the great and the good', were represented in Basingstoke Union, and this continued to be the case throughout its history. There were also in attendance six *ex officio* guardians including local gentry and churchmen. Attending was Assistant Commissioner A'Court. Magistrate Sclater was appointed chairman of the board, and Mr Blunt vice-chairman. George Lamb was appointed clerk to the union, at an initial salary of £60 a year.

The union was initially to be divided into four administrative districts but this changed the following year. The parishes and population of these four districts are given in the following table, and a diagram of their boundaries – just to give an idea of the area of the union – is given in Appendix I.

Fig. 1 Basingstoke Union Districts, 27 May 1835, based on 1831 census information (Total pop. 15,424)

			Estimated population
Bramley District 6½ miles by 4½ miles	Silchester	Parish	414
	Beech Hill	Tithing	249
	Stratfieldsaye	Par.	559
	Stratfield Turgis	Par.	232
	Bramley	Par.	429
	Hartley Wespall	Par.	283
	Sherfield	Par.	599
		Total	**2,765**

Basing District 6 miles by 4 miles	Basing	Par.	1,103
	Newham	Par.	329
	Mappledurwell [sic]	Tithing	211
	Nateley Skewers [sic]	Par.	245
	Up Nateley	Par.	153
	Herriard	Par.	426
	Tunworth	Par.	126
	Upton Grey	Par.	452
	Weston Patrick	Par.	210
	Winslade & Kempshott	Par.	134
		Total	**3,389**
Basingstoke District 4½ miles by 3 miles	Basingstoke	Par.	3,581
	Eastrop	Par.	69
	Worting	Par.	120
	Wootton St. Lawrence	Par.	847
	Sherborne Saint John	Par.	702
	Monk Sherborne	Par.	522
	Pamber	Par.	473
		Total	**6,314**
Dummer District 7 miles by 5 miles	Deane	Par.	157
	Oakley	Par.	246
	Steventon	Par.	151
	North Waltham	Par.	458
	Popham	Par.	104
	Woodmancut [sic]	Par.	92
	Dummer	Par.	383
	Farleigh Wallop	Par.	108
	Nutley	Par.	138
	Preston Candover	Par.	442
	Bradley	Par.	103
	Ellisfield	Par.	245
	Cliddesden	Par.	329
		Total	**2,956**

All situated in the County of Southampton except Beech Hill which is in the County of Berks. HRO, PL3/5/1

The first meeting then moved on to the appointment of relieving officers and medical officers (see pp. 24–25). Next a new workhouse: it was resolved that 'it was expedient' that a Union Workhouse be erected at or near Basingstoke in accordance with the Poor Law Act, and a committee was appointed to progress the construction, 'if possible during the present building season', consisting of Richard Booth, Abel Easton, William Blatch, Revd William Knight and Edward Blunt.[HRO]

Weekly meetings were to be held regularly, at 10 a.m. on Friday mornings in Basingstoke Town Hall, with Assistant Commissioner A'Court, or one of his colleagues, attending occasionally. In June 1835, auditors and treasurers were appointed; Messrs Raggett Seymour & Co., bankers of Basingstoke and Odiham, became treasurers, for a fee of £10 a year. A stationer was appointed and printed detailed instructions, official forms and books of account were requested from the PLC, who would now regularly and consistently be recorded in the minutes as prescribing nearly everything the union board did – we will see later just how strict this control became.

All 'out-door assistance', out relief (relief outside the workhouse) was now to be strictly administered by the union board through the new relieving officers, and the following month, June 1835, all poor rate assessments in the parishes of the new Basingstoke Union, the 'parochial rate', were to be controlled and supervised by the union board. The existing parish properties for the relief of the poor, cottages, allotments and workhouses, were to be sold off and the proceeds used against the cost of the new workhouse, their residents to be sent to the workhouse if they had nowhere else to go. It was all about control.

Help for the injured and unemployed, orphaned children, unmarried mothers, the old, chronically sick and infirm was now taken out of the hands of parish officials – people who knew them – and placed under the control of the new employees of the Union Board of Guardians.

The Poor in 1835

At the end of June 1835 an interim procedure was established for the making of payments and relief in kind from the union each week to relieving officers to give out to the poor, following the board's examination of the latest allowance lists. An arrangement was agreed by the board in August that, until a proper workhouse was available, the Basingstoke Poor House was to continue 'to maintain paupers sent to the poor house for 2/9*d* per head per week, not including wine and medicine'.[HRO] There were many discussions entered in that first minute book about the supply of 'relief in kind' during this period, and the method and cost of its purchase from local shopkeepers – bread and flour (both 'best seconds'), bacon, cheese, lard, salt, starch, tea, sugar and soap.

Who were these poor people in 1835, upon whom this bleak new system was to be imposed? We have remaining a single notebook detailing applications for relief in the Basing district from 11 July to 11 December in that year,[14] which gives a good indication of the problems faced by ordinary people close to the edge. It is, of course, one book, from one district, covering only six months, so it is not strictly statistically significant – but it is a useful snapshot. And its contents are typical of the problems faced by the poor for decades.

It is a simple, blank-paged book (before the formulated system of the PLC in 1836), written in the hand of the relieving officer, R. W. Mansbridge, a local tailor, with allowances in another hand, which looks like that of William Sclater, the board chairman – sometimes initialled and signed. It would have been presented to the new Board of Guardians every week, with some discussion about individual cases; some of the decisions seem quite arbitrary. The book is very detailed, with names, parishes and circumstances, and often quite sad.

An analysis of the book shows a total of 159 successful applications during the period, some of them repeated for more than one week, and sometimes initially disallowed and then allowed later. Many of the applicants were labourers without employment and with large families, and if a count is taken of the number of people supported by relief, including wives and children, the total rises to about 400, or nearly 12 per cent of the total population of Basing district in 1835.

There was a definite pattern: a labourer, married with five or six children, often only about a year apart in age, struggling with an income of 8*s* or 10*s* a week, with £3 or £4 in annual rent, a hand-to-mouth existence. If the man was unable to work, or was sick (or his wife was sick) even for a short time, it was a disaster. Only in the direst circumstances was relief allowed, often deferred if the applicant was simply unemployed and should find work.

Some representative examples are:

William White, labourer (Herriard), earnings 9/6*d* a week applies for relief having 5 children to support. Family in great distress, children's shoes and clothes very bad – 10/- to be given out in clothes.

William Easton, labourer (Nateley Skewers) aged 46 applies for relief having a wife and 5 children to support [named] … he works for 8/- a week and has £3 a year to pay for Rent. A very industrious man but his family are in a state of destitution – to have £1 5s to be paid out for his rent, the Relieving Officer to report monthly.

John Hidcoop (Newnham) aged 26 applies for relief having been ill and unable to work 11 months past … has a wife and one child – allowed 2/6*d* per week.

This was followed two weeks later by:

Jane Hidcoop Widow aged 21 applies for relief having a child 18 months old – allowed 1/- a week for the child and 2/6*d* as occasional relief for the woman.

> The Relieving Officer applies to be allowed for One Gallon of Bread and 6/- given to James Vickers (Basing) … he having 3 children under 7 years of age and no employment.

Often a poor family would require clothes or shoes, completely beyond their means, for an older child going into employment. Usually, a young girl going into service was required to have shoes and a change of clothes at her own expense. A young boy, to be employed as an under-carter, would need good shoes and a greatcoat. Usually the cost price of items was provided.

The elderly also appeared in the Relief Book. Usually not employed, they had no means of support, and were often ill or infirm:

> William May (Basing) aged 78 applies for a person to take care of his wife aged 80, who from imbecility of body and mind requires constant attendance – Allowed.

> James Cooper (Newnham) aged 70 applies for relief not having any employment. His wife aged 74 has had a Cancer in her Breast during the last 4 years – 2/6d for the man and 2/6d for his wife.

Illness or injury reduced a family to complete destitution. There are examples of families where all the children became ill with smallpox or scarlet fever, together with the mother, preventing the father from working. In one instance, one of the children's names is crossed out – obviously he had died by the time the application was presented. A father of six fell from a load of hay and dislocated his shoulder, rendering him unable to work. A mother's illness or a difficult confinement with a new baby was just as devastating, leaving several young children without care even if their father was in work.

Another circumstance which caused difficulties – there are three examples in the Relief Book – was a daughter becoming pregnant with a 'Bastard Child'. Usually, the remedy was the workhouse for the unfortunate girl. But older women could find themselves in the same situation:

> Ann Egan (Up Nately) aged 40 applies stating she has no employment … was deserted by her husband some years ago and has had two Bastard Children … – Refused.

The relief provided was minimal, often 2s or so for a family of five or six, and sometimes provided partly in bread (by the gallon) or flour, occasionally in meat. On one occasion, Richard Porter, a labourer from Up Nately, with a wife and five children, was struggling with his rent; he was described as an 'industrious man', and was given 15s to help with the arrears, but this was to be a loan, and his repayment was to be used for purchasing clothing for the children.

There was a logic to allowing or refusing relief. Anything outside total destitution and complete hopelessness, or which indicated some kind of moral shortfall, was rejected outright. Similarly, anything which assisted in finding or maintaining work was allowed. Family groups with illness were helped, but only as long as the illness lasted.

In his report to the PLC in May 1836, before the new workhouse was completed, chairman Sclater stated that relief of able-bodied poor had diminished considerably under the new system, but that he felt it was mainly due to new work available on the railway and for other public and private employers, but that bad weather had made it necessary to provide more relief for large families.[16]

> **BREAD**
>
> Bread was commonly sold in medieval and Renaissance England as the gallon loaf (also called the 'half-peck loaf'), which weighed 8 pounds and 11 ounces, or 8.7 pounds. Later, including during the Victorian period, it was nearly always sold as the 'quartern loaf', which was made with exactly 3.5 pounds (or 1/4 stone) of wheaten flour, and whose finished weight was approximately 4.33 pounds. Thus, two quartern loaves of finished bread weigh the same as the older and larger gallon loaf.[15]

The new workhouse, once built, was supposed to solve this problem for everyone. The theory was that, once the poor houses and cottages had been sold off, the choice for a pauper and his or her dependents would be to go to the new workhouse as a last resort, or find some means of support.

The Officers of the New Union

The Guardians

Each parish in the union elected at least one guardian. There are no details as to how this was achieved in Basingstoke Union, but the comments of Chairman Sclater are interesting. In his privately published 'Letter to the Poor Law Commissioners' in December 1836[17] he writes:

> It would be improper for me to comment largely on a body of men, amongst whom I am a member, '*et quorum pars magna fui*',[18] ... the Guardians in my Union have been selected out of the several ranks of Country Gentlemen, Clergymen, Farmers, and first-rate Tradesmen – that they are all men conversant in business ... without any improper influences, all of them perfectly awake to the evils of the old system, and some of them, I believe, enamoured of the new.

Sclater's publication is a revealing document about the early years of the union in Basingstoke – he obviously felt strongly enough to get it printed and distributed, and it is referenced in many modern studies. It provides a balanced, practical and somewhat critical view of the imposition of the new system. As the Chairman of the Board until he was an old man, and with continuing interest and participation to the end of his life, he obviously had great influence on the administration of the union over some time, and no doubt played a part in its relatively humane actions over the years. He would have attracted men of a similar mind to work with him.

Fig. 2   William Lutley Sclater, portrait presented to him by the Board of Guardians, exhibited at the Royal Academy in 1854 (from drawing by F.R. Say).[19]

The London to Basingstoke railway was opened in 1839, and extended to Southampton in the following year. In 1848 the GWR line to Reading was opened. The railway, its expansion and its associated trades and functions continued to provide employment to the end of the century, as is evidenced in analysis of census records for the town and its surrounding villages.

Every action and decision taken by the Board of Guardians was strictly democratic, down to the smallest item. A vote of those present was taken and the largest number carried, the chairman having the final vote where the decision was hung. There was never any deviation from this – all officers or employees were 'elected'.

Relieving Officers

The men responsible for implementing the system on the ground in the parishes were the relieving officers. They assessed applications, visited the poor in their districts, liaised with medical officers and parish officials and distributed out relief, reporting back to the board at every meeting. For the first time, these were not the local clergy or farmers and businessmen who were using their spare time and energy – they were employees, who were forbidden to take other work. Relieving officers for the districts in Basingstoke Union were appointed, at the salaries of £70 per annum for Bramley and Basing districts, and £80 per annum for Basingstoke and Dummer districts. Each relieving officer provided a £50 bond for security, his own money, and a £50 surety to be provided by a named friend in the event of his defaulting.

John B. Barrett (yeoman) was appointed for Bramley, and Robert William Mansbridge (tailor, and assistant overseer for Basing) for Basing. John Follett (blacksmith), and John Doe Pearce (tailor) were appointed for Basingstoke, and Henry Pearce (army sergeant) for Dummer.[HRO]

Relieving officers were inexperienced and untrained, but were given great responsibility, not only for dealing directly with applicants and considerable amounts of cash, but eventually the power to admit people to the workhouse:

> The most novel and important part of the machinery … is Relieving Officers. It works well when the officer happens to be intelligent, active, mild, and patient in temper, yet at the same time firm and undaunted, generally acquainted with the previous habits, characters, dispositions, and capabilities of the poor within his district; unembarrassed in his own private circumstances, a good accountant and an honest man: and we expect all these qualifications out of a class of candidates who had no previous occupation … and for a salary of about £80 per annum … In many respects I look upon this officer as but an indifferent substitute for the Assistant Overseer.[20]

Inevitably, there were teething troubles. The problem with honesty was illustrated in August 1836 when John Doe Pearce was suspended for one week pending investigation into charges of submitting false bills and receipts,[HRO] the fraud being sufficiently serious to cause the board to obtain a warrant for his arrest for forgery with intent to defraud. Correspondence in TNA gives more details: he had kept for himself relief money of over £150. Some of this was enabled by the continued use of the old 'ticketing' system, whereby paupers were given tickets for individual shops to claim food. This was obviously open to abuse, and could not be properly accounted for. The board was accordingly admonished by the PLC and instructed to use the 'new' method of tendering for provisions by suppliers, and arranging proper distribution.[TNA]

Pearce had even borrowed £5 from his colleague Henry Pearce, which was eventually repaid to him by the board. R. W. Mansbridge performed some of Pearce's duties together with his own for additional salary. J.D. Pearce disappeared. 'One of our Relieving Officers carried on a system of fraud to a considerable extent during one quarter of a year … he has hitherto eluded the pursuit of the police and escaped.'[21]

It is at this time, 1836, that the four districts of the Basingstoke Union were combined into three, partly because of the difficulty of getting reliable men. J.D. Pearce's work was distributed around the other three relieving officers: 'I declare it was partly under despair of electing any very desirable officer out of the class of persons usually presenting themselves as candidates.'[22] These districts were effective and remained for many years. Using population figures for May 1835 as a guide, Basingstoke district had approximately 6,600 people, Bramley 4,500 and Dummer 4,400, and there were two new small parishes, Andwell and Weston Corbett (which were later absorbed again).

The saga of John Doe Pearce was not over, however, and investigations continued for some time. Since he had defrauded the local parishes, the PLC had to be approached to decide whether the shortfall had to be borne by the parishes or refunded from union funds, and in November 1836 the PLC sanctioned a refund. There was the inevitable bureaucratic disagreement as to exactly how this should be done, which was still going on in January 1837.

In December 1836, Thomas Fowler, of the George Inn, Basingstoke, who had provided surety for Pearce, was asked to pay £50 to the board. This being a large sum in those days, he paid by instalments, and it is not until the following October that a full receipt is minuted, together with £3 16s legal costs to Messrs Cole & Co.

Meanwhile, doubt was also thrown upon the dealings of Henry Pearce. He was accused of receiving extra payments, incurring a board investigation. It appears that this may have been a misunderstanding on the first occasion, but later Pearce was accompanied during his work to ensure his honesty, and his salary was 'adjusted'. Whether or not there was any truth in the allegations, it all proved too much for him, and he resigned in January 1837. John Renouff was a temporary replacement, but Basingstoke Union had, for the time being, lost another relieving officer.[HRO]

Medical Officers

The other mainstay of the system were the medical officers. Their duties and stipends were decided at the first meeting: 'Resolved that any contract or agreement is to include all medicine and surgery cases and attendances on the poor of the District whether belonging to any parish in the Union or not and whether the paupers for the time being be in or out of the Workhouse.'[HRO]

This was inclusive of accidents and midwifery, but the appointed medical officers were not obliged to attend any paupers in any workhouse out of their respective districts. The stipend was £80 per annum for Bramley, £100 each for Basing and Dummer and £170 for Basingstoke.

Medical officers were not directly employed by the union, but the PLC favoured tendering by doctors, with no fixed salary and the doctor providing his own supplies – this was to discourage excessive care and 'pampering'.[23] All medical contracts, as always, had to be approved by the PLC. A committee was set up from members of the board in Basingstoke to deal specifically with the appointment and contracts of the 'Medical Gentlemen', consisting of Revd John Coles, James Holding, William Blatch, Richard Booth and Edward Blunt.[HRO] After some discussion, and a raising of the stipend, the first medical officers were appointed – 'Messrs. Covey and Nichols' for Basingstoke, Basing and Dummer, and Mr Hall for the Bramley District.

Sclater was initially impressed with this system of medical help for the poor:

> This worked well with us during our first year, when the salaries, under your sanction … compared with the expenditure under the old system, were sufficient to induce some of the highly respectable practitioners of the neighbourhood … to discharge their duties with punctuality and attention … and it was found … that medical relief was rather extended than diminished.[24]

In June 1836, a return of attendances by the new medical officers in the union to date gives a total of 2,017 visits.[TNA]

However, problems soon arose. The situation, which was directly created by the PLC, was described in detail by Sclater. The same terms with the same doctors were initially agreed in the renewal of the contract in 1836, but when this was reported to the PLC, they disallowed them and indicated that their payments be cut to 'little more than half the former salaries',[25] and if this was not acceptable, advertisements for new tenders were to be placed. Of course, the doctors did not agree, and representation to the PLC was made – no reply was received.

When one of the doctors resigned, it was necessary for the relieving officers to call in medical help on *ad hoc* payment, which inevitably cost more than the original contract. This impasse caused disruption in services and went on for some time, and the board finally advertised again for tenders. Two tenders were from the existing doctors, under the condition that their services be reduced considerably, and the other one 'was from a stranger … he was invited to attend our Board, when I must say that we were rather startled at the sight of such an emaciated countenance and such wearing apparel, as made it difficult to distinguish our candidate from the paupers applying for relief'.[26]

He was approved by the PLC, but 'the first communication we had from "our hero" was an application for a loan or advance of his wages, in order to enable him, not to purchase any thing required in his profession, but to procure board and lodging for himself'.

The Clerk

The clerk, George Lamb, was responsible for preparing the minutes of the meetings, presenting accounts and performing all the other administrative and secretarial functions that arose – including liaison with everyone who became involved in the business of the new union, from employees to purchase tenders, from solicitors to the PLC itself. Lamb, who was also the clerk to the magistrates, was appointed at the instigation of William Sclater as being 'not only an excellent lawyer, but a man of independent and honourable feelings'.[27]

'The office of Clerk is becoming more and more laborious and important, owing to the complication of accounts that have been devised by the ingenuity of the Commissioners'.[28] This was a huge and often thankless task (his salary being frequently questioned by various guardians), and even politically difficult:

> When the Clerk complies with the directions of the Poor Law Commission, contained in a letter to him of 21 Dec 1836, that he should report to them any Board proceedings outside the Board's authority, this should be considered a breach of official confidence and he should resign, and the Board immediately elect a new Clerk.

This was a notice of motion by Charles Edward Lefroy, a Basingstoke guardian, on 3 February 1837.[HRO]

It is worth mentioning that these early minute books, written by Lamb or one of his clerks, are clear, legible and informative; they are so full of interesting information that it is impossible to include it all here. However, their disadvantage as historical documents is that correspondence and reports, particularly with the PLC, are often referred to as having been read and discussed with no details, which is frustrating.

The first indication of the administrative costs of the new union establishment, £900 a year, appear in the minutes in October 1835[HRO] and are detailed later in the section on 'Paying for the Workhouse'.

Building the Workhouse

Of course, a fundamental function of the new union was to build a workhouse. Immediately after the first meeting in May 1836, land was to be acquired near Basingstoke, and a decision was needed as to the size of the building; after some discussion, the number of inmates was to be 400.[HRO]

Finding an architect was not a problem, and Sampson Kempthorne was the man for the job. Of his three basic designs (square, hexagonal and '200-pauper'), the one deemed most suitable for the Basingstoke Union was the square, or 'cruciform' design; Kempthorne was officially appointed in June 1835 with his plan being submitted for approval the following week. The design was theoretically for 300 inmates, but in the early years it was not considered by the medical officers and board suitable for more than 230 at most. This design of building was also used at Andover, among others.

The piece of land designated by the assistant commissioner was to the east of the town of Basingstoke and just inside Basing parish, south of the future railway line, consisting of '4 acres, 1 rood and 14 poles'. Like much of the land in the Basingstoke area, it was owned by Lord Bolton and the Honourable Thomas Powlett Orde-Powlett, and was valued at £277 2s 6d, the board being required to make good any loss to the existing agricultural tenant.

> ### FENCES
>
> In a detailed report from the Clerk to the PLC, it had been decided to reduce the building cost by £500 by dispensing with perimeter walls. It was believed that these could be built during the winter, from the chalk lying on the site, by able-bodied paupers.[TNA] Given the low number of such men in the workhouse over the next couple of years, and the building of a fence in July 1838, this was evidently not done. Enclosing walls do not appear on later maps.

Fig. 3   'Perspective View of a Workhouse for 300 Paupers', design by Sampson Kempthorne, from the 1835 *Report of the Poor Law Commissioners.*

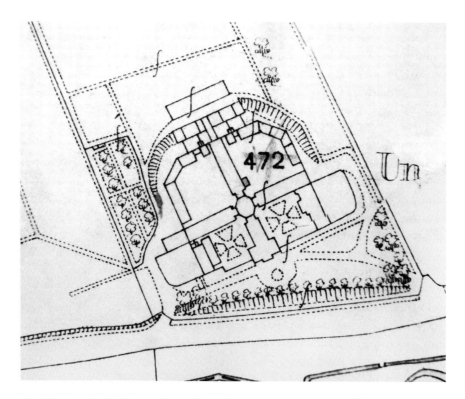

Fig. 4 Basingstoke Workhouse, from a first Ordnance Survey map in 1873.[29]

The approval of the PLC was sought, along with that for the design of the workhouse,[HRO] and this was received within the week – remarkably, within two months of setting up the union, the project was underway.

Three tenders arrived for the building in August 1835: Biggs & Ball, £5,670; Dewey & Co., £5,700; and Elliot & Co., £5,720.[HRO] Dewey & Co. were appointed, to be paid by 10 per cent instalments as authorised by Kempthorne. An application was signed by the guardians at the meeting of 16 October for a loan for £7,500 from the Exchequer, at a rate of '£5 per cent', for the total cost of building the new workhouse and land.[HRO] The PLC were approached for their opinion on seeking a remission in the brick tax (introduced in 1784), since Basingstoke had no local quarries to provide alternative building materials, enjoyed in many other unions. This was rejected.

The road running across the bottom of the map is Basing Road. This is the first image we have of the workhouse. The trees and orchard may well have been added, but the strange features are the apparent landscaped areas in the two southern quadrants – in the later drainage maps these were the Old Women's and Old Men's yards, which were almost certainly there from the beginning.

Building works commenced on the new workhouse in September, with the clerk of works, Mr Bosville, being given access by relieving officers to able-bodied labourers, initially for clearing the ground but later for more skilled work. Thereafter, a weekly payment to him appears in the minutes for a year, for paying labourers and also, periodically, for his own salary and other sundry items such as wheelbarrows. Regular payments to the contractors, Dewey & Co., are also minuted.

All the basic accommodation was there: dormitories, a kitchen, schoolrooms, a very basic infirmary area, a chapel and a laundry. There was a single entrance, with a boardroom and a porter's room. Also, rooms in the central hub for the master and matron, so that they could oversee the whole building and yards, and rooms for the other officers. In accordance with the rules, there was to be total and complete separation of inmates: men, women, boys, girls. The windows were deliberately high and small, and only on internal walls so that any view outside was impossible.

The only plans that survive, apart from the basic outline on maps, are in TNA. They are inaccurate and were drawn for drainage works in the 1890s, but appear to be loosely based on the original 1836 building. Some subsequent changes of use are not shown, and some rooms do not correspond with what happened later, but they are useful in giving us a very general idea, in spite of being a bit wrong in places. A diagrammatical representation is in Appendix II.

Kempthorne proposed the installation of a hot water heating system early in 1836; tenders were invited and a figure of £127 was finally settled, to include the heating of the 'Governors' Room' (either the boardroom or the master's room). At this time an advertisement for the recruitment of 'Bricklayers and their Assistants' was distributed by the board.[HRO]

By midsummer 1836, the building was taking shape, and insurance against fire was purchased to cover £3,000 building, £500 furniture and £200 fixtures, and a committee of three was appointed for 'ordering and directing the supply of external and internal and fitting up furnishing and completing all that may be necessary preparatory and in order to the occupation of the Workhouse by its Inmates'.[HRO] A porter was appointed, partly to keep a watch on the site, and an additional watchman was to be found if required.

In July advertisements were placed in the local press for a master and matron to run the workhouse, and the next month William Spier and his wife, Hannah, of Reading, were appointed. It was a condition of employment for the master and matron that any children they had were also to live there. The annual salary for both was £75, they were to live in the workhouse and their food was to be that supplied to the inmates. Spier and his wife could move into the workhouse whenever they pleased, but their salary would not commence until Michaelmas, the end of September.[HRO]

The first use of the workhouse appears in the minutes of 30 September 1836, when meetings of the board were held in the boardroom of the new building and no longer in Basingstoke Town Hall; bread and cheese were provided for the guardians and hay and straw for their horses. The local surveyor of highways was approached regarding the bad state of the roads around the building.

On 14 October 1836, the clerk was instructed to 'report to the Commissioners the Completion of the Workhouse, that same is now ready for reception of paupers and for their Instructions.' As with any new building, there were still final arrangements to be made, including fittings, and a temporary finishing committee was appointed to oversee the work. For example, a payment of £122 was made to Charles Simmons, ironmonger, for bedsteads. The contractors' final payment for the building was not requested until February the following year, as there were still outstanding items – 'the state of the chimneys and other defects'.[HRO]

On 4 November 1836, 'the Master … instructed to make the necessary preparations for receiving into the New Workhouse the several paupers directed to be sent there this day'.[HRO] What must it have been like for these desperate people, to be taken into this huge, bleak building, probably the largest they'd ever seen?

Paying for the Workhouse, the Poor and the Union

The new building was an expensive project. The modern equivalent of £7,500 is probably near to £500,000, this to be found and paid for by the 15,500 people of the Basingstoke Union. Of course, not all of them were functioning ratepayers. There was open concern among members of the board – where was all this money to come from? In September 1836, a request was made to extend the Treasury loan from ten to twenty years and for a reduction of the interest rate to 4 per cent. Even before the workhouse was finished, a call was made for a 'sixpenny rate' on the parishes 'for the purpose of paying a quarter's salary to the Officers, and for other general purposes', and a further two orders for a 'shilling rate' were made in October.[HRO]

The minutes of a board meeting in October the previous year had covered a full financial accounting – 'an estimate of the probable expenses for the 'In Maintenance' and out relief charges of the poor in the Union, and also the expenditure of the establishment for the next quarter'. The total amount required from all the parishes in the union amounted to £2,296 17s 4d, with a quarter to be paid each month from October to December inclusive.

The usual method of dividing rates between parishes was to allocate according to the recent average pauper costs; in Basingstoke Union the rates seem to have been divided, very accurately, in proportion to the population of each parish, with the exception of Basingstoke town. Being the market town with the highest population, it would have had to bear nearly a quarter of the amount, so an adjustment down was made. There is a table in the minutes which shows exactly how this is distributed by parish.

From now on, the assessment and collection of a parochial rate for poor relief was a formal arrangement and it continued to be covered in the minute books weekly with quarterly accounting. The rate covered the contribution to poor relief (out relief and later maintenance within the workhouse) and the establishment costs (the salaries of officers and ongoing expenses for the administration of the union and each parish's contribution against the loan for the building of the workhouse).

Fig. 5 Costs of the Union Establishment, October 1835.

	£	s	d
Clerk	60	0	0
Auditor	50	0	0
Medical Officers			
Bramley District	90	0	0
Basingstoke District	170	0	0
Basing District	100	0	0
Dummer District	100	0	0
Relieving Officers			
Basingstoke District	80	0	0
Basing District	70	0	0
Bramley District	70	0	0
Dummer District	80	0	0
Treasurer	10	0	0
Hall-Keeper	7	16	0
Stationery, postages & Contingencies	12	4	0
Total	**900**	**0**	**0**
of which ¼ for the Quarter is	225	0	0

To meet which Sum of £225 a Rate of 4d in the pound on the average assessments amounting to £222 1s 4d is required.

HRO, PL3/5/1

Throughout Britain, this is the beginning of today's rating system, as controlled from central government. As we will see later, the union boards were to become functioning and empowered local authorities, which were increasingly involved in administration over the next decades, evolving into the local government of today.

In Basingstoke, the concern over finance led to the consideration of various options for raising money. One of them was to seek loans from private individuals at 4 per cent. This was rejected as being unfeasible, and the board had to fall back on the procurement of funds by 'sale of property or raising the amount by mortgage'.[HRO] (The first repayment instalment of the Exchequer loan was made on time in March 1837, being £675, or one-twentieth of the loan including interest.)

According to the rules of the PLC, the instruction for parishes to raise a useful amount of money was to sell off the existing parish properties which were used to house and care for the poor. After all, theoretically, they would no longer be needed.

Sale of Parish Properties

Parish sales started in April 1836, the first public auctions being for Wootton St Lawrence, where '27 Tenements, with Gardens Attached' were sold off, and Monk Sherborne, with eighteen properties.[TNA] Names of the occupants were always given in the sale notices, and many of them ended up in the workhouse.

That December, Basingstoke Poor House, the existing old workhouse in the town, was sold to a Mr Ford for £440 – it was thereafter called 'Ford's Building'. In Basing, four cottages were purchased by Lord Bolton and several members of the Booth family for a total of £205. In Silchester, the parish poor cottages were acquired by Revd John Coles, one of the *ex officio* guardians. This process of selling went on to the end of the century, although inevitably slowing down after the initial bonanza.

Charles Paice, a local auctioneer, handled most of these sales for years and undoubtedly made a lot of money. There is a large amount of very scattered information in the correspondence ledgers in TNA: details of the properties for sale, who was renting them, information on outlying buildings and gardens, much of it on the pre-printed forms later produced by the PLC for national use just for this purpose. This is beyond the scope of this study, but would be of interest to parish historians.

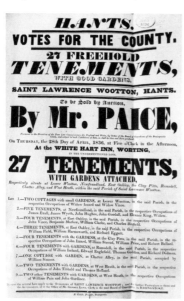

In some cases, the amount yielded was enough to pay off a parish's loan portion altogether, for example in Stratfield Turgis and Sherfield on Loddon, and the PLC's instruction was to invest the excess in bonds for the benefit of the parish. In Wootton St Lawrence and Monk Sherborne some of the money was later used for emigration expenses (£100 and £200 respectively) (see the 'Emigration' section on p. 34).

Sclater states that the sale of parish cottages made the workhouse indispensable '*as a place of refuge for the destitute*' [his italics], although 'as a substitution for the outdoor employment or

Fig. 6   Sale poster for poor houses in Wootton St Lawrence, April 1836.[30]

relief of agricultural labourers in an agricultural district, it is not merely objection-able, but execrable'.[31] He points out that, in Basingstoke, many of the cottages were purchased by 'landed proprietors who … adopted the occupiers as their tenants at reasonable rents', but in other cases the buildings were considered nuisances and demolished, their occupiers evicted.[32]

Meanwhile, various draconian changes to the provision of relief were proposed to the board, but often rejected – for example, 'that no person owning freehold, copyhold, safehold and leasehold property shall be deemed a pauper and as such entitled to relief in any shape' (proposed by George Harriott), and 'that from [the opening of the new workhouse] no Relief be given for or on account of any Bastard Child in this Union except in the Workhouse. Also that no Bastard Child under the age of eight years shall be received in the House without its mother if living and unmarried' (proposed by Edward Blunt).[HRO]

A suggestion that relief in money be given to large poor families who were unable to pay their rent, in the interim period before completion of the workhouse, was rejected by the PLC.[HRO] Only loans could be made, and after completion of the workhouse in 1836, small loans are minuted every week. Very few of these loans seem to have been paid back, and one wonders whether this was a way of getting round the strict out relief rules. In 1836, a total of £11 was loaned; in 1837, £29; in 1838, £23; but in 1840 and 1841 combined, only £5. Over the whole period that this activity appears, less than £7 is actually recorded as having been repaid.

Emigration

The other method of easing the financial burden, of course, was to get some of the poor to simply go away, the process to be sponsored and supported by the union. Two hundred copies of a printed notice were distributed in Basingstoke in 1836:

Emigration

Twenty thousand persons of the Working Classes could be provided with imme-diate employment in Canada by the Government Agent at a High Rate of Wages. Farm Labourers readily obtain from £20 to £30 a year with Board, Lodging and Washing.

Day Labourers during the Summer from 3/- to 4/- per day. Labourers about the Wharfs, Timber yards and Shipping from 3/6 to 5/- a day with provisions.

The Class of persons chiefly required are Farm and Common Labourers to any extent Small Capitalists. Mechanics. Domestic servants female as well as male.

Persons wishing to emigrate should apply for further Information to the Guardians or Relieving Officers of their respective parishes.

By Order of the Board of Guardians of the Basingstoke Union,

February 26th 1836   Geo. Lamb, Clerk [HRO]

There was a great demand for emigration at this time, both from the poor themselves and from people who wanted to get rid of them, and TNA has a great deal of correspondence between the PLC and various officials of the union and others, some of them requesting sanction for financial help from union funds for this purpose. Interestingly, one of them, in January 1836, was from W.L. Wiggett Chute of The Vyne (the local stately home) – one of the richest men in the area – asking for money to send off some of his labourers to Canada. The PLC simply said that an official resolution from the board was needed.[TNA]

Very quickly, pre-printed forms to formalise arrangements emerged from the PLC, followed by the inevitable demand for returns and figures on local emigration. Unfortunately, we do not have accurate numbers and statistics, but there are some interesting documents giving an indication of what happened. Many parishes found the process difficult; an effective and efficient flow of funds was not forthcoming for some time, and there was much of the usual nitpicking from the PLC, which did not help.

Here is a very typical example: the overseer of Monk Sherborne, William Hooper, wrote a second letter (having received no reply to his first) to the PLC in May 1836, setting out expenditure of £250 for sending some paupers to Canada. Some of this had been donated and some was from central government, and he requested that the balance be found from the proceeds of sale of poor cottages in the parish.[TNA]

This was initially refused, and Hooper wrote again, pointing out that within the last five years, Sherborne had sent seventy people to Canada 'at an expense little short of £500 and we are still overstocked'. Other 'pressure of demand on the rates' had prevented him from even being able to pay himself. And 'no payments for the present year's emigration expenses are yet entered in the Parish Book'.[TNA]

He then went on to set out a typical cost scenario from a recent batch of emigrants:

Items referred to as paid by the Overseers	
Carriage on Board Ship above sum borrowed	£24
Ditto in two wagons to Gosport	£8
Paid the emigrants for food on the road	£4 19s 6d
For a person to superintend embarkation and payments by him for emigrants	£1 17s 6d
Solicitor of the Exchequer, Bill Commission for preparing their Security	£3

After deducting 'donations in aid received', this left a shortfall of £28 in the parish budget for this single episode, and this process appears to have been continuous. From various sources, the average cost of steerage alone to Canada in 1836 was about £4 for an adult, and half that for a child.

Bureaucracy and the Poor Law Commission

Around the time of the opening of the workhouse, various changes appear in the record keeping of the union, imposed by the PLC. In August 1836 a document had been received from them, an 'Order for the Keeping, Examining and Auditing the Accounts of the above Union, and of the several Parishes of which it is composed'.[HRO]

This is an official, bound, signed and sealed document listing all the documentation to be kept and submitted by all the officers and administrators of the union, with examples and suggestions. The PLC were kind enough to suggest that all these books and forms could be purchased from Mr Charles Knight, a London publisher, at a 'considerably reduced' rate.

The minute books were to be completed in a prescribed manner, and a copy of the instructions was pasted in the front of the book for reference purposes. A new minute book was accordingly started and the strict format was followed. A subject index is provided at the front of each minute book, but it was obviously too difficult, and probably time-consuming, to keep up properly, so it is fairly useless. Some of the most important items appearing weekly are the regular payments in out relief and details of 'In Maintenance' in the workhouse, which can be analysed.

This is just an indication of the books, forms and accounts to be kept:

General Union Accounts
The Minute Book.
Ledger.
Order Check Book.
Check Book of Admissions into and Discharges from the Workhouse.
The Pauper Description Book (names, parishes, dependants, date of birth, residence, 'the Particular calling the Pauper has exercised'), disability, purpose for seeking relief.
Abstract of the Application and Report Book (Schedule D, Form 24) with Decisions of the Board.

Orders
Notice of Auditing of Quarterly accounts to be fixed to the Workhouse door by the Clerk – rules and times for preparation and presentation to Board.
Notice of number and description of paupers, expenses incurred in relief, proportions by parish of relief and Establishment charges.
Lists, of paupers, to be affixed to church door in parishes.
Quarterly Abstract of each account to be submitted to the Poor Law Commission.

There were also a large number of instructions to be followed: before each weekly meeting, 'Clerk to check Master's accounts, Provision Check Account, Provision

Receipt and Consumption Account, Out-door Receipt and Expenditure Book to
be compared with Minutes. All accounts to be submitted to Board weekly'.

Workhouse Accounts (to be kept by Master)
Inventory Book (furniture, fixtures, fittings, stock, etc.).
Admission and Discharge Book.
Register of Births.
Register of Deaths.

Weekly In-door Relief List
'The names of the Paupers, with the number of days each Pauper is in the House
in each week … the aggregate number of days in each week passed in the
Workhouse by the total number of Paupers in each Parish.'
Provision Check Account.
Clothing-Materials Receipt and Conversion Book (for made up clothing and bedding).
Clothing Receipt Book.
In-door Labour Book (description of work by each Pauper daily).

Out-door Relief (to be kept by Relieving Officers)
Application and Report Book.
Weekly Out-door Relief List.
Out-door Receipt and Expenditure Book.

Medical Relief Accounts (Medical Officers)
Register of Sickness and Mortality.
Weekly Return Book.

And it goes on … 'Under this head of the machinery of the system … be Reckoned
the Books or Forms of Accounts, not less than twenty-eight in number', says Sclater,
pointing out that not even the smallest item of relief can be given 'without a large
expenditure of Stationery'.[33] He then goes on to describe, in great detail, the procedure, the forms, the ledger entries required – the 'Application and Report Book'
containing twenty-three columns, all of which must be later transcribed to the
'Abstract of the Application and Report Book'.

The pauper had lost his local identity: 'at the old Vestry Boards, a single glance
at a pauper's face, or the mention of his name, sufficed to call to mind almost
instantaneously, his whole history … whereas to the Board of Guardians, he is
most frequently a stranger'.[34]

This must have been daunting to a group of people who were not trained or
experienced in this work, with all the problems it entailed, some of which are
reflected in the minutes as failure to present for inspection complete books and

forms, and incomplete record keeping. One gets the impression sometimes, during midwinter or particularly hard times, of there being a significant struggle simply to keep up with the paperwork. In fact, in January 1838, a truck was procured for 'conveyance and transfer of books and papers and other proceedings to and from the Clerk's Office and for other occasions connected with the Workhouse'.[HRO] At the same time, a bill for £34 9s 10d was paid 'for Registration Books'.

Everything but the minute books has gone.

There were also orders and instructions received periodically, of which a printed Consolidation Order survives in HRO from 1842. Every small decision, financial or otherwise, was to be referred for approval by the PLC, and this often appeared to be onerous, unpopular and time-consuming. For example, in November 1836 the clerk wrote to the PLC seeking their approval to provide 'some place with the addition of firing during the Winter Months at the expense of Basingstoke Parish for the use of the poor'[HRO] – somewhere they could get indoors and be warm – but the PLC responded, rather facetiously, that the 'Statute of Elizabeth' (the old Poor Law of 1601) already provided that the church 'can be used for this purpose'.[TNA]

Earlier in 1836, the board had written to the PLC requesting a change in the rule that paupers had to attend a board meeting if they wished to appeal their relief decision. It was pointed out that this was a long and often difficult journey for most poor people in a large rural area – also it was intimated that it was not a good idea for them to assemble, waiting and comparing notes.[TNA] There was no change in the ruling.

A quote from a Nottinghamshire MP in Hansard on the bureaucracy of the PLC:

Why, no human powers of either body or mind can comprehend or carry all that has been written and printed at the expense of this deluded country in support of this detested measure by its prime agents. You are erecting a Nelson monument of vast altitude. You may almost erect a Poor-law monument of equal height, though of more corruptible materials, of the reports of these commissioners … I have already got upon the English Poor-law upwards of 20,000 pages.[35]

Poor Life Outside the Workhouse

What happened to the poor in Basingstoke Union under this new system?

Every small diversion from the strict rules of the new Poor Law – and of course, in the real world there were many – had to be sanctioned by the PLC, which created the folios of correspondence in TNA. They fill in the reality, an interface, behind the minute books, difficulties and conflicts between poor relief outside the workhouse and within it. Every disagreement or perceived injustice, financial or otherwise, every tiny decision outside the rules, generated reams of letters, which was undoubtedly exasperating for the officers of the board and made decisions protracted. Some of the responses from the PLC were so turgid, written in lengthy Victorian syntax (not to mention awful writing), that they are incomprehensible.

These folios are revealing about the kinds of problems experienced by individuals. Here are three examples from early 1837:

- January: Cynthia Haydon, 32, a widow with five children, was evicted from her poor cottage in Basing when it was sold and she moved to Basingstoke to find lodging. She was offered the workhouse, but declined, not wishing to be separated from her children. Under the rule that relief could only be received within the pauper's own parish, she was now totally destitute, and was relying on private charity donations (from two or three of the union guardians), until a ruling was received from the PLC.

    The eventual decision was that she should move to an industrial area, and find work for herself and her oldest child.

- January: William Wareham, 76, and his wife Mary, 75, asked to live together in the workhouse because he was blind and she could care for him. Permission was needed for this, and it was agreed, provided the couple would be kept separate from other paupers.

- May: Grace Rampton, 30, three small children, home parish Nately Scures but residing in Tadley (neighbouring Kingsclere Union), was widowed when her husband had a seizure. She had a cottage with a garden for vegetables, and paid for the funeral with the money from the sale of a pig. She applied for relief from Basingstoke Union and was, inevitably, offered the workhouse since she would be totally destitute if she moved back home. The board considered that this would actually be more expensive than letting her have out relief in Tadley to supplement her tiny income.

    The PLC allowed the relief for six months, and then a further six months later when she became ill. What was to happen after that?

The same year, the board attempted to get the PLC to change the rule regarding refusal of out relief outside a pauper's own parish, and extend it to the whole union – many examples relate exactly to this rule, and it caused great difficulty to individual people, and administratively to the union. The board even made representation to the House of Commons in April 1837, but to no avail – the rule stayed for the time being.

In the early 1840s circumstances nationally had overtaken the insistence on workhouse admission over out relief – it was proving impractical. In the industrial areas of the country, particularly, and in times of periodic hardship there were just not enough places. The Outdoor Labour Test Order was issued, ruling that able-bodied paupers should perform labour in return for relief, which should be given only in the form of food and clothing. There is no reference to these arrangements in the minutes and out relief continued to be paid at the same level and in the same way here in Basingstoke, as we will see later.

The physical problems of actually claiming out relief were deliberately difficult everywhere under the new system. A quote from Hansard:

> One great and glaring fault is the enormous extent of the unions. Why the poor have now to travel ten or twelve miles to ask for relief, which may be refused them, and then they have to walk the same distance back with a heavy heart. I will put it to the House whether anything can be more cruel than in the extreme heat of summer or the cold of winter to drag the poor so far, while, perhaps, they may be sent back without any relief whatever?[36]

Increasingly, a common form of temporary relief for struggling families was to put one or two children into the workhouse, which must have been a hard decision for everyone, and difficult for the children concerned – it is an indication of how close to the edge these people were when the reduction of one small mouth among a family of, say, seven or eight would make a difference to the shortfall. It was a common practice for many years. It was nearly always children aged between about 7 and 12 – little ones were too much trouble to look after in the workhouse, but older ones could work.

J. Headeach, the board's auditor, in his report in 1838 to the PLC, disagreed with this practice for different reasons. He considered that it was keeping the price of labour low, and was a 'modification' of the old system of relief, in that the pauper received the same net value as he received previously. He also felt that this kind of relief led to 'improvident marriages' and more cases of 'illegitimate children'.[TNA]

Often help was provided by neighbours, local traders and farmers, and sometimes the guardians themselves. For example, in the case of Dennis Downham, a blind man of Monk Sherborne, who was sent to a special training school in Bristol in 1837, his clothes and journey were paid for by friends and neighbours; the parish and the union also paid for his board in advance (which was, strictly speaking, not allowed by the Poor Law rules).[TNA]

The rules and regulations relating to relief within the pauper's home parish, involving 'removal' back, whether it was socially appropriate or not, not to mention the usual complications of ordinary life – bereavement, illness, accident – caused difficulty for the poor themselves and consternation for the guardians, and the responses of the PLC were, as previously mentioned, often unhelpful and sometimes quite arbitrary or even cruel.

Here are some revealing and typical examples of 'removal' difficulties from 1838 to 1840, found in TNA. There are many more.

- Elizabeth Reynolds, a recent widow with six very young children, was removed from Bethnall Green and admitted to the workhouse. She had two older children, one of whom was prepared to provide housing in Bethnall Green, and she wished to return, if the union would grant her 6s a week in support. The PLC firstly replied: 'ask the date of the husband's death', and relief was later refused on the grounds that she was able-bodied and therefore fell outside the rules of out relief. She absconded from the workhouse a week later, with four of her children, whom she later abandoned. She was found and prosecuted.[HRO]
- Elizabeth Crockford, a widow of Basingstoke with four children, had been removed to Basingstoke following the sudden death in Petersfield of her husband, a horse-collar and harness maker and occasional postman. She had been surviving on the charity of neighbours but the local union insisted on her return home. Her oldest son had been left in a free school in Petersfield, following which he was to be apprenticed to a trade, and her oldest daughter was in school, where the schoolmistress was letting her stay for free. She had a mangle and had been taking in clothes for 4s a week, but her rent was 2s a week. All she wanted to do was to return to Petersfield, to re-unite her family and carry on working, with the help of out relief from Basingstoke. The guardians were directed by the PLC that they could give out relief in this case, but did not feel 'justified in sanctioning her return'. The response in the archive is long, difficult and convoluted, and their reasons for the decision were, firstly, that 'it defeats the intention of the law', secondly, she could become a vagrant (implicating the guardians in assisting her), and thirdly, she would be depriving Petersfield paupers of work. However, in their kindness, help was to be allowed for the son while still in the school.

There are further examples of hard times for large families. Those of two agricultural labourers from Pamber with no work, in November 1839, were included in one letter to the PLC:

- William Stamp of Pamber, with a wife and seven children. 'He is employed in thrashing [*sic*] wheat at 4/– per quarter and that about 3½ bushels per day is about what he can thrash.' His oldest son, 14, can bring in an additional 2s a week, and he pays 1s a year in rent for his cottage.
- John Dicker of Pamber, with six children, earning 10s a week, with 1s a year rent.

Both of these families had been given flour during the previous winter, and the board suggested that, since they were able-bodied, they might at least place one child in the workhouse. This provoked a difficult twelve-page response from the PLC. Because two of Stamp's children were twins, the workhouse option was agreed, but in the case of Dicker, a 'large family' was not an excuse for relief. The PLC would find it impossible to lay down a rule as to how many children constituted sufficient stress on income to warrant relief – 'So much depends on the industry, frugality and good management of the man and his wife … the only safe course … is to revert to the simple and efficient expedient of the workhouse' for the whole family.

Two cases were put to the PLC for 'insufficiency of earnings': Henry Abdy, of Weston Patrick, with a wife and six children, and John Carter, of Newnham, with a wife and five children, both unable to pay their rent. The PLC authorised one child of the Abdys to be taken into the workhouse, but John Carter was to be allowed no relief. This seems arbitrary.

Basingstoke Union Workhouse

In October 1836 the workhouse was declared open. William and Hannah Spier were in residence as master and matron, as was the porter, William Blunden. Provisions had been acquired; on 30 September contracts were let to local suppliers:

> John Barton for meat … Good Beef, 5½d per lb, Mutton, 6d per lb., Beef & Mutton Suet, 6d per lb.
> Moses Cook … Good Bread, 11/2d per gall.
> George & Charles Barton … Flour, 36/1d per sack
> Wallis & White … Coals, best Newcastle, £2 per ton, Coke, 50/- per ton.[HRO]

Details appear in the minutes every week of tenders and purchases of basic food, fuel and materials for the running of the workhouse, and payments made to various businesses for supplies. In November, the following orders were placed: 12 doz. pearl buttons, hose for men, women and children, 100 yards of flannel, 51 yards of 'check', also calico, gingham and hats. The inmates were to make most of their own clothes. Also ordered, 11 galls of bread, 44lbs beef, 2lbs suet, 6lbs candles, 6lbs butter, 2 tons of coal and 35cwt of coke.

'Provision Receipt and Consumption' accounts were set up and monitored closely by the board, as were contracts to provide out relief in kind. The workhouse was the biggest single consumer in the district, and these contracts would have been lucrative and much sought-after. All the big names in trading in Basingstoke appear, some of them going on in later years to become very significant players in the town and further afield.

Workhouse Rules in General

What happened to new inmates? We have no record of the process in Basingstoke, but the procedures laid down by the PLC will have been followed to the letter. So, as regards workhouse life for the inmate, a general description of the usual practice according to the rules applies here.

The first impact was the building itself – it was huge, dark and forbidding. New inmates were searched, their clothes taken from them, they were bathed and had their hair cropped, including the children – this, on the face of it, looks cruel, but most of these poor people were probably filthy, infected with lice and fleas and possessed very little useful clothing. The bathing would have been particularly alarming for some, who had not bathed or even been fully naked for years. The medical officer would make a brief examination to ensure there was no obvious infectious disease, workhouse uniform clothing was provided (which, of course, made it easy to spot them when out in the community). All personal possessions were taken from them, to be returned when they left. They could just keep a Bible if they owned one.

The general treatment following their admission was designed to be difficult. Crowther argues that because the clothing, food and shelter provided in the workhouse was very often vastly superior to anything the paupers received outside, the PLC had to make the idea repellent, and this was to be done by segregation, strict control and discipline.[37] Inmates were expected to be quiet, orderly and obedient, and mealtimes were to be conducted in silence. The food, while providing basic subsistence, was deliberately bland and boring: bread, cheese, gruel, a little cooked meat and vegetables weekly.

Another unpleasant twist was that withdrawal of food was almost universally used as punishment for misbehaviour, as we will see later, and this happened in Basingstoke. The *1st Annual Report of the Pool Law Commission* in 1835 lists the circumstances under which diet could be used as punishment at the discretion of the guardians:

Any pauper … who shall neglect to observe such of the rules …

… Or who shall make any noise when silence is ordered;

Or use obscene or profane language;

Or by work or deed insult or revile any other pauper in the workhouse;

Or who shall not duly cleanse his or her person;

Or neglect or refuse to work;

Or pretend sickness;

Or who shall wilfully waste or spoil any provisions, or stock, or tools, or materials for work;

Or wilfully damage any property whatsoever belonging to the Union;

Or disobey any of the legal orders of the master or matron, or any other superintendent.

The most controversial and difficult workhouse practice was the segregation of family members, which caused a tremendous amount of public protest, and no doubt great stress and unhappiness within each establishment. Men were separated from women, boys from girls, and children over four were separated from their mothers, with only visits allowed. The buildings were designed with this segregation in mind, with separate wards and separate exercise yards outside – some designs of workhouse even had elaborately separated stairways, so that people in different groups never saw one another at all, and this can still be seen in Southwell Workhouse in Nottinghamshire. However, elderly couples over sixty could be allowed to stay together, and this happened in Basingstoke, and double bedsteads were ordered for this purpose.

Paupers were classified into seven basic groups:

- Men infirm through age or any other cause (later, over 60s);
- Able-bodied males over 15;
- Boys between 7 and 15;
- Women infirm through age or any other cause (later, over 60s);
- Able-bodied females over 15;
- Girls between 7 and 15;
- Children under 7.

Among these, of course, there were women who had illegitimate children or were about to give birth to them. No allowance was made in the early years for the separation of mentally ill, violent or disruptive people, which must have been a source of great distress. To be fair, part of the motive for separating children was to keep them away from the bad influence of some of the adults, and in some workhouses, including Alton, there was room to keep the wayward women separate; this was not the case in Basingstoke.[38]

The day was strictly scheduled and deliberately monotonous, marked by the ringing of a bell. Typically inmates would rise between 5 and 6 a.m., say prayers and eat breakfast, work until midday, eat dinner, work until supper, say prayers and retire to bed at about 8 p.m. Tedium and boredom were the worst enemies of inmates, and this would have been particularly difficult for youngsters. Typical work throughout England was without skill or interest. Oakum picking was almost universal, stone breaking and sack making were common, and until 1846 (when it was banned following the Andover scandal) so was bone crushing, of which more later. Corn grinding by a treadmill capstan was also fairly common.

Paupers were not prisoners and were allowed to leave the workhouse, but only with permission and for a good reason. In Basingstoke, paupers were allowed out to look for work, and to walk to their parishes on Sundays to attend church services.

This is, of course, all very well in theory, but conditions varied tremendously from union to union, usually as a result of the general ethics and the interested oversight of the people in charge, the boards of guardians. Where the board was uninterested, not prepared to spend a little extra money or to supervise its staff properly, cruelty and blatant favouritism could take place, and there are too many stories of horrific treatment or simple meanness and neglect. Staff were invariably underpaid and overworked, and the job of workhouse master tended to attract people difficult to employ, ex-NCOs or policemen, often bullies. Where the board was vigilant and caring, the situation could be completely different. We will look at neglect and cruelty with the associated major workhouse problems, discipline and punishment, in Part 3.

However, it should be remembered that, given the living conditions of the poor at the time, the workhouse provided shelter, warmth and a basic diet when they were not available in the community. We have mentioned how children were left in the workhouse to get a family through hard times, and people constantly moved in and out of the workhouse seasonally, following the availability of work – the agriculture year in rural areas, factory labour needs in industrial ones. And many people learned to play the system well.

According to the rules, the minimum staff requirement for a workhouse was a master and matron (a married couple, for purposes of convenience and economy), a porter (a gatekeeper, policing exit and entry and searching for unauthorised 'contraband'), and a chaplain; in the latter case workhouse duties would be part of his general clerical responsibilities. Many workhouses (unlike Basingstoke) did not employ teachers for years.

The master's job was not an easy or lucrative one. He was responsible for general management and discipline, and every item of food and clothing used – nine different account books were required. The matron was responsible for female inmates, the domestic running of the workhouse, supervising the kitchen and general nursing of the sick. The pair had complete and total control over every tiny aspect of life, and it is easy to see how things could get out of hand under the wrong circumstances. There was also the constant conflict between being a strict disciplinarian with difficult people, but also caring for the elderly, the infirm and the very young.

Basingstoke Workhouse in Particular
We can make observations and deductions about conditions in Basingstoke Workhouse.

The list of tenders for supplies appearing quarterly in the minutes is interesting. In addition to bread and flour, it includes beef, mutton and suet, 'Good English bacon', 'Good cheese', 'Good butter', sugar, tea and coffee, oatmeal, peas, potatoes and lard – the basis of a sustaining diet. Tenders for quantities of port, wine and brandy began to appear in 1837, for distribution to the sick and elderly under medical supervision. From late 1838, inmates were allowed a choice of coffee instead of cheese at supper. There are several cases of inferior quality food being returned to suppliers for replacement, and in 1842 it was stipulated that bread delivered should be no more than a day old – later that year each relevant baker was required to enter into a bond for £50 to cover his performance.

Within two months of opening, at the medical officers' suggestion, a better diet regime (Dietary No. 2) was substituted for the basic Dietary No. 1, along with tea for nursing women. This was increased again in 1838 to Dietary No. 3.[HRO]

Dietary No. 3 officially consisted of three meals a day, based on gruel (oatmeal boiled in water or milk), bread and cheese. Breakfast was half a pint of gruel with 5oz of bread; dinner consisted of bread and cheese, with meat, bacon and vegetables twice weekly, soup once weekly (instead of the bread and cheese); and supper was bread and cheese. This amounted to approximately 1lb of bread and 3.5oz of cheese a day, plus a few extras, with women receiving slightly less, and small variations for children and the elderly.[TNA] To a modern person, this is not much food, a subsistence diet and lacking many nutrients. However, more enlightened workhouses like Basingstoke did supplement this wherever possible with additional meat, fruit and vegetables when available, grown in the workhouse grounds. Potato supply appears in the minutes in February 1843. The 1843 basic diet appears in Appendix IV.

Also appearing in the supplies and tender lists are hair brooms, shaving equipment, mop heads, scrubbing brushes, yellow soap and starch, indicating a reasonable standard of cleanliness and hygiene. In early 1837, George Hussey was the first barber of many hired to shave and cut the hair of inmates. Shoes and boots in a selection of sizes were purchased in these early years, as were articles of women's and men's underwear and linens, caps and bonnets, stockings and handkerchiefs. A cobbler, George Eckett, was a recipient of regular work and payment for repairing footwear (later this was done within the workhouse). There were purchases of gingham, frocking, 'stout callico' in two widths, buttons and fasteners, 'house flannel', 'Drabette for stays', a range of different fabrics, so that inmates could make their own clothes. It seems that inmates were warmly and adequately dressed.

A visiting committee, people who could drop in at random and inspect the workhouse, consisting of various guardians, was established shortly after opening, and reported to the board weekly. This became a problem since it was obviously not a popular task – sometimes there was no visiting committee at all, and various ways of distributing the job fairly were tried, from drawing lots to rotating through the guardians alphabetically. After the first few months, the visiting committee is barely mentioned and from what follows, we can assume that it was not functioning for some time.

In March 1838 there was a serious outbreak of typhus in the workhouse, which ran until June. Correspondence throughout this period describes sickness and many deaths, and rather sad details of clothes belonging to the deceased, their only possessions, which would have been either destroyed or put into store to be recycled for future use. Of the fifteen deaths reported in April and early May that year, nine were from 'fever' and complications, most of them elderly and children. The master, matron and porter bore the brunt of the extra work, as nobody else wished to become involved, but there are indications that people were cared for and comforted as much as possible – all three were later given a bonus. Of course, nobody had any idea what caused the disease. Windows were opened, walls were whitewashed, and, more usefully, rations were temporarily increased, with children given milk at breakfast. It was suggested that confinement in 'the House' did not help, and that inmates might be allowed more exercise outside.[TNA]

A schoolmistress, Mary Carpenter, was employed early in 1837 at 7*s* per week, and, early that summer, was instructed to take the children for exercise outside the workhouse for one hour a day, weather permitting. Children were taught reading, writing and arithmetic, with up to four hours a day in the schoolroom, and the necessary materials were purchased – this is many years before there was a legal compulsion to educate poor children, and there was a general feeling among many at this time that education did them no favours, giving them ideas and aspirations above their station. Later, in October that year, knives and forks were purchased specifically for the use of the children in the workhouse.

Windows were ordered to be repaired when broken or leaking, and left open at mealtimes for ventilation; bedsteads were repainted and covered with sacking, the heating system and the kitchen were maintained, a man was employed permanently in a janitorial/maintenance role.

In July 1842 there was a new initiative on getting the visiting committee working again, with a proposal that guardians living near each other should be selected, to ease travelling.[HRO] Visiting committee reports begin to reappear, with many complaints. The kitchens were dirty, paupers appeared idle, bedding was not folded properly and the porter's dog had been allowed into the schoolroom. The schoolmistress was reported for being 'disrespectful' and a 'disunion' between the staff was noted. There were worries about the 'good order and discipline' of the workhouse – things had slipped![HRO]

It is also worth noting that attendance of guardians at the board meetings became sporadic, with sometimes only three or four there, including the chairman and vice-chairman – harvests needed attending to, and the weather could be awful. Late in 1842, there was a reduction to only one truss of hay per week provided for the guardians' horses, which confirms this.[HRO] Under these circumstances, it can be assumed that the general conditions and care of the poor fell upon the chairman, William Sclater, who usually turned up, and who, fortunately for Basingstoke Union, seems to have been a reasonable and caring man.

Inmates were allowed six hours' absence a week to look for work, and to attend their parish church on Sundays (this was controlled, with withdrawal of the privilege for abuse), and there was an arrangement for the 'occasional absence of aged and infirm persons'.[HRO] This did not go down well with the PLC – it was against the spirit and idea of the workhouse – and there was some correspondence with the assistant commissioner, but it seems that nothing changed. In fact in many unions, it was common for the boards to quietly ignore the rulings of the PLC, for better or worse. where they did not fit into local practice. The PLC did not, after all, have any legal right of compulsion. It was pointed out to the PLC that the conditions in Basingstoke were 'not as elsewhere', and there was less danger of serious disappearances and abscondments, and they were requested to modify the rule. For example, in 1837, a PLC order was given that a visitors' book be obtained, and visits to the workhouse could only be allowed by ticket obtained from the guardians, at certain times and in the presence of the master. This was completely ignored by the board and nothing more was said – except that we know the visitors' book did become a fixture.

Life and death went on in the workhouse. There are many minutes relating to funerals paid for by the union, with funeral expenses from 1*s* for a baby to 12/6*d* for an adult, and there are tenders and quotations for elm coffins ('1 inch and pitched' specified in 1842) to be delivered to the workhouse in different sizes. The price in December 1836 was under 12 years, 8*s*; over 12 years, 12*s*. Also, a bier for the coffins was acquired. This purchase of coffins became a permanent regular tender for the workhouse and the parishes.[HRO]

There is a preconception that pauper funerals were stark and associated with mass burials in some parts of the country, but Hurren and King found that 'many nineteenth-century Poor Law officials recognized the customary and moral rights of the dependent poor to their perception of a "decent" funeral';[39] paupers were returned to their home parishes for burial at the expense of the union.

In the absence of other instructions, the clothes of deceased paupers were kept by the master for re-use:

Joseph Clark, July 1837, 'Funeral expenses 12/8d, clothing retained'.
Barbara Epes, September 1837, 'Deceased, leaving small items'.
Catherine Beckett, April 1838, 'Deceased, left 2 gowns, 1 underpetticoat, 1 old cloak'.
Lucy Hamsworth, April 1838, 'Deceased, left 1 frock, 1 upper and 1 under petticoat, 1 shift, pair stockings, 1 bonnet, delivered to child's mother, who asked for them'.[HRO]

Other individual items, such as bibles, were often passed to relatives.

BURIALS

Those inmates who died without any clear place of origin were buried in the local parish churchyard, St Mary's Church in Basing. A brief study of the Burial Register, which exists as a typed transcript from 1813 to 1875, shows the first workhouse funeral on 3 May 1837, Martha Page, an infant, 'of the Union Poor House'. Each page then shows several entries, simply labelled, 'Union', and the majority of them were for infants or the elderly.[40]

A midwife, Ruth Bunniston, was employed regularly by the union in the early days, her fees appearing in the minutes for several years; we will meet her again in Part 2. A note of names that appear can often reveal difficult stories. One typical example is that if Isaac Moody. In February 1841 he was allowed to leave the workhouse because his wife was ill; in April there was a midwifery charge of 7/6d for Mrs Moody, followed by the funeral, for 1s, of 'infant' Isaac Moody, and then for his mother, at a cost of 3/6d.[HRO]

Problems with Staff

The appointment and retention of workhouse staff was a problem, as was their co-operation with each other. Life was confined, veering between stress and tedium, with little spare time or facilities for leisure. Indeed, the staff were as confined and controlled as the inmates: 'they came to constitute a fraught community living together but remaining alone, sharing little except the exercise of power over a captive audience just as the master exercised power over them. Truly, they made the institution as they were made by it.'[41] Crowther puts it very well: 'under these monotonous conditions, surrounded by inmates whom it was their duty to discipline rather than to aid, the workhouse staff existed in a manner which awaits the pen of a Chekhov to describe.'[42]

In January 1838, the master and matron were called before the board and admonished. There are no specific details but it is suggested that discipline had become too lax. They resigned and a new couple were considered for appointment: John Cunningham and his wife, on the recommendation of Assistant Commissioner Hawley. Lacking any experience, Cunningham and his wife were sent to Andover Workhouse to assess what the job involved, and his subsequent letter to the guardians is telling:

> I saw sufficient at Andover to convince me that I could not perform the duties imposed on me as well as my wife being in a delicate state of health. You must get a strong, robust man and woman, and I think Mr McDougal would be most likely to obtain one from his old corps [the Artillery], as there are 3 or 4 Sergeants now about to be discharged.[TNA]

We should perhaps note that the master at Andover, Colin McDougal, was responsible for the bone breaking scandal in 1845 (see the 'Bone Crushing' section on p. 53), and also for numerous acts of cruelty and violence towards inmates.

William Duffy, a sergeant major in the Royal Artillery, and his wife, Margaret, applied for the posts of master and matron and their application was accepted. Since they had no experience, as with Cunningham, it was again 'ordered that they proceed to Andover for the purpose of inspecting and acquainting themselves with the state of that House and the system there pursued', expenses paid by the union.[HRO] They were to start work immediately, but they did not like what they found at Andover and they, too, cancelled their application the following week. A Mr Sutton and his wife were among the applicants for the posts, and they were contacted by the clerk with a proposal that they should start work in June 1838. We do not know whether they were sent to view Andover first. Meanwhile, Spier, the original master, complained about the uncertainty of his position, and asked for additional payment in respect of extra work arising from illness and fever in the workhouse.

Sutton's daughter, Charlotte, applied to be considered for the job of schoolmistress (Mary Carpenter had resigned through ill health) and was employed to teach the girls at a salary of £16 a year; it was to be understood that she would also teach boys for the time being, 'there being now but few and those very young'.[HRO]

In September 1838, porter William Grant was charged with 'gross misconduct towards some of the female children'. He was arrested and committed to trial on charge of 'carnally knowing and abusing Lucy Dibley and other inmates of the House, being a child between 10 and 12 years of age'.[HRO] He was sentenced to 18 months' imprisonment with hard labour – he had originally been appointed following the firing of his predecessor for drinking and absenteeism. His replacement, John Parsons, was also writing master for boys and girls, at a salary of £20 a year, but he resigned within two months.

When Master Sutton's wife died early in 1842 his daughter, Charlotte, was appointed matron after a failed attempt to find another woman, but this was deemed unsatisfactory by the PLC, in that the couple should be man and wife – so in April that year father and daughter 'resigned', although offering to stay until alternatives were appointed. He complained bitterly about his treatment to the PLC in a letter: '[I] request your attention to the way I have been treated … I have served nearly four years … not aware of any fault found with the manner I have conducted the business of this establishment … against my wish and inclination to give up a situation'.[TNA]

Sutton pointed out that there had been no complaints, and many favourable comments by visitors, and he requested compensation for the loss of his employment; the PLC merely concurred with the decision of the board. He continued to write to the PLC and the board, and in 1843 asked to be reconsidered for a position, having suffered with ill health in the north of England in the intervening period. He gives a written list of comments from the visitors to the workhouse, particularly the 'great and the good', by way of reference for his good work[TNA] (see the section 'Conclusion, the First Ten Years', p. 59).

Charlotte Sutton remained in post as schoolmistress but was deeply unhappy. She wrote to her father complaining of 'insults and indignities', along with constant interference. Both she and the porter, Samuel Winscome, resigned, due to 'insulting and unhandsome treatment' by the new master and matron.[TNA]

It is under new master James Ellis and his wife, Getty, that we see the only instance of corporal punishment of an inmate, of which more in Part 3. Ellis did not last long, and the couple were replaced later in 1843 by the Pulestons, Philip and Elizabeth.

There was a long catalogue of arguments and friction among the small workhouse staff. In October 1843 a bitter dispute appears in the record between the master and the schoolmistress, Mary Ann Collins. Many letters and statements from various people, including inmates, survive in TNA. They are particularly fascinating because they give a rare glimpse into the daily life of the workhouse: cleaning and maintenance, employment of children, procedures at mealtimes, distribution of clothing, and much more – the basic texts read like a Victorian novel.

Collins was eventually dismissed and the matron Elizabeth Puleston disappeared in November 1843, leaving her husband, who became drunk and frequently absent. A temporary matron was appointed and resigned within four months, and Philip Puleston was forced to resign in 1844. At this point the guardians were absolutely desperate, immediately appointing Mr and Mrs Waters from London – shortly thereafter Waters left the workhouse one evening and was eventually found drunk in the Castle Inn in Basingstoke. They were both put on a train back to London.[43]

Disharmony was continual and constant, often to the complete exasperation and annoyance of the board, particularly since things were often complicated by the interference of the PLC. Similar difficulties were found even in appointing and maintaining a chaplain.

This was not a happy place to live and work.

Work in the Workhouse

People in a workhouse were expected to work, and inmates were to provide any service that was required for the running of the house or to assist in its maintenance: gardening, laundry work, cooking and cleaning, groundwork, building maintenance, anything that was needed in a self-contained environment containing up to 300 people. Those who did not become involved in these activities were to do other work, even work of little value, on the principle that nobody was to be idle unless they were physically incapable.

Oakum picking first appears in the minute books in March 1837, the fire insurance being increased by 1s 'on account of oakum being picked'.[HRO] In August, the clerk was asked to ascertain whether a 'better price' for oakum could be obtained in the neighbourhood, followed by various communications with Messrs Van & Co., and the actual prices are mentioned. Oakum picking then seems to have lapsed, because, nine years later, when the board was looking again at additional occupation for paupers in 1846, it was reintroduced (see Part 2) and continued thereafter for decades.

There were further discussions about providing other useful work for the inmates, and in February 1838 Revd Harrison (guardian for Oakley) gave notice of a motion that the area around the workhouse, over 3 acres, should be cultivated, areas for exercise laid out and work sheds erected so that work was not done within the building itself.[HRO]

In May 1839, a pigsty was built under the direction of Mr Eaton and Mr Blatch (guardian for Nutley), a farmer.[HRO] In January 1840 pigs were purchased, five from William Turner for £2 7s 6d,[HRO] and similar numbers were then bought every three or four months. At this time salt was being bought by the hundredweight, and it can be assumed that this was used for preserving meat. By 1843 pig-keeping, breeding and trading was so successful – after all, there was plenty of agricultural knowledge among the inmates and officers – that it became a mainstay. Provisions for the pigs were included in regular tendered supplies.

A problem did occur in 1842 when seven of the pigs died, apparently from poisoning. A committee was formed to investigate (Sclater, Blunt, Curtis, Powell, Portsmouth, Hassell, Herriott – the names of these worthies indicates its importance), and authorised to liaise with the police and offer rewards for information. This turned out to be an overreaction when a vet's investigation revealed no evidence, and an iron furnace was installed in the pig house for boiling their food. A year later there was sickness in the workhouse, which was blamed on 'indifferent meat' caused by contaminated salting tubs.[HRO]

Baking bread within the workhouse was also an experiment for just over a year. In September 1840 It was considered to be a useful and economic exercise, and Charles Barton (a guardian for Basingstoke), a miller and baker, was brought in to set up the process. The master estimated a saving of £30 a year, and since the porter was supervising the actual baking, and having to acquire clothing for himself, he was paid £10 a year additional wages. This was not completely successful and a local baker, Mr Steer, offered to attend or send a 'competent man' for 5s a week.[HRO] The man did not carry through, however, turning up at odd hours or not at all and causing some inconvenience to everyone. The agreement was withdrawn. In December 1841 baking attempts in the workhouse ceased (the additional wage, of course, no longer paid to the porter).

OAKUM PICKING

This involved the unpicking of old used, tarred ship ropes (called 'junk' and usually made from hemp) into separate fibres which could be sold on and used for other purposes, ship caulking, building, plumbing insulation and the like – hence the phrase, 'money for old rope'. It was one of the universal tasks of inmates of workhouses and prisons throughout the country, the commonly used phrase 'on the spike', meaning a stay in the workhouse, deriving from the use of a metal spike to split the thick ropes. It does not take too much imagination to see that this would be dirty and hard on the hands, and, more importantly for the workhouse system, time-consuming and tedious. It was also work that could be done while sitting by the elderly and less able-bodied.

Brewing beer worked better. The necessary equipment was purchased in December 1840 and, again, the porter was offered supervision duties for £13 a year. This arrangement continued until September 1842, when a brewer, Frances Cullum, was brought in to run the brewery for 1s for each bushel of malt used. This continued for a year or two, since malt and hops became part of the regular supplies.

Bone Crushing and the Andover Scandal

The most controversial work, as it turned out, was bone crushing. This had become a mainstay of many rural workhouses, since the end result could be sold as farm fertiliser at a considerable profit. It is difficult, without the accounts, to track the financial progress of this lucrative venture, but conclusions can be drawn from the minutes.

In June 1840 Basingstoke investigated the purchase of the necessary equipment. Initially, two bone boxes were bought, and by November it was necessary to build a shed and other buildings for crushing and storing bones and dust, at a cost of £2 13s. Bones were acquired by Master Sutton at £5 to £10 a load. At first he was also selling the dust for about 6/6d per cwt, the first major sales yielding a total of about £26. In 1841 the bone shed fell down and needed to be shored up.

By early 1842, the throughput of bones had dramatically increased. With a direct supplier being used, Messrs Bower & Co., the total cost in February was nearly £20, and continued at a similar rate, with additional costs for carriage. The quantity of bones processed and dust produced quickly moved into tons – in February 1843, ten tons of bones were bought, and many of the guardians bought quantities of dust for their farms at a price of £4 per cwt. Later that year a further ten breaking boxes were ordered, and the dust was advertised for sale locally and by tender in the national press, with an expected yield of £80 per ton.[HRO] It was an incredibly profitable business.

Bone crushing in Basingstoke Workhouse was now strictly quantified and regulated: '1cwt 14lb of bones to be broken by every able-bodied pauper in the Workhouse between 20 and 45 years of age, 16 to 20 years of age at the discretion of the Master, but no such pauper to break less than half a cwt or more than 1cwt.'[HRO] Unsurprisingly this met with resistance, with inmates refusing to work – Charles Hunt, for example, was ordered to appear before the magistrate if he continued to refuse, and he was not the only one.

> **BONE CRUSHING**
>
> This was done by hand, with a crushing rod, either iron or with an iron tip, in a box made of wood and iron-bound for strength.[44] The worker would stand and crush the bones by hand, which would have been very hard on the hands and back, and he or she would have been splattered with debris and dust. The bones were crushed to a consistency to pass through a sieve. They would be from any animal, including humans, and were not always fresh or dry, which made the job even more disgusting.

There were genuine concerns. There was a suggestion from David Bransby (a guardian for Basingstoke for three years) to substitute gypsum for bones, and there were increasingly concerned letters from the PLC regarding hygiene, ventilation and adequate facilities. Longmate reports on evidence given by the local assistant commissioner, Henry Parker, relating to an outbreak of fever in Basingstoke, thought to be due to the handling of old bones: there were, he explained, 'bones and bones' … that is, 'bones of commerce', which were boiled to make soup or soap, before being dried and pulverised, and 'green bones' straight from slaughterhouses and kitchens, which still contained marrow and had fragments of meat clinging to them. The crushing of the latter sort of bones in workhouses should, he suggested, be banned, or else be done in an enclosed mill and not by hand.[45]

All this came to a halt with the infamous Andover Scandal. In August 1845, Henry Parker, on a visit to Andover Workhouse, found the rumours of hungry inmates picking and chewing the bones for food to be true, in addition to other incidents of exceptional cruelty and degradation perpetrated by the master. There was a huge national outcry, of which more in Part 2 – England was upset. The best description of actual bone crushing at Andover comes from a parliamentary debate reported in Hansard:

> Mr. Mundy stated, upon oath, that, accompanied by two guardians and medical men, he examined ten paupers; all, with the exception of two, admitted that they were constantly in the habit of eating the marrow and gristle from the bones. They eat it from old bones, meaning those that had some moisture remaining in them, but still were in a state of decomposition; and some had been in heaps two or three months – they eat it from these as well as from the fresh ones … though it was supposed to be the principle of the Andover Union that dry bones alone should be crushed, yet there was no instance on record where fresh and clean bones were furnished, whether received from a distance or collected in Andover and the adjoining villages. When a beef bone, or chine bone, was turned out of the heap, there was a scramble for it, described like a parcel of dogs, and the man who got it was obliged to run away and hide it until he had an opportunity of eating the marrow. One man fetched two bones, which he had eaten that very morning in wet ashes; a portion of muscle very offensive was adhering to the ends of the bone. The men said that it was a considerable time before they could make up their minds to do so, but after they had once taken to it they preferred that description of labour to any other, because they could get bones to pick.

Mr Mundy is described as a guardian and magistrate.[46]

In the same debate it was stated that old bones from a renovated churchyard were sold to Andover Workhouse, and that part of a human skeleton was suspended in the yard. We do not know whether any of the bones crushed in Basingstoke were not animal, but we do know that the process was inspected and regulated, and the inmates were not starving – this is the difference.

John Arlott, in an interesting article in *Hampshire* magazine, wrote that Revd Christopher Dodson, the chairman of the Andover Board of Guardians, was 'the worst type of sin-detecting, sharp-tongued, autocratic 19th century parson. He was stubborn and a bully ... most damagingly of all, he refused to admit error when he made a bad appointment'.[47] This is an excellent example of how the people in charge of a union could affect its whole ethos and function, and the quality of provision for the poor. An exhaustive and fascinating description of the whole affair is given in Ian Anstruther's book *The Scandal of Andover Workhouse* (see the Sources section on p. 181).

The Andover Scandal led to the complete banning by the PLC of all bone crushing in November 1845, a practice being used by 200 unions in England at the time.[48]

In Maintenance and Out Relief: Some Numbers

Analysis of the figures given week by week in the minute books in this early period, in conjunction with occasional statements in correspondence and returns to the PLC, enables us to draw some interesting conclusions.

The first indication of numbers of inmates in the workhouse is a letter to the PLC in December 1836 reporting only one able-bodied pauper in the workhouse, a man of 26, and his two young children.[TNA] As mentioned above, there was no fixed number of people in the workhouse – many of them came and went with seasonal variations in agricultural work, often for a brief period of relief when times were particularly hard, and often only parts of families, the children or the elderly, to provide a small safety valve for very challenged incomes. And there is no doubt that over the years the poor learned to play the system very effectively.

It is interesting to note that in January 1839, the accumulations of chalk round the workhouse building site could not be cleared, because there were not enough able-bodied inmates available, and the job had to be contracted out. Previously, in the early summer of 1838, there was a temporary delay in appointing a school-mistress, since there were not enough children to warrant the cost.[HRO]

In the years between 1837 and 1840, accurate quarterly in maintenance tables, showing number of paupers by parish, number of 'pauper days' and cost were written in the minutes. This also gives us a fairly accurate assessment of cost of about 6*d* per day for food and clothing. During these years, the average number of inmates rose from 86 to 159. In the June 1841 census, there were 130.

A return to the PLC in February 1842 gives a total number of inmates of 181. Ninety-four (or 52 per cent) of them were children under 16,[TNA] once again

indicating the common practice of putting 'extra mouths' in the workhouse to
help out during a difficult period. At the same time, a report by medical officer
Edward Covey suggested that the total population should not exceed 230, 'inclusive
of double and a few treble beds for girls and boys'. He also stated that 'there is general
illness at present prevailing. The children do not continue long in a state of good
health. The schoolroom is densely crowded and <u>very inefficiently ventilated</u> [his
underlining]. The ventilation throughout the House is insufficient and irregular'.[TNA]

From 1841, we only get the cost (by parish) in the minutes, but we can work out
an estimate of the number of 'pauper days' – hence the number of paupers – using
this rough calculation: the average number of inmates in the workhouse in 1845
had risen to nearly 200. There were peaks in the difficult months, January to March,
and a record number was reported to the PLC in 1843 of 254, half of them being
children.[TNA] Extra bedding had been provided and space appropriated for a new
'day room'. The steady cost of in maintenance is indicated in the graph.

The other side of the equation is out relief. Each week, the three totals by district
paid in out relief are given in the minutes, allowing us to calculate the cost paid out
in cash over the period. This does not include payment in bread and flour, since
this is not comprehensively entered into the minutes except for a brief period from
1848. However, we can see trends, and there is very little change, and certainly no
decrease, which should have happened if the poor were all being tidied away into
the workhouse.

Fig.7   In Maintenance and Out Relief costs, 1837 to 1845.

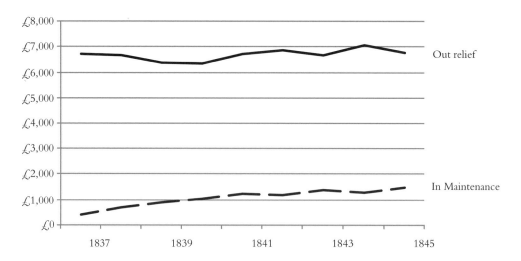

Our Basingstoke figures do not tie in with the statistics given by the PLC of a 22 per cent drop in the overall national cost of poor relief, from £6.3m to £4.9m between 1834 and 1845.[49] We can fairly safely assume that, with the workhouse rarely filled to capacity, the Basingstoke guardians were willing to support many of the poor in the community.

The 1841 PLC's 'General Order for the Prohibition of Outdoor Relief' caused consternation, protest and argument among the members of the Basingstoke board, and then it was effectively ignored. The PLC, and its successors, attempted this prohibition periodically in subsequent years, with the same result on the ground – it was harsh and impractical. Most of the modern books and articles about the Poor Law system indicate that this was the case in nearly all other unions throughout the country.

> The principal unions in the agricultural counties of Berkshire, Buckinghamshire, Hertfordshire, Kent, and Middlesex; from which it will appear that in that quarter, the aggregate number of persons who received relief within the walls of the workhouses of those unions was 8,349 whilst the number who received out of door relief was 39,894; showing that the proportion of those relieved in the workhouses, as compared with those who received relief out of the workhouses, was only as one to five ... to the sick, the aged, and the infirm, relief is now given in an immense proportion – in the proportion of five out of six out of doors, I contend, that even with respect to the able-bodied, relief in the workhouses is the exception, and not the rule ... In-door relief is the test applied to see whether the wants of the applicant are really great, and whether the complaint of want of work and employment is not merely a pretence. It is resorted to as a mode of ascertaining the truth as to the real condition of the party applying for relief.[50]

In Basingstoke, an average annual amount of about £6,500 in cash payments was roughly maintained over the period. If we consider that a typical claimant was receiving a couple of shillings (and a few loaves of bread) and the total payout weekly was about £130, this amounts to several hundred claimants.

The totals, too, are absolutely consistent when taken seasonally; when averaged in Fig.8 they show no surprises as to what time of year was the most difficult for the poor.

The other interesting information which can be drawn from the minute books is the entry starting in October 1840 of a weekly listing of 'Out Relief Special Cases'. This listing was stopped a couple of years later, for no apparent reason. There are too many names to give here, but a six-month analysis reveals that they were nearly always the temporarily sick. Sometimes there are only a couple of names and sometimes three pages, but one can see the ebb and flow of minor epidemics of measles, whooping cough, colds and influenza, as well as consumption (tuberculosis) and more serious problems. There were also injuries and infections.

Fig. 8   Average seasonal Out Relief costs, 1836 to 1845.

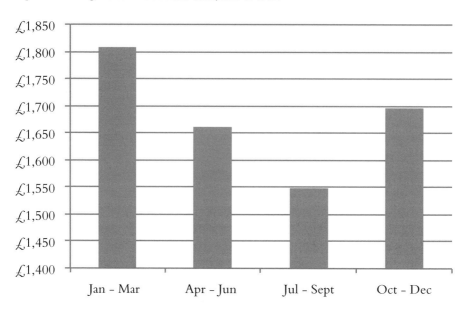

The terms 'fever' and 'debility' predominate throughout, and is it likely that some of this was due to general malaise from bad diet and living conditions, and some of it was possibly malaria.

The Union Outside the Workhouse

Of course, each union itself became a significant organisation in local affairs. It was increasingly involved in medical services, maintaining land valuation and statistical information and controlling local rates. It took over functions previously per-formed by the justices and other local bodies, and new ones were created. The Poor Law Union was a new, powerful administrative body, inserted between the parish and the county and becoming immensely useful to central government.

In September 1837, the Basingstoke minutes begin to describe the process of professional surveying and valuation of parishes for the purposes of assessing the rates, often with accurate maps prepared. This was paid for by the union, with most of the work going to Thomas Hasker of Messrs Hasker & Cousins, often from £50 to £100 per parish, sometimes more. The PLC suggested using one firm of surveyors, for the purposes of uniformity. There is, again, a considerable amount of correspondence in TNA detailing this process, which goes on for months.

Many people were unable to pay the rates on grounds of poverty, and had to be officially exempted by a magistrate. This became a weekly entry in the minute books from 1838, often about twenty or thirty people – in April that year 272 persons in Basingstoke parish alone. Collectors of rates began to be appointed in various parishes in 1838; the parishes had to agree, and there was some resistance.

The 1840 Vaccination Act made vaccination against smallpox freely available to poor people, funded by the union, making this effectively the first free organised health service. Basingstoke Union, following instructions from the PLC, accordingly negotiated and entered into tenders with their medical officers for this to be done, and vaccination notices were posted in every parish and issued for every child baptised and registered. The initial cost was 1/6d per person, which rose to 2/6d in 1844, and all these transactions were minuted. The doctors were not required to attend each house, but were to arrange for paupers to collect in convenient places for this to be done.

The 1836 Births, Deaths and Marriages Registration Act required the appointing of local deputy registrars and acquiring offices for them, which was the responsibility of unions, and this process in Basingstoke is minuted over the ensuing period. Payments of registration fees for births and deaths of paupers appear in the minutes, along with notices of marriages (only the middle-class ones) which were read at board meetings three times.

The *12th Annual Report of the Poor Law Commission* gives expenditure returns for the year ended March 1845, and shows Basingstoke Union as having received £13,300 in income and having spent 83 per cent of it, or £11,000, in direct relief of the poor in the area, including medical expenses.

Conclusion: the First Ten Years

The overall impression on researching these early years is that Basingstoke Workhouse was a comparatively humane and well-run establishment, in terms of Victorian morality and customs, and the union's dealings with local poverty were usually sympathetic to the poor; they did what they could, what they thought best, under a harsh and restrictive system.

In a request for a reference from the guardians, Master Thomas Sutton, whom we met earlier, included extracts from comments in the visitors' book between 1839 and 1842. Although these entries are undoubtedly selective, they are telling, particularly those from visitors from outside the union:

- John Colvin, Ludlow Union (1840): 'Inspected this House to see the arrangements that I might compare them with the Union to which I belong. All I have seen here is very satisfactory shewing great attention to cleanliness and the comfort of the inmates.'
- Lord Northampton (1840): 'Was much pleased with the order, cleanliness and regularity which I observed in it and the good behaviour of the Children at School.'
- Edward Ashley, Staines (1841): 'Having been very politely conducted through the … departments of this establishment by Mr Sutton I cannot leave without

recording my satisfaction at the general good order and comfort witnessed here and was much pleased with the school children considering the advantage they derive.'

- Duke of Wellington (1841): 'I was much pleased to find ... in such good order and so comfortable arranged for accommodation of its inmates the provisions which I saw were excellent of their kind. I heard of no complaints.'
- T.R. Sheppardson, Vicar from Northumberland (1842): 'I visited this Union for the purpose of comparing it with the workhouses of the North of England. In every thing very superior, cleanliness great, the inmates appearing happy and contented, and the children exceedingly well-taught and clothed.'[TNA]

Though the New Poor Law may have been considered cruel by many of the poor and a few well-to-do sympathizers, it is difficult to detect a conscious intention of this among those charged with implementing the statute. Few guardians set out to grind the faces of the poor – their concern was to strengthen the social fabric of the countryside, in as cheap and efficient way as possible. If this task often seemed to require the adoption of a harsh line, it was sometimes manifested in benevolent attitudes and policies.[51]

Part 2

Consolidation, 1846 to 1871

Moving on From the Early Years

The next period takes us from the end of the PLC, through the years of the Poor Law Board (PLB) to 1871, when it was absorbed into the new Local Government Board (LGB), of which more later.

Between the first minutes in 1835 and a return of medical districts in 1860, the population of the Basingstoke Union only increased by about 1,400, half of this in the town of Basingstoke itself.[TNA] In a rural area, the huge urban upheavals of the industrial revolution and urbanisation taking place in the rest of Britain largely passed it by for the time being, although it was becoming a thriving and important market town with the coming of the railway, and local trade and industrial activity were increasing.

This period for the Basingstoke Union and its workhouse is one of consolidation, and one gets the feeling that the organisation, and the workhouse, had settled into its role. We will deal with the history of the union and workhouse over the next twenty-five years by looking at each aspect of its life, the building, conditions for inmates, schooling, sickness and the provision of out relief, staffing matters, plus the gradual shift into the role of an early local government authority.

The PLC was in its last days in 1846. As well as internal unrest, squabbling and political intrigue within the Commission itself, there was the problem of bone crushing and the shocking, highly publicised conditions at Andover, which had become symbolic of all that could be cruel and oppressive in the workhouse system. Complaints were made by individual paupers and members of the public, and even the Home Secretary himself, Sir James Graham, 'disapproved of that mode of employing the poor'.[1] The result was a Select Committee in parliament in March 1846, which ultimately led to the workings and conduct of the PLC being examined, and heads inevitably rolled. The overworked assistant commissioner for the Andover area, Henry Parker, became the scapegoat and was forced to resign.[2] The vicious master, Colin McDougal, was forced to resign, too, but the tyrannical and bullying chairman, Revd Christopher Dodson, stayed in post for many more years, because they could not find anyone else to take the job.

The end of the PLC came in 1847, when it was disbanded and replaced by the Poor Law Board (PLB), which consisted mostly of Members of Parliament, and therefore had more legal control and responsibility, ostensibly with greater public involvement, although many MPs saw the changes as merely cosmetic. The same people were effectively in charge and there was little fundamental change in the system for several years. However, there was more control and oversight, which made overt abuse less likely, and conditions for inmates everywhere were more consistent.

There are some interesting comments in the parliamentary debates in 1847 relating to the change in Poor Law administration, and it is very clear that the whole system was unpopular and a subject of intense and sometimes vitriolic controversy. Ralph Etwall MP stated his opinion that he was 'satisfied that there was something so rotten in the present Poor Law, that, however it might be carried out … it would never be administered satisfactorily … for the benefit of those for whose relief it was intended'.[3]

William Ferrand, MP for Knaresborough, pointed out that the Poor Law had created a huge bureaucracy, in which only one eighth of relief was administered in the new workhouses, and '590 unions, 590 masters of workhouses, 590 schoolmasters, nearly 2,000 relieving officers, and probably 3,000 medical officers; then there were 590 clerks to the boards of guardians'; all now were subservient in their offices to central government. He stated that women were sometimes drowning their new-born babies and passing them off as stillborn to escape their being taken into the workhouse, that elderly people were often imprisoned in their quarters on meagre rations at the mercy of 'some sergeant of dragoons or discharged soldier'. He had himself visited a workhouse where the master had increased rations when he saw the poor becoming weakened, without informing the authorities. He described a poor woman living just over the official boundary of her parish and being refused help by a relieving officer who was strictly applying the regulations – she starved to death.[4]

Returning to Basingstoke and its records, there were changes in the format of the minutes from 1848, with the new regime. This format was prescribed by the PLB and thereafter remained fundamentally the same, with only minor differences, for the next sixty years. There were changes in accounting and reporting, indicated in the minutes, but we do not have these documents. As would be expected, hand-writing changes periodically, and sometimes there is one hand for routine matters and another, possibly the clerk himself, for other notes. The type of content also changes from time to time, with periods of more details and naming of individual paupers, events and decisions, contrasted with periods of basic, dry minutes, which is frustrating. It is often confusing to follow through exactly what was happening. There is little here relating to day-to-day life inside or outside the workhouse until the reports of the visiting committee begin to appear in the minutes in early 1871 (see p. 104), but only for a time.

The prescribed format for the minutes was as follows, and shows the variety of matters now being administered by the board:

- 'Examination of Books' and financial matters: relieving officers' out relief payments, and the supporting cheques paid to them. The master's estimate of ongoing expenses, often followed by note of a 'balance in the Treasurer's hands this day'.
- 'Other Business': various items such as notices of marriage at the registry office, general cheques made out to suppliers – mostly provisions, expenses, vaccination costs, adverts for staff, payments to casual staff and so on. Also regular payments and receipts involving other unions relating to paupers living outside Basingstoke, or outside paupers being supported here, and payments to lunatic asylums and hospital donations.
- Tenders for goods and services were listed quarterly, along with estimates for local rates and details of 'nuisances'.

Only after all this, or slight variations thereof for every meeting, are there occasional specific and different items. Frustratingly, complex receipts and payments of money are impossible to follow without the supporting documents.

However, from 1847, in the MH 12 archive at TNA, and roughly every six months, are stored the official PLB inspectors' reports. While fairly brief and dry, they are very revealing about what was going on; comments were entered on a pre-printed form with set questions indicating comprehensive standardisation in care and oversight.

The role of assistant commissioner changed to that of inspector and Mr Piggott was the first inspector from 1847. He was followed by Lord William Reginald Courtenay (11th Earl of Devon), who performed this task for the next two years, until he became secretary of the PLB in 1850; seventeen years later he became its president. The next inspector was former assistant commissioner W.H.T. Hawley, a man of privileged background, who had been part of the system since the beginning; he served until 1874.

The system became even more bureaucratic with reports and returns on a range of matters such as the care of lunatics, vaccination, orders for school books and so on in addition to reams of correspondence. Unfortunately, although there are many enclosing letters for such documents, including financial and statistical statements, most of the enclosures are not there, undoubtedly filed elsewhere and lost. There are many hundreds of letters from the board of guardians to the PLB, requesting sanction for relief in various forms, sometimes involving people under the most difficult of circumstances, to whom great sympathy and support was shown; this was often

INSPECTION REPORT QUESTIONS

To be answered by Inspector in 1860 (Revised Form H&G 1000 11/59)

1. Date of last previous visit.
2. Is the Workhouse generally adequate to the wants of the Union, in respect of size and internal arrangement?
3. Is the provision for the sick and/or infectious cases sufficient?
4. Are the receiving wards in a proper state?
5. Is the Workhouse School well managed? Insert a copy of any entry in the visiting Committee's or other book, made since your last visit, by an Inspector of Schools.
6. What is the number of inmates in the Workhouse not in communion with the Church of England, and what arrangements, if any, exist for affording them the religious consolation and instruction of ministers of their own separate persuasion?
7. Are the provisions of the 19th Section of the Act of the 4 & 5 Wm. IV. c.76, duly and systematically observed in the management of the Workhouse? [Note: this relates to vagrants]
8. Are there vagrant wards in the Workhouse, and are they sufficient? Are the arrangements for setting the vagrants to work effective, and is the resolution of the Guardians under 5 and 6 Vict., c.57, Sec.5, duly observed?
9. Does the Visiting Committee regularly inspect the Workhouse? Do any of their answers to the queries in the Workhouse regulations suggest the propriety of any interference on the part of the Commissioners? Insert a copy of any entry made since your last visit in the visiting Committee's book, or other report book, by a Commissioner in Lunacy.
10. Has the maximum number of inmates in the Workhouse, fixed by the Commissioners, been constantly observed since your last visit?
11. Are the proper extracts from the Poor Law Amendment Act, and the Regulations of the Commissioners, hung up in the Workhouse?
12. Have all appointments of new officers, and changes in salaries and districts, since your last visit, been reported to the Commissioners?
13. Is there any officer whose appointment has been sanctioned provisionally? If so, state your opinion of his fitness.
14. Have you any reason to believe that any of the books or accounts prescribed by the Commissioners are not properly kept?
15. Have you observed any illegal practice, or any departure from the Regulations of the Commissioners?
16. State whether the terms of the Contracts for Vaccination are generally fulfilled, and whether there is any defect in the Vaccination arrangements, upon which you think it desirable that the Board should communicate with the Guardians.
17. Has any marked change taken place in the state of the Workhouse, the number of inmates, or the general condition of the Union, since your last visit?
18. Observations not falling under any of the preceding heads, and points (if any) upon which it is suggested that the Board should communicate with the Guardians.

unrequited by the PLB, who seemed intent on expending as little money and effort as possible. Their lack of sensibility often led to their decisions being ignored by the guardians – with criticism from the auditor later – but assistance was given anyway:

* James Hussey, whose wife died giving birth to twins in 1853. Although he was earning 10/- a week, the guardians applied for sanction for 5*s* a week for a nurse, so that he could work. Unhelpful note in MH 12, the signature unclear: 'I object if this application is, I presume, to enable this pauper to obtain a nurse for the 2 infants, and it does not appear whether he is to support such nurse or whether he is to find his own livelihood out of the 5/- proposed to be granted. It further does not appear whether the infants are to be farmed out for [?] ... if so it will be placing the man (who earns the regular wages of the District) in a better position than other labourers who have a wife and four or five or more children to keep out of the same means – I think these points should be explained before the relief is sanctioned.'
A grant of 6*s* a week was subsequently made by the guardians.
* In 1861, Elizabeth Hall, a widow with several children, was returned by Battersea Union to her home in Steventon. The guardians overrode a PLB decision and paid relief to her in order to keep the family together and out of the workhouse.

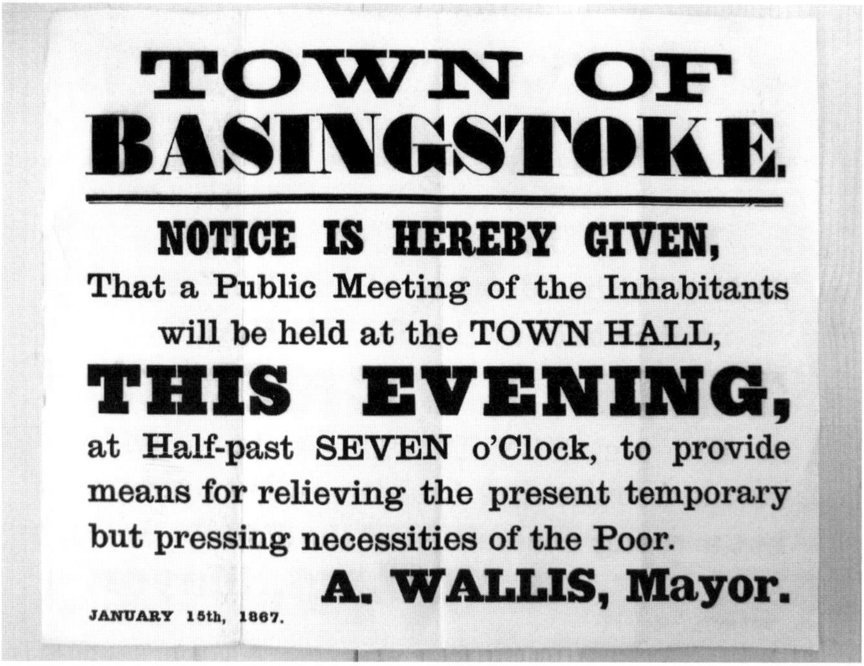

TOWN OF BASINGSTOKE.

NOTICE IS HEREBY GIVEN,

That a Public Meeting of the Inhabitants will be held at the TOWN HALL,

THIS EVENING,

at Half-past SEVEN o'Clock, to provide means for relieving the present temporary but pressing necessities of the Poor.

A. WALLIS, Mayor.

JANUARY 15th, 1867.

Fig. 9   Notice of Public Meeting for the Relief of the Poor, Basingstoke, 15 January 1867. (HRO 10M57/Z76)

The Board of Guardians in Basingstoke was so exasperated with the PLB in July 1860 that chairman Sclater presented a petition to the House of Commons 'against a continuance of the present powers of the Poor Law Board beyond the period of one year'.[TNA]

The people of Basingstoke seemed sympathetic to their poor. During unusually severe weather in January 1867, there was a sudden distressing increase in people struggling to survive, many of them out of work. The mayor, Arthur Wallis, called a meeting at which a 'public subscription' was opened under the control of the leading citizens in the town. Donations of £90 were received, handbills were distributed and the town crier called desperate poor to the town hall on the two following evenings. Relief was given by ticket for food, fuel and clothing and it was estimated that 400 families received help. To quote the newspaper report: 'it is highly creditable to the public spirit and liberal benevolence of the inhabitants of this little town that so large a sum … should be collected and dispersed in two days'.[5]

Basingstoke Poor Law Conference, 1870

In February 1870 an important Poor Law Conference, lasting seven hours, was held in the town hall in Basingstoke and was attended by about 100 officers of various unions in Hampshire and Berkshire. It was organised by Sir Wyndam Spencer Portal, who 'knew very well the difficulties there were in the administration of the Poor Law Relief' and who called the meeting with a view to 'devising the best measures for improving the present system'[6], in the hope that communication between boards would increase the consistency of approach. He remarked that for a time nationally out relief was reduced but that it seemed to be returning to previous levels, due to the practice of using relief to support low wages, and poor people applying for relief 'on every petty occasion' rather than when they were experiencing genuine hardship. He had apparently attended several such meetings across the country and they had been found useful.

There were 'about 50' chairmen and vice-chairmen present, with Sir Michael Hicks Beech MP, of Oakley Hall, and Inspector of Workhouse Schools, T. Carleton Tufnell.

WYNDHAM SPENCER PORTAL

Wyndham Spencer Portal, a member of the influential Basingstoke family of banknote paper manufacturers, became 1st Baronet Portal of Malshanger House, Hampshire in 1901. He was a captain in the Hampshire Yeomanry, chairman of London and South Western Railway and deputy lieutenant for Hampshire, also a JP and an MP. He was educated at Harrow and RMC Sandhurst. He frequently stood in as chairman in the later years of William Sclater, before Sir Nelson Rycroft was elected, and appears throughout the records. He was actively involved in poor relief all his life and wrote an interesting, temperance-inspired pamphlet in 1869 about the conditions and treatment of the poor, which is held in the Hampshire Archives.[7]

Fig. 10 Sir Wyndham Spencer Portal, 1st Baronet (1822–1905).[8]

In addition to Portal, the other Basingstoke people attending were Sir Nelson Rycroft as chairman, the vice-chairman, the clerk, two of the relieving officers and two medical officers, and the master, Mr Humby. William Sclater also attended; he was evidently still interested, although he had retired as chairman that April. There were also several Basingstoke guardians present. Four subjects were covered: 'The Training of Pauper Children', 'Vagrancy', 'Out-Door Relief' and 'The Internal Management of Workhouses'. This important conference was extensively covered in the *Reading Mercury*, the *Oxford Gazette*, the *Newbury Herald* and the *Berkshire County Paper*, some of which are available online in the British Newspaper Archive Online. They make fascinating reading with a good indication of attitudes towards the poor and the system at the time, and comments and extracts will be included in the various subjects below.

Fig. 11 Sir Nelson Rycroft (1831–1914), 4th Baronet of Kempshott Park and Dummer House, County Magistrate for the Basingstoke Division and a JP. Chairman of Board of Guardians 1870 to 1885.[9]

Some of the most telling comments came from Revd J.G. Joyce, guardian of Statfieldsaye: 'In treating of the internal management of workhouses we are bound to recognise at starting how grave a subject we enter upon. It has long been an acknowledged blot in English life'. He pointed out that 'inmates of the house are infinitely more at our mercy'. Since he was one of the major speakers at the conference, it can be assumed that he was expressing the general attitude and views of many within Basingstoke Union administration.

He spoke critically about the fundamental difference between relief outside and within the workhouse:

> Recipients of relief out of doors have homes of their own, frequently have occupations … and they have opportunities for some little diversion of thought and exercise of feeling amongst relations or friends. The case of inmates is totally different; their only home is the house. Many are there only to die; many are in incessant suffering. None are masters of themselves, but are … under strict rule, and under the eyes of many masters. Many are in helpless childhood, and will pass the life of childhood without love – will never know a mother's caress or a father's fondling – will grow to maturity with no ideas of right or wrong, no habits of thought, no notions of happiness or misery, except such as they have drawn from the Workhouse.

He also remarked that 'there is a constant desire to show good-will towards the inmates, but the Boards are checked by many things'.

The Workhouse Changes

In August 1847, significant work on the building was undertaken following an inspection report: 'that a separate Infirmary be erected under the superintendence of a Committee … for reception and treatment of the sick and other useful purposes'. It was noted that no vagrant wards were available. Vagrants, for the time being, were provided for in the town (see p. 72). Increased accommodation was also recommended: 'this is one of the regions in which cottage accommodation has not increased with the population & during this winter several persons have been obliged to come to the Workhouse for want of house room'.[TNA]

Infirmary provision and the accommodation of vagrants would continue to be major items of discussion at the guardians' meetings for many years. The work was financed by an additional Exchequer loan of £2,000 and tenders were invited in the usual way, being won by a Mr Gover of Winchester, the only provision being that the clerk of works was to be employed by the board and not the contractor.

Other work was done at the same time as the new vagrant and probationary wards – improvements to the schoolrooms and infirmary, the laundry and wash-house, two new play yards for the children and a large room specifically for dinner service. There is little detail in the minutes, and we do not have plans of these works, but the above alterations appear in a visiting report by the inspecting commissioner, Mr Pigott, in 1848, the work having been recently completed.[TNA]

His report was favourable: 'the discipline, order… & health of this Workhouse … incalculably improved … by means of the recent additions … especially of School Rooms and an Infirmary for 40 beds'. On his inspection day, there were 426 inmates in the workhouse (an unusually high number), of whom forty were in the infirmary and eighteen were vagrants. He remarked that the officers' apartments, day rooms and receiving wards were 'liberally provided', and there were now 'two capacious rooms', one for meals 'and the other reserved for religious worship'.[TNA]

In March the following year, Lord Courtenay's inspection comments were mixed. He remarked that the tailors' and shoemakers' shops were very cramped and that the female receiving ward was being used 'temporarily for the dead', which was to be discontinued immediately.[TNA]

In 1856, we have the first relatively detailed description of the internal organisation of the building with an accommodation return in TNA, with sizes of rooms and numbers, but no plan. Each of the four adult categories of inmate – young and elderly men, young and elderly women – were designated as having a room for day occupation and three rooms for sleeping, four in all. These rooms were 30ft by 17ft, and there are notes that the day rooms were mostly unoccupied, as one would expect with the inmates being at work. The day rooms were assessed as being able to hold about thirty people, with each dormitory holding about sixteen.

Boys and girls, separately, had a schoolroom and a couple of dormitories, of similar size to the rooms above, with the schoolrooms themselves able to accommodate forty pupils in each. There were three male and three female infirmaries, of which more later. Unfortunately, we do not have details of any of the other rooms. Diagrams of the floor layouts may be found in Appendix II.

Various other works were carried out over the period in addition to regular painting and plumbing repairs, as would be expected in a building now several years old and in heavy use – space was a constant challenge. There was an ongoing battle with damp walls. We do get some indication from the minutes of what was going on and general conditions, and here is a selection:

- Works to update the hot water system, new floors in the Mill Room and baths lined with 'thin lead sheet' (1847). There was also a proposal to install a tank for 'refuse' water instead of a 'drain across the road'.
- Pipe to the 'steam engine' installed (it is not clear where this was) (1848).
- New pigsties built, and the establishment of a new Committee for Cultivation to deal with farming matters (1852).
- Works to the cesspool (which was overflowing into the boys' yard) and increased division between inmates and vagrants (1856), followed by maintenance of palisades on walls two years later.
- Wash house and laundry erected for girls, at a cost of £39 10s – 'it will prove to be of essential service to the girls when they leave the House and take situations' (1857).
- Walls between able-bodied men and vagrants increased to 6ft and topped with glass (1859) and upgrades to existing fences and palisades – this so that 'small articles only can be introduced between the palisades'. Strict separation was to be maintained: 'there is no doubt the present fence presents the opportunity of conversation between the boys and adult inmates at work in the Garden … the adults employed in the garden are generally old men set to perform light work.'
- '15 feet of new building to the boys' school for the purpose of enlarging it', at a cost of £59 5s (1859).
- Privies provided in each ward (1868), followed the next year by a trial of 'Moule's Earth Closets', which were later approved and installed.
- Purchase of new kitchen range and scullery furnace (1870).

There were also a couple of relatively expensive purchases of equipment: new and innovative laundry machines, 'Thomas Bradford's Washing & Wringing Machines', at a cost of £14 16s 4d, and a new copper furnace for £4 2s 6d, both in 1866.

Outside the building itself, of course, there was the land allocated for agricultural use. From a letter to the PLB in 1869:

> The Guardians … have for several years past, rented about 5 acres and 2 rods of land adjoining the Workhouse, the greater part of which has been used as garden land, cultivated by the Paupers, the produce being consumed by the Inmates. A very small strip is meadow and in this is [kept] a cow … which supplies the Inmates with milk. The land will be sold by auction <u>on the 4th January next</u> [their underlining], and as it is most valuable for the purpose of the Workhouse, I am directed to ask the favour of an opinion from the Poor Law Board whether the Guardians have [legal] power … to purchase, and if so, from what fund the purchase money can be raised.

There is a plan of the land, directly to the west of the building, in TNA together with the sale notice, one of several lots being sold in the town that day.

This became, as usual, fraught with complexity, and in the end Lord Bolton stepped in, bought the land and rented it back to the union at the previous rent. In their usual way, the PLB requested all kinds of orders and undertakings, which the guardians did not pursue, since Lord Bolton had 'behaved so handsomely' they felt 'reluctant to ask any further favour of His Lordship', particularly since they could now rent the land indefinitely.

In March 1871 there were seventy-three children being educated, and at that time there was much enlargement of the girls' and boys' sleeping accommodation, along with increases in the schoolrooms – and, again, no real details, except that one part of these works cost £189.

Sadly, full architectural plans of the workhouse drawn up in 1871 have gone missing. There were again extensive building works in that year, some of which were needed because the union was unable to 'offer the house' to applicants during the winter months. There are written descriptions of the works in MH 12, but they are incomplete. The works were so extensive as to prompt the PLB to request a meeting with the architect, a medical officer and a guardian in London.

THE EARTH CLOSET

Designed and patented by Henry Moule in 1860, the earth closet was basically what we call now a composting toilet, where earth and ashes were added, using a lever, to a seated receptacle after use. It required that supplies of soil and ashes be maintained, and that soiled material be removed periodically, the produce being useful for garden and agricultural fertilisation. It was the system almost universally in use within buildings, but eventually became superseded by the water closet later in the nineteenth century.

Fig. 12 Sale Notice, adjoining land, 1869.

Lot 3 (coloured Pink on the annexed Plan)

AN EXDEEDINGLY VALUABLE ENCLOSURE OF
FREEHOLD ARABLE OR GARDEN LAND

With a strip of
FREEHOLD MEADOW LAND
opposite

Containing together 5a. 1r. 38p.,

In the Parish of Basing, and divided by the Public Road from Basingstoke to Basing, to which both Inclosures have long lines of Frontage.

THE MEADOW LAND IS BOUNDED ON THE SOUTH BY A STREAM OF WATER
The whole Property is in the occupation of the Basingstoke Board of Guardians, as yearly tenants at the Rent of

£16 10s. 0d. per annum

THE SITUATION OF THIS LOT IS REMARKABLY GOOD.
THE LAND IS OF FIRST RATE QUALITY with Southern Aspect

Commanding beautiful Views of Hackwood Park & the picturesque Scenery of the Celebrated Old Basing Ruins and the interesting country around.

SCHEDULE OF LANDS.

No. on Plan	Description	Culture	A.	R.	P.
620	Cowderoy's Down Close	Arable	4	3	6
624	Cowderoy's Down Meadow	Pasture	0	2	32
			5	1	38

TNA, MH 12/10682. Marked in pencil 'Lord Basing £570'.

Dealing with Vagrants

The 1834 Poor Law Act did not specifically deal with 'vagrants', casual poor or tramps. These were people with no fixed address who walked around the countryside looking for food and shelter, and the workhouse system provided them with places to rest within walking distance of one another. They were not allowed to return to the same place within thirty days.

At the Basingstoke Poor Law Conference in 1870, Mr Barwick Baker (secretary of the Gloucestershire Conference of Guardians and member of the Manchester Historical Society) estimated there had been an increase of over 3,000 vagrants nationally in the previous ten years – although he accepted that statistics were difficult.

He was not sympathetic. He felt that a period of hard labour after a night in the workhouse would discourage the 'vagabond life', along with the difficulty of walking a full day between stops. He also felt that feeding and bathing them was not helping the disincentive. He stated that since 1869 'several counties' had been sending anyone begging straight to prison for ten days, which diminished the number of vagrants: 'the larger number of tramps who used to pass my lodge on the road from Bristol to Birmingham, have diminished by more than half, and the nuisance of poor dwellers by the roadside is almost entirely abated'.

In Basingstoke itself, there is hardly any mention of vagrancy in the first ten years of the union. In the early 1840s there were only a small handful of vagrants noted in returns. Vagrants were sometimes sent to the workhouse by the local authorities (the minutes state about four a week), but the master complained that there were no facilities for them – theoretically, they should be kept strictly separate from the usual inmates, there was no food ration allowed for them and there was no provision made for them to do the prescribed few hours' work for their keep. In fact it was specifically stated on one occasion that there were very few vagrants, and special provision was not considered necessary: 'the House in this Union not being in a high road and away from the town they have but little to complain of as respects an evil which elsewhere no doubt is expensive'.[TNA] This changed by mid-1846 with an increase in vagrants arriving in Basingstoke; this correlates with the national increase in destitution at that time, 'The Hungry Forties', brought about by a combination of economic slump and bad harvests.

In 1846 a house was made available in the town at the expense of the Basingstoke overseers; the guardians provided £2 for rent of 'a small cottage and two apartments' as a temporary measure, and there were meetings with the local constabulary and the town watch committee regarding supervision. There was heated argument with the PLB about whether the union should contribute for food, bedding and maintenance – 12/6*d* had been paid to a woman taking care of cases 'with contagion', 6*s* for coal, and £4 1*s* for replacement of bedding ordered burned by the medical officer.[TNA]

The PLB never agreed these payments, for various legal reasons, in spite of personal appeals from the overseers. In November 1846 there was exceptionally bad weather, and whole families were turning up 'almost in a state of nudity' with no food. The overseers calculated having received nearly 600 people, often arriving late at night, having found no shelter in the workhouse. They were issued with a ticket for bread and a bed for one night only. It appears that finally the union simply defied the PLB and gave assistance. There appears to have been some sympathy for these poor among the guardians and they were referred to as 'casual poor', 'wayfarers' and 'trampers' rather than 'vagrants'.

When facilities were built at the workhouse shortly thereafter, as with everything else, there were rules. In a letter to the PLB in April 1848, the regulations regarding the employment of vagrants stated that males were to 'turn the corn mill' or 'break 42lbs of stone in four hours'. Females were to spend four hours picking oakum or cleaning the vagrants' wards – no person should be made to work more than four hours, or not at all if they were old, weak or incapacitated. Vagrants in Basingstoke also pumped water. Once a vagrant had done his or her allotted work, they could leave the workhouse and move on. The PLB suggested that a notice be printed and displayed around the workhouse setting out the rules and conditions of their stay – there is the one for Kingsclere in MH 12, probably used as an example, but the Basingstoke one is missing.

'A case of singular character occurred a few days since in this Union Workhouse' in February 1848, when two 'trampers' were discovered naked in their bed one morning, having completely destroyed their own clothes in a bid to be given better ones. They were given some old clothes from the store, without apparently being disciplined apart from the normal work task.[HRO] This is the only mention in Basingstoke, but this attempt to upgrade clothing was described by Mr Barwick Baker at the Poor Law Conference in 1870, referring to his Gloucester union: 'a sack was procured; a slit was cut in the bottom for the head, and one slit on each side for the arms, and then the sack was placed over the man. [Laughter] The practice of tearing up clothes has never been repeated'.

But between 1846 and 1850, from a return to the PLB, there were relatively few vagrants taken into the workhouse. The highest number was thirty-six in 1848. Inspector Hawley's report in 1851 stated that 'there are Vagrant Wards which are in good order, but no able-bodied are admitted. None are relieved but the sick & actually destitute, and they make an application in the first instance to a police officer who is appointed Assistant Relieving Officer'.[TNA]

The officers of the union were not popular among the travelling poor. Relieving officer Ellis had his windows broken in May 1848 by resentful vagrants seeking relief and the PLB ruled that the cost of repair should not be found from union funds. There were other problems with vagrants, particularly when they brought proscribed items into the workhouse, and a constable was employed, with a payment of £4 a year to the superintendent of police, to examine them upon entry. In 1850 William Sparshatt, superintendent of police for Basingstoke, attended the board, and it was agreed that:

> All Vagrants and Wayfarers seeking relief by admission into the Union Workhouse must first apply for and obtain from the Superintendent of the Hants Rural Police residing at the Police Station in Oat Street, Basingstoke … tickets for that purpose as on production only of same to the Master will admission be given.[TNA]

Segregation from the normal inmate population was considered essential, and changes were made in 1856 when Inspector Hawley noted that wood was stored in a room in the male vagrants' accommodation, enabling communication between them and inmates fetching wood. Around 1860 – it is not clear exactly when – vagrants were denied food but were not made to work, the accommodation being shelter only. This seems to have been some sort of ruling, but in Basingstoke vagrants were given the remains of food from the previous day for breakfast, and the sick were given medical attention.[TNA] However, between 1863 and 1869, this changed again, and able-bodied vagrants were set to work picking oakum. We have no details of how all this happened because the relevant ledger in TNA is restricted.

Often, of course, they died; in 1869 a very sick vagrant was brought into the workhouse, having lain in a barn in Beech Hill for four days. We know this because when he died there was argument as to whether his funeral costs should be borne by the parish or the union – the union paid.

Children in the Workhouse

The most significant group of inmates in the workhouse were the children. They were considered to be the one group of paupers who were not responsible for their circumstances. Although the census returns from 1841 to 1871 do not directly support this (they are, after all, snapshots taken on one day) there are many interim reports and comments indicating that at least half of the continuing population were children aged 14 and under. A single return of orphans in March 1844 (incomplete), arising from a House of Commons investigation, showed that eighteen inmate children had lost one or both parents and twenty-five had been deserted. At the same time out relief was supporting fifty-seven widows with 137 dependent children.[TNA]

The census information indicates that most of these young inmates were not in any family group, or perhaps only with a sibling. In the gap between census returns it is suggested from the scraps of information we do have that this was fairly normal. One return to the PLB in March 1847 gives details: of the total of eighty-three, twenty-one were 'illegitimate' (seven without their mothers), twenty-two were orphans, ten were deserted, and the remainder were children of able-bodied paupers inside or outside the workhouse.

Putting one or two children from a large family into the workhouse by way of relief became more and more routine, to the extent that by January 1847 a pre-printed form was being used to request sanction from the PLB, giving the names of the family, their parish, the children's ages and a brief description of their reasons for struggling. There are many of these forms throughout the MH 12 archive in this period, some of which are quite heartbreaking. It is evident that the workhouse would not take very small children, who might be difficult to manage, or older children, whom the PLB believed could find their own work – although quite how a probably illiterate 12-year-old in a tiny, impoverished village in the middle of rural Hampshire could find work is difficult to imagine. It was usually the children aged from 7 to 11 who were taken in, who could work outside their school hours, performing simple tasks like cleaning, and meanwhile they were educated and taught basic skills for future employment.

The PLB was not happy about this, and finally stepped in to stop the practice in 1853, not on moral or sympathetic grounds, but on financial ones:

> This is in support of wages and the Guardians are not legally justified in propos-
> ing it unless there are some special grounds to warrant their doing so. No reason
> is stated why the applicants are unable to obtain the usual wages of the district,
> and if they are able-bodied and able to do so, they are not proper objects for relief
> at the expenditure of the poor rates.

Ten years later the guardians tried again to get sanction for taking two of Benjamin Cook's children in, following his widowhood and reduction in farm wages, but it was refused.[TNA]

Since all inmate children were put into school from a very early age, this leads us to another important part of workhouse life.

Schooling and Education

With so many children in residence, schooling was a vital part of workhouse life, and the subject of considerable attention by the guardians and the PLB. This led to frequent questions and returns, fortunately for us.

In this period prior to the 1870 Education Act, there was great interest in the provision of education for poor children within the union system; then, as today, the only way out of poverty was literacy and consequent flexibility of work. In 1848 there was a proposal from Whitchurch Union to set up a joint district school, which was rejected. The subject re-emerged two years later with a direct instruction from the PLB to seriously consider a district school, and they sent a Poor Law inspector, Lord Courtenay, and the government inspector of pauper schools, William Ruddock, to a board meeting. There was a proposal to unite the Basingstoke school district with Farnham and Hartley Wintney; this was unpopular among the guardians – we do not know why, probably on grounds of money – with twenty-five votes against, so it did not happen.

District schools were again mentioned, critically, by Wyndham S. Portal at the 1870 Poor Law Conference. He felt that if the school within the workhouse was 'run effectively' there was no need for the additional capital outlay of building new schools. Considering that perhaps much of his experience of workhouse schools was in Basingstoke, his comments are important here:

I believe that if a return were called for … showing the number of children who have received full benefit from workhouse training, a very large proportion of them will be found to be depauperised, and no difficulty whatever is found in procuring situations, especially for the girls.

The secret of success is this: – Obtain a master or matron who have their heart in the work – good, kind, Christian people, but who do not come to the situation altogether for the sake of the salary that goes with it, but who will look after the orphan, the friendless, and the (otherwise) destitute child as if it were their own – who teach the children to look to them not as their master, but as their friend – who will advise them as to their clubs or their savings banks – who will entwine themselves into their confidence.

It is unlikely that he would have made these comments if these were not the prevailing attitudes in Basingstoke.

From the late 1840s, the schoolmaster and schoolmistress were formally tested for competency by an officer from the Board of Education, and, if satisfactory, a grant against their salary was made yearly. Some of these reports are in MH 12; they were tested for religious knowledge, spelling, penmanship, arithmetic, grammar, history and geography, reading and industrial skill, along with basic teaching skills. Even if a teacher was a religious nonconformist, they were to teach the Church of England catechism.

As educational requirements became more specific, advertisements were placed widely (and frequently, as we shall see later) for new teachers, in *The Times* and papers in 'some northern counties'. The applicants needed to be 'capable of teaching reading writing and arithmetic and competent to train pauper [children] in general habits of industry and usefulness'. Successful applicants would not be just teachers, in the modern sense of the word, but they would be involved in the day-to-day life of their charges, including supervision at mealtimes and bedtimes, distribution of clothing and so on. Emotional support was never mentioned.

The frequent comments and reports gleaned from the records build up an interesting picture of what life was like for these poor children. Within the workhouse school, conditions were often crowded and difficult, and discipline was a perennial challenge. By far the biggest problem was the great difficulty in keeping teachers in the job, as will be seen in the later section on staff. The constant changes were often remarked upon by the inspector as being detrimental to continuity for the pupils.

In January 1847 the boys' schoolroom was very cold. The chaplain reported:

The boys are suffering a great deal from the coldness of their schoolroom where they are generally kept six hours a day on a paved floor and without any fire, and to suggest their being taken by the Schoolmaster into the other schoolroom which is large enough to accommodate … both boys and girls … there is an angle in the old school room which is at present not used where I think the boys might take their lessons without interrupting the Mistress or her pupils. Of course they could not be together except during school hours.[HRO]

This was agreed by the board and the schoolmistress, and a fire was allowed.

Mr Piggott remarked the following year that 'the children are better instructed here intellectually than in any other WH in any district, with one or 2 exceptions. There is a pupil teacher under the regulations of the Council of Education, and the Schoolmaster & Schoolmistress are intelligent and zealous'.[TNA] He did, however, criticise the lack of formal industrial education, which came a little later.

The younger children under 7 years old were taught in the girls' school, which must have been chaotic. In 1848, the schoolmistress (Martha Wilson) wrote to the board, the letter later forwarded to the PLB. She stated that a 'poor little boy', Thomas Cleave aged 6, 'who is an idiot' with 'dirty habits' and 'unconsciousness of control' was causing problems in the schoolroom. Lord Courtenay was sent to investigate, but in the meantime Thomas was to be removed and placed under the 'supervision of some well-conducted female' (an inmate). He was later confirmed by the inspector as unfit to associate with other children, and that 'if possible, some cheerful and airy room should be assigned to him, and to any other children similarly afflicted, where they might be placed in charge of some respectable female'.[TNA]

The inclusion of very young children reached a crisis point in 1850, as indicated in medical officer Covey's report to the board of 'eruptive disease' in girls. Lord Courtenay had suggested that one of the rooms on the first floor of the girls' wing, easily accessible by the matron, should be set apart as a schoolroom for female children under 6 years old, and that 'some able-bodied woman in the House should superintend' under supervision. If this could not be done, Covey reported, then the visiting committee suggestion should be considered: 'the girls' schoolroom might be enlarged by taking in the private sitting room of the school-mistress and allowing her to sit … for her meals up stairs in the Little Room adjoining to her bedroom'.[TNA]

The next visit from Lord Courtenay was a special one, indicating bureaucratic concern: the younger children were now being cared for in a separate room. He stated that the situation in the regular schoolroom was 'much relieved' and that ventilation was 'actually at present the best in my district'.[TNA] Remember that ventilation and whitewashing were considered the greatest tools in controlling infectious disease.

The report of W.H.J. Hawley in January 1852 is interesting in its indication of standards of education, although it is primarily criticising the current schoolmaster, John Matthews:

The Girls School is very well managed but the Boys School is in a very unsatisfactory state. The Master who has been lately appointed … appears to be
incompetent, and since he had had charge of the school it has retrograded considerably. None of the boys are now taught Geography, although the first class
consisting of 16 boys was far advanced in that study under the late Master, they
were also in many of the higher branches of Arithmetic but have been put back
to compound multiplication & reduced to the level of the present Master's
ignorance. The boys are very disorderly & their Yard dirty and dilapidated …
He carries a stick which from its appearance seems to be frequently used, which
is contrary to the articles which relate to punishment of the boys … I beg to
advise that the Guardians be written to on the subject of the most unsatisfactory
state of the Boys School.[TNA]

The visiting committee also complained to the board that the schoolmaster had
allowed 'the boys (particularly their heads) to get in a very dirty state'.[HRO]

Sensible and responsible children were often used to help in the schoolrooms,
and this is mentioned regularly in inspection reports. Very occasionally, there was
a star pupil who might go on to better things. It was recognised that exceptionally
bright and intelligent children were completely failed by the workhouse system
of schooling, designed to teach only the basics and get youngsters into work as
soon as possible. In 1848 William Henry
Cox, a pauper youth, was noticed for his
ability, trained and later certified by the
PLB and the Council for Education as
an assistant teacher. The guardians were
'desirous to adopt any suggestion that
may be offered in furtherance of the
boy's advancement' and confirmed that
he should have 'separate sleeping place'
and 'have a suit of strong cloth made of a
different pattern to distinguish him from
other boys'. He was also to sit at one end
of the table during mealtimes and 'assist
the Master in keeping order'.[TNA]

Considerable efforts were made on
behalf of another gifted boy. In 1851 a
letter to the PLB from Joshua Ruddock,
inspector of schools, regarding pauper
Henry Oliver of Oakley, stated:

LIST OF BOOKS ORDERED FROM THE
SET LIST IN JULY 1853, FOR 46 BOYS
AND 44 GIRLS IN THE SCHOOLS

Reading and Composition: The Young
Composer, Part 1 by Cornwell, 1 copy

Writing: Manual of Mulhauser's
Method by Parker, 1 copy

Arithmetic: Arithmetic Theoretical and
Practical by Chambers, 1 copy

Geography: Epitome of Geographical
Knowledge, Irish Board, 1 copy, Hughes
Physical Geography, 1 copy

History of Scotland: History of
Scotland, 2 vols by Scott, 1 copy

Vocal Music: Wilhem's Method of
Teaching Singing by Hullah, 1 copy

TOTAL COST: 13s 9¼d

The principal of the Training Institution of the national society is willing to receive him as an articled pupil for one year, at the reduced charge of 9/- a week instead of the usual 12/- ... lodging, board and training thus amounting to £23 8s 0d, or with the addition of extras probably £25.

Ruddock himself was prepared to donate £10 if the rest could be raised – he was confident that Oliver would eventually be able to earn a good salary, and he could help in assisting him in such employment. Ruddock also noted, in a later letter, that Oliver would need 'a sufficient outfit, say new suits and three changes of linen', to enter the institution, and he was also prepared to help with this.

A former guardian from Oakley, Revd Matthew Harrison, was keen to raise money to help the boy and hoped the union could assist: 'if not, we must take some other means of raising the money, subscription is objectionable because the parties seldom pay in proportion to their means and their responsibilities'.[TNA]

Books and maps for the schools were purchased regularly, and this became more systematic over the next twenty years. A syllabus was developing and there was an established order form with items supplied direct from the Committee of Council on Education, no doubt to ensure that workhouses were buying the correct books. According to Fowler, from his research at TNA, this is relatively unusual: 'although the Poor Law Board allowed unions to buy textbooks at a substantial discount, few unions took up this offer'.[10]

Resources and space in the schools were always under pressure. In 1850 the schoolmistress reported seventy-four girls under her care, and in 1852 Schoolmaster Carter applied for an additional capitation fee, there being an average number of forty-eight boys in the school – surprisingly, the PLB agreed. Later, in March 1871, there is a minute of school space being considered insufficient, with seventy children in space for only about forty-five.

With the difficulties in obtaining regular teaching staff, in 1867 a proposal to combine the boys' and girls' schools under one teacher was made, and agreed 'in principle' by the PLB. In fact, the last schoolmaster, J.F. Turner, was only employed for a year, from 1865 to 1866, and was not replaced – his duties were covered, informally, for a year by one of the master's sons. This raised the question of supervision of the boys, especially at night, when the porter could not be expected to fill this role, and it was proposed that 'superintendents' be engaged to teach the boys 'useful occupations' along with their 'spade husbandry', such as clothes mending and knitting. Formal industrial training had arrived.

Industrial Training

Of course, the main purpose of educating poor children in the workhouse was to prepare them for work. It was therefore thought necessary that appropriate trainers should be used to teach the boys, particularly, in the skills and techniques of agricultural labour. It is not clear from the minutes exactly how this was achieved some of the time, but commitment to the idea is indicated by the expansion of arable land around the workhouse, and an inspection report in 1851 stated: 'the boys are instructed in agriculture in the large field which the Guardians have lately [added] to the Workhouse premises'.[TNA]

The porter was involved in training the boys in 1855: 'under the superintendence and instructions of the Porter ... [boys] ... be employed and instructed in agricultural work for four hours every day weather permitting and Sundays excepted, and that ... the Porter be paid £1 10s 0d per quarter additional to his present salary in consideration of such services.'[TNA]

Boys also received some training as cobblers, and there are indications of other people supervising needlework for the adults, in which the girls would probably have been involved – again, it is not clear how this arrangement worked, or whether these people were existing skilled inmates or people brought in from outside. The problem of boys working at shoemaking in the men's day room gave rise to alterations in 1851, with aged couples sleeping nearby being moved and a dedicated workshop being arranged.

Other people were formally employed for this purpose. Lucy Louisa Gosling, described on her registration form as experienced in the 'management of a farm house and dairy',[TNA] was employed for about a year from 1858, on £14 per annum, followed by Agnes Forder, a relative of the master. There were also facilities for teaching tailoring. Leonard French was formally employed for four years from 1867, and tools for repairing boots and shoes were purchased, although it is not clear that this was his speciality. He was followed by Frank Fiander in 1871, an ex-artilleryman and previously a workhouse porter.

This practice is the prevailing one for the area. Inspector Hawley, in his correspondence files to the PLB, gave details of industrial trainers throughout his district, consisting of Dorset, Southampton, Sussex and Wiltshire. The skills mainly consisted of shoemaking, tailoring and spade husbandry, with sewing, knitting and domestic tasks for the girls.[TNA] There are a few – very few – instances of children being apprenticed from Basingstoke workhouse; one boy, John Bulpit, was apprenticed to cordwainer William Goddard of Sherborne St John for four years in 1856.[HRO]

There is no detail of formal industrial training for girls, but from occasional comments in the records this was aimed at domestic service, training which could be achieved in the regular running of the workhouse itself, involving them in cleaning, cooking, laundry and needlework, and work in the dairy.

Girls were commonly found work in domestic service, and they needed clothes and shoes to start. Payments for these were officially disallowed by the PLB at the time, as in the 1848 case of Jane Keep, aged 14, from a large family in Stratfieldsaye, but it appears that the guardians quietly went ahead, and simply informed the PLB of the cost – in this case 15s.

Later that same year, the guardians again applied to the PLB for sanction in the similar case of Ann Gold:

Application was made for relief to this pauper an Inmate in the House aged 14 years for clothes to the value of 30/- to enable her to take a place now offered in a Tradesman's Family in Southampton. The Girl has been in the House the last two years and her Father is also an Inmate in the House and the parties have no other House or Residence. Ordered that the Clerk do write to the Poor Law Board for their sanction in the present case and also in similar Instances if and when required. The Clerk is also directed to state that the party offering to take the pauper makes the offer on the condition that she is provided with Clothes.[TNA]

A few children were sent away to the new industrial schools. These and reformatory schools were started after 1850 to take in difficult and disruptive youngsters under 14 years of age, sometimes vagrants, or neglected or destitute children, with the idea of educating them in a formal environment and training them for work. Girls usually learned domestic work and boys a trade – agricultural skills or military training with drilling.[11]

Louisa Kent, 'a child' from Pamber, was allowed £3 0s 8d for an outfit for admission to 'the Industrial Home' in 1863 (which one is not stated), and 3s a week was to be allowed for her maintenance there. Similarly, four years later three girls, Elizabeth Duckett and Mary Ann and Elizabeth Lucas, were sent to the industrial home 'in London', their clothing and travel expenses provided.[HRO]

However, there was no systematic programme in Basingstoke for sending these children out of the locality to work, as was the case elsewhere in the country, particularly in the industrial areas. Among these it is worth noting the infamous case of 'Mr Drouet's Establishment for Pauper Children' in Tooting, specifically established for taking children up to the age of 14. It was run by Bartholomew Peter Drouet, which, like Andover, caused a scandal and condemnation in parliament. There was severe overcrowding, an awful diet and bad sanitary conditions, all of which inevitably led to disease with 180 children dying from cholera. Charles Dickens stated in *The Examiner* in January 1849 that 'the cholera, or some unusually malignant form of typhus assimilating itself to that disease broke out in Mr Drouet's farm for children, because it was brutally conducted, vilely kept, preposterously inspected, dishonestly defended, a disgrace to a Christian community, and a stain upon a civilised land'.[12]

Basingstoke workhouse children were not subjected to this, but Wyndham S. Portal commented in 1870:

We, as guardians, want rather more freedom and discretion afforded us in the matter of educating our pauper children than the Poor Law Board at present allows us. It would be well to give us permission to put out, either on loan or hire as day-workers, either on a farm or elsewhere, those who are preparing for their first situations in life, allowing them to come home to the workhouse as their natural, and, indeed, only refuge.

He also had an interesting idea to expand the use of the workhouse school: 'again, as children in the small workhouses go out to the neighbouring village or national school, so let the ordinary labourer send his child (if he should live near, and wish to do so) to the school in the workhouse, on payment of the ordinary fee'.[13]

In conclusion, reading and exploring the records relating to the Basingstoke Workhouse schools, the impression is created of a system continually under pressure of one sort or another, numbers and mixes of ages and abilities, undoubtedly involving constant changes with children coming and going. The accommodation was often barely adequate, discipline was difficult and there were regular episodes of rapidly spreading infections; at the same time there was bureaucratic supervision and, occasionally, interference within the organisation. It is no surprise that there were problems with keeping staff (see the 'Staff' section on p. 105). It is to the credit of the Board of Guardians that there appears to have been some success in educating these poor children.

The Problems of Health and Disease

Victorian Life and Illness

Health was an immensely important factor in the life and times of the poor and the unions, to the extent that it cannot be separated from a complete view – it is a continual thread that runs through any description of this aspect of the social history of the times. Illness often caused poverty, and poverty caused illness, a vicious circle, which became a significant function in the running of unions and, later, local government.

Life was difficult and grim by modern standards for many in the Victorian period. This was a time when the population, and particularly the poor, were continually threatened with typhus, typhoid, cholera and smallpox, along with all the conditions and diseases associated with poverty, bad diet, overcrowding – particularly in the new industrial towns and cities – and lack of hygiene. Bathing was uncommon, flushing toilets were yet to arrive, drainage and sewers were inefficient and porous with seepage into muddy roads and ditches, and water supplies were often communal. Even middle- and upper-class homes were damp and cold for much of the year.

Tuberculosis and diphtheria were common and malaria ('bad air') was endemic, often diagnosed simply as generalised recurrent fever and debility. The exact mechanism for infection was not known for many years, until in 1854 John Snow found a bad water supply to be the agent in the spread of cholera. Attempts were made to remedy sources of suspect water, as we shall see later.

Children, poor or rich, died in large numbers from diseases we rarely see now: measles, whooping cough and scarlet fever. Women often died in childbirth, together with their babies, the poor ones sometimes not wanting to apply for medical help from the local union for fear of being stigmatised.[14]

Like most other local unions, Basingstoke made an annual subscription, about 10 guineas a year, to the County Hospital in Winchester so that one pauper could be sent there for treatment, and this amount was steadily increased over the years. It is indicated in a letter to the PLB in 1855 that sometimes the senior officers of the union would personally provide funds for the care of additional paupers, 'which has been of considerable saving to the Union'.

In addition to the infirmary in the workhouse, of course, medical officers continued to work all over the union providing very basic emergency care to the poor, vaccinating against smallpox and taking part in gathering information for the government. Later, from the middle of the century, many of them were finding it necessary to employ assistants, funded by the union, and in 1860 the number of medical districts in Basingstoke Union was increased to six.

Firstly, we will look at provision for the sick and elderly within the workhouse, followed by what happened outside in the rest of the union.

The Workhouse Infirmary

There is little detail of what went on within the workhouse infirmary in terms of inmates, numbers and practices. However, we can glean bits and pieces. We know from an inspector's report in 1848 that there was accommodation for forty people in the infirmary, and the 1856 Accommodation Return shows three male and three female rooms designated as infirmary space – they were 16.5ft square, and apparently could accommodate six to eight people each, which roughly corresponds with the 1848 report. These separate rooms also enabled some degree of isolation when there was infectious disease.

A dedicated 'dead house' was built in June 1848, at a cost of £14 10s, but there is still mention in 1849, from another inspector's report, of the dead sometimes being kept temporarily in the female receiving ward, probably as a result of an epidemic. Following 'several' deaths from smallpox in the workhouse that year, an order was given that all bodies not removed within 24 hours by relatives would be speedily buried in Basing churchyard.

A SUITABLE HEARSE

In January 1868 Chairman Sclater was displeased with the usual method of moving the cheap, rough coffins on a farm cart and proposed that a 'suitable hearse' be obtained, and a horse and driver service be contracted on tender – there was unanimous agreement to this proposal and advertisements were placed.[HRO]

There were two known cases in 1847 of the workhouse building being used as an emergency centre. We only know about these because they were taken out of the hands of the attending doctors once the patients were in the building, which caused complaints by the doctors to the PLB. In the first case a railway worker had a serious accident on the line and was carried down the hill to the workhouse, whereupon the master informed the surgeon that the case was now in the hands of medical officer Covey. The latter declined to attend and the man died.

In the second case, another serious accident to a railway worker, the man had both legs amputated by a non-union surgeon, after consultation with two other doctors. The man was not aware that he had lost his legs until he was told. As he started to recover, a call was made by 'someone' for medicine from the doctor, but he was told at the workhouse that he was no longer caring for the patient. The argument the doctor made to the PLB was that the man was not a pauper, but merely taking advantage of 'better living conditions' while he recovered.

There were several items of maintenance works and alterations involving treatment of the sick: in 1859, there was a tender for painting and 'destroying bugs', and for 'two rooms set apart for the poor afflicted with chronic disease' with associated chimneys. There are indications that plans for proposed alterations to the infirmary and sick accommodation were drawn up in 1867, but, frustratingly, there are no details.

By 1871, we know from a report regarding the separation of infectious cases that a dedicated infirmary building had been erected: 'a detached building, contains 4 wards upstairs and 2 downstairs with nurses' rooms and surgery separating the two lower wards. There are two staircases conducting from the lower to the upper storey and the doors of the wards open on to the landing in the usual way'. This building clearly appears on the drainage maps of the 1890s, to the north of

STANDARD PRE-PRINTED WORKHOUSE MEDICAL OFFICERS' STATEMENT, 6 JANUARY 1869

1. Is there sufficient ventilation and warmth?
2. Has the accommodation during the preceding six months for the several classes of sick been sufficient?
3. Are the arrangements for cooking and distribution of food, as regards the sick, satisfactory?
4. Is the nursing satisfactorily performed?
5. Is there a sufficient supply of towels, vessels, bedding, clothing, and other conveniences for the use of the sick inmates?
6. Are the medical appliances sufficient and in good order? Are there any water-beds or rack bedsteads, and, if so, are they sufficient in number and in good order?
7. Are the lavatories and baths sufficient and in good order?
8. Are the supply and distribution of hot and cold water sufficiently provided for?

> **ANNE NEWELL**
>
> Anne Newell stayed in post
> for ten years. In 1875, now
> elderly, she applied to return to
> the workhouse, paying for her
> own care from the £20 annual
> pension she was receiving
> from the union. She died in
> the workhouse in 1886.

the main building (see Appendix II). Interestingly, it does not appear on the 1873 OS map, although the vagrancy wards do; possibly it was not there when the survey was done.

A medical officer had always been assigned to the workhouse, to visit regularly and be on call for emergencies – the boardroom was assigned for consultations in 1864 – and an inmate, Ann Newell, was employed formally as a nurse in 1851. She was allowed staff rations along with lodging and an annual salary of £4. She was allowed an extra 5*s* in cases of midwifery attended by her. This was the usual practice throughout England at this time, and in recognition of its limitations (the inmate nurses in question often not being able to read or write) the PLB proposed formal training for nurse inmates in 1856 – nothing was done about this in Basingstoke for several years.

Midwifery was a significant element of medical care; the midwife employed from the first days of the workhouse, Ruth Bunniston, continued to receive occasional but regular payments for the more difficult cases, and her last mention is in 1851, 'a poor widow', being provided with £5 for emigration to Montreal with Henry John Bunniston, who may have been her son.

Nursing in the Workhouse

A formally trained nurse was first employed in Basingstoke Workhouse in November 1861, and this led to a serious reconsideration and upgrading of conditions in the infirmary. Mrs Prudence Pugsley was elected at a salary of £20, with accommodation and rations, and her start was postponed for a fortnight, on the recommendation of medical officer Wells, to allow her to gain experience in Guy's Hospital in London. A committee of guardians (Sclater, Chute and Joyce, the most senior men) was set up to 'make the necessary arrangements for the reception of the Nurse and her accommodation and also for transferring to her care the Infirmary Linen'.

Their full report with recommendations two weeks later is an interesting picture of that time:

> In the wards of the Infirmary that the articles of furniture, bedding and utensils entered in the Inventory … in 1858 … be replaced … the roller blinds throughout the Infirmary to be put back into their fittings and made good where decayed. In the Nurse's Kitchen the large deal table formerly in use there to be restored to its own place, the Boiler to be put in order (… being defective), a small table to be provided which the Nurse can move about as required and an arm chair for sitting up at night. A new coal scuttle, 4 yards of cocoa nut fibre matting,

a small set of tea things with tea pot and coffee pot, 6 metal tea spoons, 6 plates and 2 vegetable dishes, a set of jugs and 2 saucepans, 2 large and 4 small drinking glasses. The Nurse's sleeping room to be plastered and papered, a window curtain, a wash-hand stand and ware, a small dressing table and looking glass, a chest of drawers, a towel horse, a small bedside carpet, a wooden rack with pegs to be provided. In the Water Closets of the Infirmary lids to be fitted where absent. In the Surgery the Medical Officer requests that a small stove be put up, a bell to communicate with the House to be hung. [Note: this early mention of 'water closets' is puzzling!].

Copies of a Sick Dietary Table in the form directed by the Poor Law Commissioners … be hung in the Wards and in the Nurse's Kitchen. That the Nurse be allowed what coal she may require for use proportionally to the persons in the Infirmary and that she have such assistance from pauper inmates as has been heretofore and is at present allowed.

The Committee recommend that when the Infirmary is ready all pauper inmates of the House who require a Nurse, with the exception of Idiots, be placed in the Infirmary under the Nurse's care.[HRO]

It did not take long for problems to emerge – a month after Mrs Pugsley started work there was a complaint against her by medical officer Wells, relating specifically to two pauper women: 'I found Ann Duffin much worse and in a great danger. She was ordered into the Infirmary that she might be attended to during the night, which the Nurse in a most impudent manner refused to do'; and 'Mary Keep in Labour pains since Saturday, sent for Sunday as the Nurse felt herself incapable of undertaking the case'.[HRO]

Mary Keep later died, incurring an additional fee for a doctor called in from outside. She had convulsions, and four other pauper women in confinement were temporarily removed from the workhouse to prevent possible infection – they obviously had no idea what had killed her.

Mrs Pugsley's shortcomings were referred to the PLB inspector for his opinion, whereupon she resigned, desiring 'to be relieved of her duties at once'. Pauper nurse Ann Newell was put back in charge immediately pending replacement.

There followed a series of nurses who did not stay for long, and inevitably the quality of care suffered. Revd Joyce mentioned, in 1870 at the Poor Law Conference, a young man dying of consumption who asked for cold water to drink by his bedside, which was not provided over two days. The difficulties with staff morale and retention will be described in greater detail in the later section.

The workhouse nurse had become an essential member of staff. Revd Joyce stated in 1870 that:

One trained nurse, adequately paid, should have general charge of the hospital and infirmary. Whether engaged by the Board to act as midwife or not, she should be capable of doing so, and, if possible, certified as an accoucheuse, because labours are continually occurring in her wards, and often when medical officers may be difficult to find. In a workhouse more depends on the nurse in skill and temper than on anything else for the alleviation of the sufferings which are inseparable from such an institution.

The Sick and the Old

It is impossible to say what medical conditions were being dealt with within the workhouse itself – we will move on to the wider union later. Apart from confinement and diseases relating to old age, the commonest relatively minor conditions mentioned are the spreading of 'eruptions' and itchy eyes among the children; 'itch' is often mentioned and is probably scabies or fungal infection. In 1854 problems with the boys' heads was deemed to be 'filth' rather than sickness. There is occasional mention of scarletina, which was endemic, and scrofula; in 1866 two paupers with the latter were considered so serious as to be sent to Margate for sea bathing. One of them was Anne Appleton, a girl appearing in the census of the workhouse in both 1851 (aged 13) and 1861 (a 'general servant') – we do not know whether she had been in the workhouse for all of the fifteen years.

It was not until 1869 that 'dirty' cases were segregated from the general population on admission, although it is not clear exactly what 'dirty' means; there was always a risk of families with severe infections or non-specific fevers bringing them into the workhouse. That year, the soft soap used in the workhouse was replaced by carbolic soap.

There were genuine attempts to make the sick more comfortable and to help the disabled. The administration of cod liver oil and quinine had become routine by 1866, both inside the workhouse and in the parishes. Similarly, there are several cases of a water bed being borrowed, and a couple of cases of blind paupers being sent away for better care, one of whom was Henry Ansell, who was sent to Bath Institute for the Blind in 1854 at a cost of £10 a year, plus clothes and expenses; he was later moved to the Bristol Institute. James Whatmore behaved so badly at the Blind Institute in Birmingham that he was sent home and later admitted back into the workhouse.

Another concession to the sick and elderly was the allowance of beer and brandy prescribed by the medical officer and distributed by the nurse. We know this because brandy was regularly purchased for the workhouse in quantity, and that there was controversy over its distribution involving staff members (see pp. 103, 108).

The elderly were always a very significant part of the workhouse population; census information from 1841 to 1871 shows about a quarter of inmates were aged

60 and over, with several people over 80. The old were very much at the mercy of the times; diseases of malnutrition and bad living conditions were common, as were rheumatism and arthritis, for which nothing could be done to relieve the disability. Many of them were in the workhouse for the remainder of their lives, and appear more than once in the remaining records.

A return of inmates 'receiving beer, elderly and infirm' was prepared in 1846, and ten of them appear in the 1841 census and the 1846 return, demonstrating their long-term residence. Hannah Combs, in her 80s, is noted as receiving beer, 'aged and infirm' in 1846, was still in the workhouse the following year and was joined by her husband, William, an agricultural labourer, in the 1851 census. William alone was still in the workhouse in the 1861 census. The couple were evidently regulars in the workhouse for over two decades. Samuel Clark, an agricultural labourer from Mapledurwell in his 70s, appeared in both the 1851 and the 1861 census returns.

Mental Illness

The mentally ill and mentally challenged poor were another group of unfortunate people who needed support from their local unions. The three words most commonly used in the records for Basingstoke are 'idiot', 'imbecile' and 'lunatic', the first two being vague in their definition and often apparently interchangeable, and they were cared for either in their parishes or in the workhouse. A 'lunatic' was defined as someone of danger to him/herself and others and of difficult social habits, and who was usually assigned to an asylum (the word is later, however, used throughout in official documents relating to mentally ill in the workhouse). In the early years, a mentally ill pauper was not otherwise considered to be any different from the rest of the needy population, and those confined in workhouses, with no specialist care, undoubtedly had difficulties themselves and with other inmates – they could suffer from anything from basic learning challenges to depression or paranoia. This huge and difficult subject is beyond the scope of this book, but we will look in a little detail at how these people were dealt with in Basingstoke.

It is not until the mid-1840s that the mentally ill appear as a specific category. Around this time some returns to the PLB turn up in the records following the Lunatic Asylums Act of 1845 which made the provision of county lunatic asylums compulsory. Previously, a request from the PLC in 1843 had asked for details of paupers needing asylum care, and the response was that there were none at that time[HRO] – the mentally ill did exist, of course, but there seems to have been no formal administrative procedure in place.

Later, lunatics needing asylum care were placed in various nearby institutions until the opening of the Hampshire Lunatic Asylum in Knowle, Fareham in 1852. Among the asylums to which Basingstoke lunatics were sent in the intervening years were Dr Twynam's Asylum in Winchester, Littlemore Asylum in Oxford and Camberwell Asylum in London; the arrangement in all cases was that regular payments were made by the union for their care. At this time it is often the only way we know about the individuals concerned.

There are some interesting events surrounding the sudden closure of Dr Twynam's establishment. Notice was received to remove Basingstoke lunatics immediately in October 1846. This evidently caused great consternation, with relieving officers being approached to inform their home parishes and request advice 'where they would wish them to be removed to', but eventually all were moved, temporarily, to the workhouse. Dr Covey assessed them and recommended 'which of them ought to be removed and if any and which of them can be with safety and propriety detained and provided for in the House'. The chairman, vice-chairman and auditor, Mr Headeach (the seniority of these men showing the board's concern), were appointed to 'treat with the proprietors of some fitting lunatic establishment … upon the best practicable terms'.

Dr Covey's report is summarised in the minutes:

- Solomon Allen, Thomas Appleton, Elizabeth Gardiner, Leah Sackley, Sarah West and Elizabeth Instrell, each he considered 'lunatics' and 'a fit person to be confined to an asylum'.
- Henry Foy was a 'dangerous idiot … to be confined to an asylum'.
- James Keens he was not sure about – 'I am not sufficiently clear on. Possibly it might be well to give him a trial in the House for a short time', he 'is not of sane mind' and Dr Covey suggested that Dr Twynam's opinion should be sought.

A month later, Camberwell Asylum offered to take them at 11s each per week, and measures were taken to transport them.

The minutes during this period contain many cases of mentally ill paupers being assigned to an asylum, but also of occasional discharges, where there had been a remission and the person was sent back home for local care. It is also evident that there was a reluctance to consign to an asylum, and not only on grounds of the cost, which was not mentioned in comments on individuals (the cost of maintaining a pauper in an asylum was about 11s a week, against 2s to 2/6d in the union).

There are many notes in the minutes regarding the most appropriate care of individual mentally ill people. One incident in 1864, arising from events on a train involving Maria Newport, created some correspondence. It is not clear exactly what happened, but her sister and son-in-law appeared before the board and a statement of facts was submitted to the railway company, eventually ending up with the Secretary of State. Mrs Newport was ultimately sent to Hampshire Asylum.

And there were instances of the local 'worthies' taking a personal interest – in 1871 Mr J.P. Jervoise of Herriard House had been regularly visiting Thomas Randall, who was suffering from 'incurable idiocy' and he was concerned as to whether Randall was getting a nourishing diet.

The two useful records remaining are the annual Lunatic Returns from 1847 onwards and the reports of the lunacy commissioner or inspector, who visited and inspected the workhouse from 1845. These are both in the MH 12 archive in TNA, but, unfortunately, this series is not complete and many are difficult to read. The returns were pre-printed forms and contained the following information: Name, age, sex and parish, whether they were being maintained in an asylum, in the workhouse or with friends and relatives in their homes, their weekly cost, whether they were dangerous and/or of 'dirty habits', and how long they had been of 'unsound mind'.

A study of what exists of eleven years of Lunatic Returns from 1847 to 1857 is interesting, particularly in respect of some of the names mentioned above:

- Thomas Appleton, a young man of around 30, from Oakley, disappears from the record from 1850.
- Elizabeth Gardener, from Stratfield Turgis, in her 60s, is in the asylum throughout, as is Leah Sackley, from Basingstoke, in her 50s, the only person described as 'dangerous with dirty habits'.
- James Keens, from Farleigh Wallop, remained in the workhouse from 1837, frequently absconding throughout the period. From a 1858 letter from the Lunacy Commissioner: 'strongly of the opinion that if the frequent escapes of James Keens from the House, always involving necessarily great misery and destitution, and likely to end some day in starvation and death, cannot be prevented by the Workhouse authorities, it is absolutely essential to the safety of this poor imbecile that he should be removed to an asylum'. The guardians resisted, based upon Dr Covey's report that he was 'distinctly not of sound mind, but he is inoffensive and his conduct mild and tractable'. There is a brief note in 1860 that he had died.
- Henry Phillips, a tailor by trade, is another man frequently mentioned in letters and reports, firstly in 1842 when he absconded. He was imprisoned for a period for indecent assault on a boy, and was briefly assigned to the asylum on a couple of occasions, from where, in 1855, he wrote to the Queen, parliament, the Duke of Wellington and the PLB (his letters are in MH 12). A Henry Phillips, aged 70, appears in the 1871 census for the workhouse. It is interesting that, despite all his problems, he was not left in the asylum permanently.
- Several seriously challenged members of the Goodwin family from Sherfield, and the Goodyer family from Nutley, are registered as being cared for in the parish by friends and family throughout.

The total number of registered lunatics in Basingstoke Union was fairly consistent at around thirty-two, with about a third of them being resident in the workhouse, about half in their parishes and the remainder in the asylum. Fragments of accounts remaining suggest that the union spent between £700 and £1,000 a year on care for the mentally ill.

As for their care in the workhouse itself, we turn to the lunacy commissioners' reports. An early report in October 1848 that fifteen people were of 'unsound mind' is fairly typical for the period; their conditions being:

> Same as those of ordinary Paupers but the Idiotic Clothing & Bedding, Females have Tea … not separated but interspersed … house clean and having a dry site and pleasant aspect – restraint never used – some of the males work at the pump … When seen were tranquil and comfortable and appeared to be tractable and harmless.

From later reports, the more able were allowed 'to leave the house with a view to earn their living by easy harvest work, gleaning, hop picking etc.' They were described as 'harmless imbeciles capable of doing such work under a supervisor. After the demand for such labour is over we were told that they usually came back to the Workhouse.' The care of these unfortunates within the workhouse often caused problems: in April 1863 we are told that:

> There is an old man named William Appleby who is very troublesome, and noisy at night, greatly disturbing the other inmates, requiring two men to look after him. Were it not for his great age … [he is] not a fit object for a Workhouse. If he is retained here I think he should have a full diet with porter daily.

A new lunacy inspector at that time recommended they have extra diet and 'that seats with backs, or armchairs, be provided for the use of the feeble and epileptic cases'.[TNA]

Evidently, there was stress in the workhouse/asylum system elsewhere – in December 1869 Inspector Hurley enquired whether the union would be 'prepared to take a limited number of harmless lunatics' from some of the London workhouses and the asylum. This was quickly refused, there being 'neither sufficient spare rooms nor accommodations'. We wonder whether he considered this because Basingstoke workhouse was a suitable environment for this purpose?

Life and Health in the Parishes

The way people lived is intrinsically relevant to the history of every union. The factors of social and economic life, as well as the prevalence of diseases and their control, were a large part of the administrative work of the union, and it again needs mentioning that a period of workhouse life would provide regular food, clothing and shelter against conditions which could be impossible outside, even though life inside was boring, tedious and regimented.

Living Conditions

Conditions for agricultural labouring families at this time are worth looking at here, if only for comparison with what was available under the relief system and within the workhouse, since these were the majority of the poor throughout our history in Basingstoke Union. The census returns for the workhouse during this period, before the growth of the town, show that the majority of inmates, where occupation is given, were labourers, usually agricultural or in associated trades, or in service of some kind, and it is likely that the remainder, particularly children, were members of families supported by these occupations.

This extract from Waller's excellent book on agricultural labourers is interesting:

Internally a typical farm labourers' cottage of the Victorian era was comprised of two bedrooms often no more than about 12 feet square. The walls were uneven and the ceilings generally low. The small windows did not permit much daylight to enter and because they were very often ill-fitting they were draughty. The entrance doors were usually of oak hung on a couple of iron hinges. The doors were often warped. Downstairs floors were usually brick or flagstone, uneven and in the absence of a suitable damp proof course were permanently damp or even wet in the winter. Because of the size of the family that needed to be accommodated, the bedrooms were usually divided by two curtains, blankets or old smocks. In one bedroom the labourer and his wife slept with the younger children whilst in the other the older children would sleep with the room divided for the sexes. It was not unusual for several children to be accommodated in a single bed. In some cases the older children would sleep on a makeshift bed made of straw pallets downstairs in the parlour. Alternatively some children would be boarded out with extended families that had fewer children or some may have already left home to serve as apprentices or domestic servants.[15]

Waller states that the average spend of wages in 1861 was primarily on food, bread and meat (about 3lb a week for a family) with a little cheese, followed by soap and rent, then fuel – these were the basics. If cash was available, tea and sugar, candles and treacle would be purchased, along with a little tobacco. School fees for the children were a few pennies. The labourer generally had to provide his own tools, such as a scythe, and he needed good boots, which cost about 15*s*.[16] The average national wage for a working week was 13*s*, but the average in Hampshire was nearer to 9*s*, less than the north but slightly more than the south-west.[17]

EXAMPLE SANITARY REPORTS, SEPTEMBER AND NOVEMBER 1866

<u>Basing</u>. The health of this parish is better at the present time than it has been for some months past; diarrhoea prevailed to a considerable extent during the early part of the Summer, but during the last fortnight it has been steadily decreasing. Within the last five days only two cases have occurred, there has been no case of cholera. Typhoid fever has prevailed very much during the last six months, and there are still some cases in the village. Cases of diphtheria and other strenuous diseases are very numerous. Basing is naturally a very unhealthy place being situated in a low and swampy position and surrounded by water, the house accommodation in several parts of the villages is bad, there are not sufficient bedrooms for the size of the family, and the area of the rooms is too small, the ventilation is indifferent, and in an overcrowded state. Many of the houses have the privies close to the back door, others have no cesspools but open ditches into which everything runs, this in hot dry weather becomes very offensive. The well water is pretty good, many of the inhabitants drink the river water.

<u>Kempshott</u>. The bad condition of the privies ought to be at once remedied, and in many cases they ought to be removed as far as possible from the cottages and at as great distance as possible from the wells. All refuse matter should be removed as far as possible from the houses, and the drains near the houses looked to and where possible disinfected. Overcrowding should be prevented and too many persons ought not to use the same privies. In cases of severe diarrhoea or cholera persons ought to be directed to mix the evacuations immediately after being passed with chloride of lime, wood ashes or anything which may be at hand at the time and then to bury them at a distance from any dwelling and cover them well with earth as dry as possible; all refuse water in which limbs soiled by the cholera patients have been washed ought to be mixed with some disinfecting fluid and also buried.

<u>Tunworth</u>. Water supply good. The houses are clean, well ventilated and not overcrowded. The privies at Kings Piper and Smiths very offensive, night soil deposited in an open ditch. Privy at Porters and Hutchins full and offensive. Population 118. Mortality during five years ending March 1866, nine.

<u>Mappledurwell</u> [*sic*]. The houses are clean, well ventilated and not overcrowded. Water supply good. The well at Purdays is out of repair, cover and curb broken. The privy is in a most disgraceful state close to the sleeping apartment. There is a large quantity of filthy night soil, with a few old boards placed over it, this is very detrimental to health. Population 223. Mortality during 5 years ending March 1866, twenty. 3 deaths from senile decay, 2 from consumption, 3 from scarletina, 1 from diphtheria. Analysis of mortality, 2 deaths from senile decay ages 79, 93, 1 from diphtheria.

<u>Worting</u>. There exists an almost universal defect in the wells of the District, it is that the mouths are too low, being generally on a level with the gardens thus facilitating the ingress of snails, toads, etc.; during rains the surface water frequently pours into the wells carrying with it numberless impurities. This might be remedied at a trifling expense by raising the mouth of the well somewhat above the garden level, say one or two feet (by means of a brick or flint wall would I believe be as good and inexpensive a plan as any) and closing it with a well fitting cover.[HRO]

Poor Law Unions were responsible for the control of environmental 'nuisances', and they had legal authority to enforce remedies. They dealt with everything from foul drains, bad water, dead animals being left in ditches, problems with filthy pigsties, communal privies and deposits of garbage, mainly things that smelled bad.

In 1866 there was a national epidemic of cholera, and medical officers were required to report on the accommodation of the poor in their respective parishes, with particular regard to the provision of clean water and basic sanitation. Their full reports, copied into the minutes in Basingstoke, are striking. Even the fact that they were accurately copied there, word for word – a rare thing – indicates the seriousness of the situation; there were also comments relating to mortality and other prevalent diseases. These reports led to the permanent appointment of a sanitary committee within the Board of Guardians and the addition of the (paid) role of 'inspector of nuisances' to the duties of relieving officers.

Many of the parishes were very sparsely populated and isolated, which prevented the spread of disease. Some of the houses were crowded, cold and damp. In most places, privies with open cesspools were shared by many families and were close to houses and water supplies, themselves basic wells which were also communal. Drinking water was often found to be dirty and contaminated, sometimes containing snails and toads. There was no system for the collection of refuse, so it built up around the houses and in ditches, and basically stank all summer. Pigs were often kept in pens directly attached to houses and occasionally inside the houses themselves.

In Basingstoke, things were no better. The reports for the town appear much later, in MH 12 in September 1871. They are there as the result of an effort to improve the truly awful drainage and sewage conditions in the town at that time, and are included in a huge amount of associated material and correspondence. The same conditions as in the villages existed, undoubtedly exacerbated by the communal concentration of housing, animal husbandry, slaughterhouses, drains and wells.

The sewers are evidently not constructed for the purpose of carrying off what they may receive from the privies, and they doubtlessly become clogged with the solid matter, and this is doubtlessly the cause of the very offensive effluvia, constantly coming through the gratings which receive the surface drainage. As we have stated before we believe the water to be very impure in many parts of the town which we have examined, in many cases it is doubtlessly polluted with sewage matter. This is more particularly the case in the more central and lower parts of the Town and there can be no doubt but that the quality of the water will continue to deteriorate in a direct ratio to the increase of wells and cesspools. In all parts of the Town where water is liable to become mixed with even the smallest quantity of sewage matter it would prove (in the event of Cholera invading the Town) an active medium by which the disease may disseminate itself very rapidly amongst large sections of the inhabitants.[TNA]

In fact, appalling conditions were so prevalent throughout England that a national attempt was made to clean things up with the 1875 Public Health Act. But endemic cholera and other waterborne enteric diseases were not properly controlled until the arrival of modern drainage and plumbing.

Healthcare

The job of medical officer was, to say the least, challenging. In 1860 a union doctor could expect to earn about £85 a year, with an additional £40 for covering the workhouse, a job allocated to Edward Covey until 1861 when he died; he had been the principal medical officer for the union since its inception.

Medical officers still had to tender for their employment every year. The salary covered basic healthcare for the poor; drugs and equipment were provided by the doctor and claims could be made for additional care or surgery. The claim process, however, was not easy – application for sanction, as with most things, had to be made to the PLB, and, as usual, their decisions often seem arbitrary and contentious, since emergency care had already been provided when the PLB later disallowed payment.

In 1856, unsurprisingly, disillusionment among medical officers in many unions led to a meeting of over a hundred union doctors in London, chaired by the Earl of Shaftsbury, presenting a petition and asking for 'redress of grievances'. The writer has been unable to find any information about this, only the note in the minutes, but it was probably about money, as these things usually are.

The correspondence in MH 12 is littered with claims and arguments, often with the guardians supporting the doctor concerned. There were claims for amputations for gangrene and infection, setting of compound fractures, operations for cancers and hare lip, urgent internal surgery, birth complications, even treatment for shrapnel injuries following the bursting of a gun. Complaints against doctors were frequent, from the patients for late or non-attendance, or from the authorities for incomplete returns.

One example that created much correspondence in 1861 is Edward Covey's claim for an additional £20 for the provision of trusses, two midwifery cases and examination of 'pauper lunatics'. In spite of the fact that the master stated that the midwifery cases were 'protracted and dangerous', the PLB declined to sanction payment, in addition to requesting further details of the lunatic examinations. This claim went backwards and forwards to the PLB for months, even after Covey's death, and eventually they agreed to a payment of £14 which went to his estate. This kind of thing did not improve the morale of the doctors.

Midwifery fees caused the most problems, which also rumbled on for months. The PLB initially insisted that doctors be present for all confinements, which the Board of Guardians thought ridiculous and impractical. The PLB also criticised the union for not ensuring their doctors lived within their districts, but it can be seen that the demographics of the Basingstoke area, with its central town and tiny out-lying settlements, made this impossible. Doctors were often called upon to attend patients miles from home, sometimes in atrocious weather and on indifferent roads, and it is not surprising that there were cases of criticism when they failed to attend or gave what was considered by the patient to be cursory care.

A letter to the PLB from John Green Bishop, of Monk Sherborne, gives us much detail of how these doctors worked, along with a prescient suggestion for increas-ing their effectiveness. He noted that he himself had been a doctor for nearly fifty years before retiring, and continued to give medical advice to local paupers one day a week. He firstly criticised remuneration:

> The rate per case is so miserably low, that I have no hesitation in affirming that estimating the time, distance & medicine at the lowest value, a loss is sustained in every case. I beg here to observe that a … fallacy exists, respecting the advantage of being a surgeon to the union, in regard to private practice whereas the circum-stance militates against the Medical Officer in many ways – some patients think they shall be treated as paupers – others fear that their surgeon being constantly in contact with all the epidemic diseases and contagion may be brought into their families.

These doctors inevitably lost some of their other patients as a result of union work.

He went on to suggest that, for a fee for the doctor of, say, 7/6*d*, a local house or schoolroom be made available for the poor to visit the doctor and various basic medicines could be available there, thus doing away with constant regular visits to the chronically sick – a precursor to a GP surgery.

This suggestion arose from the time-consuming and convoluted system of treat-ing the poor. Firstly, the relieving officer had to be found to issue an order for the medical officer to visit, whereupon the medical officer may then have issued an order for medicine, which often had to be acquired from elsewhere. Given the distance from the patient to the relieving officer and the distance to the medical officer (an average of about 5 miles), Green Bishop maintained that treatment could often take up to three days. This increased the patient's suffering, could cause death in acute cases, and lead to complaints of tardiness and neglect on the part of the doctors. He suggested that the first point of contact in an emergency could be a churchman or a guardian, to save time. The PLB's response to his letter was that 'it does not appear to be necessary to do more than acknowledge and thank the communicator'.[TNA]

An interesting fact worth mentioning with regard to the continual battle to improve public health was the first purchase in January 1867 of three gallons of cod liver oil from Willwood & Hopkins in London, to be distributed around the parishes for use by the medical officers. Before the discovery of vitamins in the twentieth century, this supplement had already been found to be invaluable in the treatment of many diseases, particularly those related to poverty and malnutrition, such as rickets.

Smallpox and Vaccination

Vaccination is a major and frequent subject in all the records. In 1853 legislation was extended to make it compulsory for all infants under 4 months old to be vaccinated against smallpox, and children in a workhouse could be vaccinated without parental consent. Since it was paid for separately, it inevitably caused great controversy and argument regarding the awarding of contracts to doctors and their payment. Sometimes doctors from outside the union administration were brought in, which caused even more difficulty. Octavius Workman was hired in 1854, but later complained of interference from Edmund Covey and resigned. When a claim was made by Covey, who had taken over the work and been refused payment because he had not signed the right form, Chairman Sclater himself wrote to the PLB in support – it is not clear what the outcome was, but, again, it did not help morale.

Many vaccination returns are to be found in MH 12, and show the number of live births each year in each district and successful vaccinations, and there are also other documents showing where and how they took place and the usual fee – between 2*s* and 3*s* per successful vaccination, which involved an inspection a week later.

In spite of these efforts, since many people were being missed and protection was not permanent, there was a major national epidemic in 1870 to 1872, which inevitably arrived in Basingstoke. Urgent measures were taken to increase vaccination and re-vaccination, but there were many cases. Initially, sufferers were taken into the workhouse in an effort to segregate them, but this did not work – there was even a suggestion that a wall should be built to separate a kitchen for smallpox victims. A specialist trained smallpox nurse from London was hired for the workhouse infectious ward at a fee of £2 2*s* a week, and this later became the usual practice. Eventually, following some rather urgent discussion, it was decided to stop admitting any more cases – for example, four cases in North Waltham in 1871 were specifically refused entry and had to shut themselves off at home.

Emigration

We cannot move away from life in the union without mentioning emigration – people still wanted to leave, although judging by the records this was less frequent than in the first decade of the union, for the poor at least, with only a handful of applications from parishes for help. Among them were ten paupers from Herriard, going to New South Wales in 1849, for whom a loan to the parish of £5 a head was made; two brothers, Nathaniel and Emanual [*sic*] Wheeler from Beech Hill emigrated to Sydney in 1850, the £5 each being £2 for passage and £3 for clothes.

Predictably, the PLB objected to the expense of emigration in 1856, following application for sanction of emigration assistance for Henry Thorpe and his family to New South Wales. The whole exchange is an illustration of just how out of touch the PLB was to conditions in the country:

> As the present condition of the Australian Colonies is such as to offer much attraction to able bodied male labourers and thus to render unassisted emigration more probable than heretofore, the Board think that there should be some special reasons to induce Boards of Guardians to render assistance from the Poor Rate to that class of persons to enable them to emigrate to any of those colonies.

This engendered a difficult and convoluted report from Inspector Hawley:

> The population of Preston Candover in 1841 was 481, inhabiting 97 houses, being about 5 to a house. The acreage is 3430 and the number of adult males above the age of 20, 133 – under 20, 121. This will give about 4 adults to the acre above 20, of whom a large proportion (say one 4th) will be old men past work. Half of those under 20 will be boys incapable of working – so that there will be … more than 4 workers to the acre – 3 men and 1 boy considered sufficient for one hundred acres of arable land. If so, the parish is overpopulated – in an oblique degree – but not as much as to justify the encouragement of emigration. In the previous census there were 98 families occupying 101 houses. The cottage accommodation appears to have decreased while the population has increased from 442 to 481.
> Query? Will not the encouragement of emigration encourage also the demolition of cottages? And on that ground should not the application be refused?[TNA]

John Lunn, a guardian for Preston Candover, wrote a response in June 1856:

> It is desired to encourage emigration from Preston Candover … the parish has more poor than it can accommodate with cottages … some have emigrated at their own expense … those could not do so not having the means … the Parish being heavily encumbered with poor, would gladly encourage them to emigrate, by taking the pecuniary burden on themselves … If this is done by rate through the Union Board, it falls on all to help, according to their means … If not, a private subscription must be raised in this case; but such inequality as that would produce, would deter those, who assist now, from assisting in the same way again.[TNA]

In the end, the Board of Guardians provided the necessary funds, and in August that year the Thorpe family sailed for Australia, the PLB leaving it to the auditor to sort out. The total cost was £36 18s, covering everything from railway fare to help with clothing, and including 2/6*d* to refund John Lunn for out of pocket expenses on the day – he was obviously there helping them.

Harriet Collis, a 16-year-old from Stratfieldsay, 'her family and home being of the vilest character' (Revd Joyce, July 1858), and an ex-convict from Winchester Gaol, having stolen beans and broken into a house, was found a position with a family emigrating to Australia – even the chaplain of the prison thought this a good idea. She had been moved to Allesley Farm Reformitory (near Coventry), where a Queen's Pardon had been obtained for her by the superintendent, Mrs Bracebridge, so that she could go. In spite of all this effort to help one troubled girl, the PLB refused sanction, but, since there was a time limit because of the sailing date, the necessary £4 was provided by the guardians. The auditor objected, but Inspector Hawley eventually thought 'the disallowance may be remitted'.[TNA]

Life in Basingstoke Workhouse

Work

As before, the mainstay of the life of an inmate in the workhouse during this period was work, both in maintaining the institution itself and providing constant occupation for all inmates who were able. We may recall that the majority of inmates were children and the elderly, with many of the others probably not particularly fit for hard physical labour; but everybody had to work.

The banning of the highly lucrative work of bone crushing in 1846 caused a good deal of consternation to the officers of the union, with the auditor casting about for ways of cutting costs and increasing income – nothing changes. It is clear from the minutes that the guardians were also looking for new ways of keeping able-bodied inmates occupied. In May of that year a committee of guardians was set up to look into the 'whole economy of the Workhouse'. Following an apparent lapse of several years, the possibility of oakum picking was again raised.

In August 1846,

> The Master … be directed to go to the Dock yard at Portsmouth to ascertain the terms upon which Junk can be obtained to be picked, to make himself acquainted with the process of picking, for obtaining a Model of the Block, Mallett & other instruments used and to obtain such further information as may be useful.

At the same time, the clerk was to write, along similar lines, to the authorities at Deptford, Woolwich, Chatham and Sheerness dockyards. A purchaser for the 'finished' product was also to be found. Exact details are difficult to find, due to the convoluted involvement of the auditor, but an initial order of an amount 'not exceeding 2 tons', at about £5 a ton, was ordered.[HRO]

In the absence of all but four balance sheets, dated between 1856 and 1865,[18] we have only one definite indication of the proceeds of oakum sales: in 1867 there were receipts of £4 in a half-year. There was a dedicated room for oakum picking, with a storeroom on the floor above, as shown in the late nineteenth-century plans (see Appendix II), and the practice continued from then onwards.

Another hard and relatively useless task that was undertaken, when there were enough fit paupers, was stone breaking. In 1848 male paupers were to break 42lb of stone in four hours, but by 1871 an order for flints from the highways surveyor could not be fulfilled since a supply could not be found – this is unexpected in an area where flint is plentiful in the ground, but no explanation is given.

Of course, it was always preferable for people to be employed in useful and lucrative work, and this seems to have been generally the norm in Basingstoke, with the make-work tasks only employed in the absence of anything more appropriate – and for casual vagrants, of course. Local landowners were approached to see if they could find work for the able-bodied.

In September 1846, a mill for grinding corn was purchased from a supplier in Reading, and a year later a stone floor was provided in the new mill room. At the same time the contractor who supplied the mill was consulted regarding the appropriate amount of labour on the mill. There is an indication here of the design of the mill from its use: sixteen men were employed a day at a time, six on and two off on each crank. The men worked 15 minutes on and 10 minutes off, and were supervised by an overseer. Later, able-bodied women occasionally worked at the corn mill. There is something relentless about this schedule. The charge for the finished product was 9*d* per sack.

Another way of employing inmates was in making and repairing shoes: a contract for the purchase of materials was placed in May 1853 for different kinds of leather and various hob nails, between 1/2*d* and 1/8*d* per 1,000. It is not clear how these skills were taught or passed on to inmates – certainly nobody was employed specifically for this purpose at this time – but it was undoubtedly a useful skill for younger boys to learn. This was still going on several years later, as indicated by the continued purchase of shoe leather; however, in 1864 there was a tender for the repair of boots in the workhouse. Perhaps the person or inmate responsible was no longer there, or the task was too large. Tailoring is also mentioned several times, but with few details, apart from some industrial training provided for boys. Also, of course, particularly for women and girls, there was the continual making, repairing and laundry of clothing and bedding.

So considerable use was made of diverse skills of inmates coming into the workhouse. Boys, nominated by the schoolmaster, could also be employed by the master on particular tasks, and running errands for him. And, as before, girls and women were consistently employed, and trained, in domestic duties, in the kitchen and cleaning the various rooms, as well as helping in the schools. As many of them as possible were found work in service so that they could move on.

Many hands were employed in the 'garden', the land adjoining the workhouse used for growing various foods, and eventually keeping a cow. This was also considered part of the training of boys, with the older ones sometimes employed for half a day much of the week in a busy growing season, superintended by the porter. Girls were taught dairy duties. From a completely unrelated letter about staffing problems,[TNA] it is evident that elderly men were also to be found working regularly in the 'garden'. The rare balance sheets and accounts, and a couple of comments in the minute books, reveal that surplus vegetables were regularly sold, occasionally up to £60 worth a year. Pigs continued to be bred, butchered, bought and sold. Altogether, this brought the workhouse close to self-sufficiency seasonally in some fresh foods, which leads us to the next topic of diet.

Diet and Supplies

There was an improvement in the basic diet provided to the able-bodied in the second decade of the workhouse. The breakfast gruel was still there, but there was an increase of a couple of ounces in the bread allowed, both then and also at dinner. There was slightly less cheese, but more cooked meat, and the content and quality of most of the diet items had improved considerably. The diet of the young, old and sick could be, and was, officially altered at the discretion of the medical officer.

From the fact that surplus vegetables were being sold, we can assume that inmates generally received their full ration and more. On occasions when potatoes and other vegetables were scarce, seasonally or because of crop blight, additional bread was given to make up.

Officers' rations, at first the same as those of the inmates, were improved, although on a few occasions they preferred to receive cash instead and purchase their own food – about 6s a week in 1860.[TNA] They did receive slightly more sugar, tea, milk, beer and butter than the inmates.

Outside these bland tables, it does appear that there were variations in what was actually given to inmates. Beer, for example, was frequently purchased – a second attempt at brewing within the workhouse was made in 1859 and continued for several years, but 'good wholesome table beer' was still included in the tenders, so we know it was being consumed in quantity. We know that the elderly were given beer, from a dispute with the auditor which ended up with the PLB – their disapproval was ignored. We also know that in 1865 women working in the laundry were allowed a pint of beer a day.

> SOUP INGREDIENTS
>
> 1849: Soup included 2 pints of pease, 2oz of flour and 2oz of rice. Gruel contained 8oz of oatmeal. (Quantities unclear).
> 1853: Soup contained 5 pints of pease and 6oz of ham per gallon. Gruel contained 16oz of oatmeal per gallon. Coffee contained 1oz of coffee, 3oz of sugar and ¼pt of milk.[TNA]

Brandy and port, too, were given as a matter of course to both the elderly and the sick. In fact, in December 1871, there was an enquiry when brandy in the infectious ward was found to be 'very much adulterated'. This was during the time when 'an inmate called Percy' was delivering the brandy to the ward in the absence of the porter, whose job it usually was.[HRO]

Medical officers often prescribed extra rations, despite sometimes being criticised by the auditor for doing so. From Dr Covey's report of 1850, referring to cases of skin disease and inflamed eyes in some of the children: 'The diet ... has little to do with it, as it consists of meat with plenty of vegetables twice in the week, bread and cheese the other days, which is a far better one than could be procured for them out of doors'. He mentioned that their general health was good.[TNA] He later commented, in a letter to the PLB of 1856 regarding the children's diet:

> I have taken into consideration the dietary table for children as forwarded by the PLB as also the present one in use in Basingstoke Workhouse ... The gruel as made in this establishment is of the best kind and exceedingly nutritious and consequently preferable to the milk that would be procured, to which many of the children object ... I do not think cheese wholesome for young children, have therefore substituted Suet Pudding and also Soup and Bread for that of Rice without Sugar or Butter. I consider a small allowance of Butter a great [his underlining] desideratum and have added it to the supper.

There appears to have been little change in the official diet over the next few years – at least judging from the records – but there is a circular, in 1871, of Australian instead of British meat being sanctioned by the PLB to be included in 'potato hash or stew', although it appears that this was not done in Basingstoke.[HRO]

The quality of supplies was evidently carefully monitored, with unsatisfactory items being returned. There are many references to poor-quality or underweight bread or cheese being delivered. Remembering that bread was being supplied to the poor throughout the union, this was a serious business, and in 1869 the police were involved. As the largest single consumer in the area for these basic goods, the union had considerable local power and often changed supplier.

The tender invitation letters which appear in the local papers are interesting in themselves, in the range of goods and services being purchased – from candles to coffins, brushes and brooms, soap and salt, boots and stockings, drapery and fabrics, buttons and threads, chimney sweeping, shaving and haircutting, to mention a few. Each quarter, payments were made to suppliers and minuted in detail, fascinating information but beyond the scope of this book.[HRO]

All the important local tradesmen feature. The subsequently internationally famous Thomas Burberry became a long-term supplier of haberdashery, clothing and fabric supplies in 1858, and even he was criticised the following year for supplying goods 'not to contract'. When coal supplied locally was found to be substandard, it was shipped in direct from Cannock Chase in the Midlands by the Cannock Chase Railway Company.

Workhouse Visitors

It was important for appropriate people from outside the strictly isolated environment of the workhouse to visit regularly, watch for problems and listen to the inmates, and this became enshrined in the rules and suggestions emanating from the PLB in London. In a letter in 1847 they stipulated that a weekly visiting committee should report on 'any abuses or irregularities in the treatment of the pauper inmates, or in the general management of the House.'[TNA] But it was difficult, as before, to get guardians to perform this task and there were repeated reminders and entreaties for them to turn up; in 1850 the board actually had weekly printed notices of the latest schedule or rota prepared and distributed. Eight years later, the minutes note that two guardians were to be elected every fortnight, and evidently the system was still having problems.[HRO]

In the late 1850s there was much middle-class interest in the conditions of the poor and workhouses in general, and one result was the belief that suitable ladies could have a positive influence. In 1859 the Workhouse Visiting Society was set up by a member of the Twining family, with the intention of influencing 'moral and spiritual improvement of workhouse inmates in England and Wales'.[19] This organisation only lasted a few years, but it obviously made an impression on the great and good in Basingstoke, and in 1860 a Ladies Visiting Committee was set up, although their access was confined to the schools in the early years.

The first committee consisted of 'Mrs Hunter, Mrs Keale, Mrs Loveday, Miss Catherine Sclater, Miss Lefroy, Miss Blunt, Miss Huddlestone, Miss Brocas, Mrs Joyce, Miss Booth, [?] Rycroft [pencilled], Miss Keate, Mrs Workman'. These were mostly female relatives of the current Board of Guardians. Members were to visit each week, the boardroom being at their disposal and a key provided. It is not clear what influence they actually had, but presumably a visit by suitable 'ladies' and a report back to the board was bound to have an effect on both morale and discipline. In the words of Revd Joyce in 1870, the system 'appears to supply, in aid of the bare law, some elements of human love and pity, which have been greatly wanting, and without which any workhouse is liable to become, and to continue, only a receptacle of vice and suffering'.

When the guardians' own visiting committee reports were transcribed in the minutes in 1871, we catch for a frustratingly brief period a few glimpses of the small details of life in the workhouse. A couple of examples from that year:

• January: 'clothing supplied was insufficient' … 'underclothing, caps etc. had to be worn for a month at a time without change, and that while the said underclothes were being washed the women and children were compelled to go without'. Also that on a certain day 'there was an insufficiency of milk for children's breakfast'.

- May: the wringing machines were broken and the women standing in water while washing – a frame was recommended for them to stand on. A stove was to be put in the old men's dayroom since '43 old men [were] endeavouring to sit round one fire, and this was attended with considerable difficulty'. 'Both the stone breaking and oakum rooms were empty at 10.30 a.m., 42 able bodied in the House'.[HRO]

There were many remarks throughout about the insufficiency of 'chamber utensils' and the fact that privies were offensive – the new earth closets had evidently not yet been installed everywhere. The other perennial complaint was insufficiency of clean clothing and bed sheets, and recommendations were made for increased ventilation in certain areas, along with painting and whitewashing.

Staff

The workhouse continued to be a challenging place to live and work for employees. In the trawl through the minutes it is evident that very much more time was devoted to various staffing issues than to almost any other single subject – from disputes and arguments to the simple frequent turnover of people. And this is also reflected in the correspondence archives at TNA.

It was almost impossible to keep schoolteachers, to such an extent that it becomes more and more difficult actually to keep track in the records of who came and went. Some teachers only lasted a couple of months, one or two walked out almost immediately – between 1846 and 1871 there were between twenty-seven and thirty teachers appointed. In 1855 the difficulty of getting a schoolmaster was so great that the board applied to the War Office 'to ascertain if a Sergeant on half-pay could be found to undertake the office'. The resulting appointee, Mr R. F. Gore, only lasted two weeks. In 1856 the board examined the actual living conditions of the teachers, to see if things could be improved, but little was done beyond adding a few mats and painting the walls. There was the general low ambience of living in a workhouse environment – and often being virtually as imprisoned as the inmates. One unfortunate schoolmistress found herself locked out after returning to the workhouse after dark. Finally, in 1860, a teacher who fitted in was found: 19-year-old Matilda Augusta Smith, from Liverpool, was appointed and she lasted thirty-seven years. We will meet her again later.

Maybe the problem was the recruitment method. Later in 1870 Revd Joyce said that 'really good officers are difficult to get and keeping them is difficult'. He criticised the method: advertisement followed by election, 'perpetually without the slightest enquiry as to candidates … when the hour of election arrives the

Board finds itself totally at sea, and its vote is turned almost by a mere whim at times. No candidate should be elected without being seen'. He went on to suggest a fourteen-day period to make enquiries about an individual, but this was seldom actually done, probably more out of desperation to get someone in position quickly than anything else. So perhaps some of the problems were simply caused by the quality of the staff employed; many teachers came and went to and from other workhouses, so there was perhaps a subset of schoolteachers who existed in the Poor Law environment.

A couple of examples of this fast-track method of appointing teachers were John Matthews and Thomas Carter. Matthews, appointed in September 1851, was fired the following January, the board having found out that he had no experience or qualifications. Carter, the next appointee, had charges brought against him at his previous placement in Chippenham Workhouse: Ann Hudd, who had 'lately left his service' accused him 'of having taken liberties with her & of having exposed his person'.[TNA]

As for the working environment, discipline in the schools, particularly with the boys, is often mentioned in a negative way, and it makes sense that the children in the schools were a challenge. Not only were they of mixed ages and abilities, but they often had difficult backgrounds and some were likely to be emotionally troubled, orphans or children deposited to support family finances. The occasional child was virtually feral.

Was it the diet? The staff diet in Basingstoke was certainly much better than that of the inmates: in 1858 one weekly ration consisted of 7lb bread, 7lb meat, 8oz cheese, 8oz butter, 8oz sugar, 3oz tea, 2oz coffee, 1.5lb flour, 1qt (2pts) milk (staff children receiving slightly less), and often vegetables from the garden. Several of them still opted to receive cash instead, to purchase their own food.

Other frequently reported difficulties with being a workhouse officer, in Basingstoke as elsewhere, were complaints of interference, overt rudeness and 'improper language' relating to the master and matron, and there was evidently constant bickering going on – on more than one occasion Master James Forder was asked, by the Board of Guardians, to be more courteous to his subordinates. The previous master, John Harbor, also came in for criticism, being accused by the then schoolmaster, Henry Bull, of deliberately undermining his authority with the boys. But one of these boys was in the hospital for several days, having been severely beaten by Bull, who, incidentally, only lasted in the job for four months.

Typically, it is very difficult to work out what was happening here, with so many claims and counterclaims between personalities. There is one copiously documented series of complaints starting in November 1858 involving nearly everyone, which led to a full PLB enquiry. The schoolmistress, Anne Whitehorne, was accused of cruelty in leaving a 2-year-old boy, who was suffering from severe diarrhoea, half naked in the yard – it is quite obvious that she could not cope with keeping him clean. At the same time, she was accused of having walked in the garden with the schoolmaster's (Charles Leaborne) arm around her, together with Leaborne's brother, James – but it was revealed later that all three had known one another since childhood. There were also problems with the girls being 'in a dirty state, both as to their bodies and clothing', an unfair accusation when clean clothing was apparently not always available. The situation goes on and on. The porter, John Chamberlain, was accused of numerous failures: refusing to supervise cleaning, refusing to assist in whitewashing the kitchen, not supervising the weighing of coals and using insolent language. There are pages of statements and reports in MH 12, and it is as if every staff grievance now emerged in one go, and many of the problems appear to have arisen from simple personality clashes.

All three – the schoolmistress, the schoolmaster and the porter – subsequently left the workhouse. It is interesting that a few months later Leaborne's new employers, Abingdon Workhouse, wrote to the Basingstoke Board regarding his employment, in view of 'the unsatisfactory manner in which the management of the school in the Abingdon Workhouse appears to have been conducted'.[TNA]

When all this was over and things had settled down, the workhouse was inspected by Inspector Hawley:

> Both schools [were in a] fairly satisfactory state, the children appeared clean and orderly … the boys were addressed about their disorderly conduct … I have no reason to complain of the manner in which the mental instruction of the children in both schools has been conducted … of the other parts of the workhouse I am enabled to make a commendatory report. The wards are all in a more clean and orderly state than I have ever yet found them, and the inmates appear more decent in their persons, and more respectful in their behaviour; many alterations and improvements have been made for their comfort by the Master [Forder], and more are in contemplation, and between him and them the best feeling appears to prevail … he is mild and respectful in his demeanour and address, has a perfect knowledge of his duties, which he carries out with firmness combined with kindness.[TNA]

Another fairly typical dispute erupted in November 1867, when the nurse, Anne Ward, accused the master of getting too involved in infirmary affairs – he had allegedly moved beds around, 'controlled' the fire and accused her of lying. She also claimed that he had not passed on instructions from the doctor and ordered her to remove a child from the infirmary. The minutes note that, in view of the disputes between Forder and the rest of the staff over the years, the board again requested his 'forbearance and command of temper' so that the 'efficiency' and 'general discipline are not disturbed'.

Things continued simmering and came to a head again in May 1868, resulting in a full PLB enquiry, where it was found that Master Forder was involved in hiving off some of the wine and spirits intended for infirmary patients, using a different measure from the nurse's, and falsifying the books relating to supplies, presumably for his own benefit.

The master and matron, and the nurse, were asked to resign immediately. The new master and matron were Mr and Mrs J.J. Humby, and the nurse (who only lasted for four months) a Mrs Clarke.

Outside, in the union, there were also occasional difficulties with controlling relieving officers. In 1854, John Barrell, who had been employed from the outset, was found to have a shortfall of £128 in his account. He was unable to pay this back, was declared insolvent and his surety, Mr Clift, was pursued through the courts. Similarly when James Ellis died, leaving an outstanding amount, the legal case involving his surety, Mr Smith, went on for two years. All these proceedings were minuted month by month.

Again, Some Numbers

In the absence of regular accounts, it is difficult but not impossible to work out what was going on in Basingstoke Union as regards numbers and costs. We do have different episodes and scraps of information throughout this period, and various methods of noting figures in the two main archives: cheques paid to relieving officers, estimates of rates to be charged, notes of inmate numbers in inspectors' reports, odd returns to the PLB and so on, and from all these we can fit together the puzzle and see roughly what was happening. And we have, of course, the three census returns from 1851, 1861 and 1871, although these should be viewed with caution (see Appendix III).

It is simply a matter of putting all the information available into one spreadsheet and looking for patterns. For example, we have an eleven-year run of average half-yearly costs of in maintenance and out relief between 1854 and 1865, and, looking at the trends and random pieces of information in the other numbers, we can reliably assume that this period is typical for this part of our history.

The reduction in out relief from the late 1850s is probably due to improving economic circumstances in Basingstoke itself, and this era marks the beginning of a long movement from the dominance of agriculture to industry and services. The town had become a railway hub from 1848, with links to more towns in the region, and a transformation was taking place, which we will look at a little more closely in Part 3. More people found steady work, and this was bound to provide a spin-off improvement in local trading and services; there would be provision even for the unskilled or semi-skilled labourers who were the majority at the receiving end of the Poor Law system.

So, how typical is this in the wider picture? A paper presented by Mr Julian B. Yonge, of Hursley Union, at the Basingstoke Poor Law Conference in 1870, noted that many unions were 'finding that the proper administration has difficulties in practice' – being the requirement to put as many claimants as possible into the workhouse. He noted that in 1869, according to the PLB, £3.68m had been spent on out relief, and £1.56m on in maintenance – a 70/30 split. In fact, the government officially allowed the re-introduction of out relief in 1871, because the preferred practice of refusing it had become untenable.[20]

Looking at the figures behind our Basingstoke graph we see that the split between in maintenance and out relief was 84/16. At the same time, although the workhouse could officially house over 400 inmates at any one time (from various correspondence), this figure was very rarely reached – there was clearly a reluctance to 'offer the house' unless absolutely necessary. This 'maximum number' is in itself confusing, since the accommodation return of April 1856 in MH 12 gives the maximum number allowed as between 320 and 350 (the inspection report of 1848, previously mentioned, verbally gives a number of 426, but this is unique).

From the numbers we have, and as would be expected, there was a marked and consistent increase in the late winter months and there would often be quite a drop in the summer. The number of inmates only went over 300 once, to 304 in March 1851, which created anomalous census information for that year.

The Census
The three sets of information for 1851, 1861 and 1871 are not very useful for detailed analysis; the problem with census data for such a small group of people, once a decade and on one night, is that it is only a very tiny sample, and does not

Fig. 13 In Maintenance and Out Relief costs, 1854 to 1864.

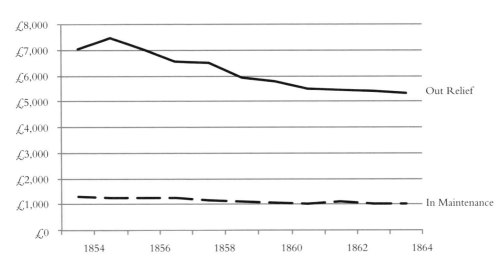

really give us any significant information to work with – but it is interesting to view in the absence of anything else.

Looking at the birthplaces of the inmates, we can see that there was a slight decline in strictly local people and an increasing number from further afield within England, but, at the same time, we don't know how many were simply overnight vagrants. In 1851 one woman, Jane Jinkstooke, 91 and a beggar, came from Boston, America. Another beggar was from Ireland, Daniel Sullivan, 50. In 1861 there was just one Irishman, Thomas Cavanagh, 36, a brazier from Cork. In 1871, the oldest two of the four Soper children in the workhouse are described as having been born in Odessa, Russia – one of them marked as a 'British subject'.

The age distributions need care, since they do not always correspond with reality – we know that there were often relatively few people capable of significant work in the workhouse. But we can see families. In all three returns there were several apparently single females with a baby or very small child. There were small families consisting of just the elderly and the young with working-age adults absent. There were a few disabled, blind, deaf or 'idiots'. This is a pattern and ties in with what we know from other records. There is a full age breakdown of all the census data in Appendix III.

As far as their declared occupations were concerned, again the sample is too small, but it is interesting. In 1841 nearly all the inmates were agricultural labourers or in service of some kind, and these occupations remain at about 80 per cent or more for the next three returns.

Administration and Other Matters

The unions and their workhouses were increasingly important local organisations. As powerful bodies, encompassing large areas consisting of towns and cities, parishes, farmland and industrial areas, the Poor Law unions had become immensely useful for central government both in acquiring information and in implementing national initiatives for social and financial control – a new tier of local government was emerging.

In Basingstoke, requests for information and returns from central government, usually via the PLB, were constant – details of any transported convicts and their families (none), the number of French lunatics being supported (none), the numbers of families of militia men receiving relief, religious accommodations in the workhouse, and so on. In 1854, detailed agricultural statistics for the whole union were requested and the Board of Guardians initially refused, saying that they had enough work to do, although they complied in the end. Information was also required by other government bodies: returns of cultivated land, returns of surplus labour, returns of cholera deaths, returns of removal orders. A German judge, studying the English Poor Law system, noted that 'English poor law statistics surpass those of all other countries both in their scope and in the time over which they extend'.[21] Unfortunately we do not have any of this information for Basingstoke, just the requests and covering letters.

The union was responsible for property valuation in the parishes and the collection of Poor Law rates, the precursor of modern council tax, as well as continuing sales of old poor properties. The assessment committee formed annually from the guardians worked constantly considering rating claims and appeals. Unsurprisingly, the estimates for rates received by the union climbed from about £3,500 in the late 1840s to over £6,000 in 1871. Further groups, or committees, were set up as required over the years – a sanitary committee, a schools attendance committee,[22] a finance committee, a farm committee. Responsibility for 'Nuisance Removal and Disease Prevention', which came under the various Public Health Acts, continued to show up in the minutes as being a frequent and regular activity.

Most of the liaison for all this work fell on the clerk. In 1849 the first clerk, George Lamb, resigned, having provided nearly fifteen years of service. He mentioned the 'kindness' of the board, and 'especially appreciates the most friendly and considerate bearing and assistance which have all along been extended to me by your most worthy and able Chairman and Vice Chairman … whom I am satisfied no Union in the Kingdom can boast of better'.[HRO]

His place was taken by William Challis, another solicitor, who stayed in the job for twenty years, until 1869, when George Lear, who initially worked for Lamb Brooks Solicitors, took over – his handwriting was awful, although that of his clerk who wrote out the routine minutes was better.

Who were the guardians behind the union? Outside Basingstoke town they continued to be mainly yeoman farmers, with the occasional clergyman or 'gentleman' farmer. For the Basingstoke parish, they were often tradesmen and merchants – John Lodwidge, ironmonger, 1856 to 1860 (he later became mayor in 1881); George Franklin, grocer, 1853 to 1858; William Pistell, plumber and glazier, various years between 1845 and 1861. It was difficult to acquire and keep guardians, parishes often going without or temporarily combining with each other for representation on the board. In view of the awesome task and responsibility, with men often having to go against their conscience and empathy to apply the rules, it is hardly surprising.

This wide area of activity, beyond strictly caring for the poor, was eventually reflected in 1871, in changes in central government, when the PLB was abolished, its responsibilities absorbed into the new Local Government Board (LGB), which remained the governing body for the Poor Law Unions until 1929.

All that appears about the change to the new LGB in the minutes is a circular letter and a brief note; a new correspondence folio is started in MH 12 in 1871.

Part 3

Challenges and Changes, 1872 to 1900

Situated in a rural part, the Basingstoke Workhouse presents a pleasant appearance. The walks are kept well-gravelled; the flower beds are carefully attended to; and an air of neatness and cleanliness pervades the various surroundings.

Hants & Berks Gazette, 'Festivities at the Workhouse', 10 January 1880

I will not say more of it than … that [it] is one of the ugliest structures it has ever been my misfortune to see.

Hants & Berks Gazette, 'Two Hours in the Workhouse', 30 July 1881

This section takes us from the establishment of the LGB to 1900, when we lose an enormously important part of our records, MH 12.

England was changing dramatically in the last quarter of the nineteenth century. Basingstoke was reaching the height of its prosperity by 1875. The arrival of Thomas Burberry in 1856 started a long run of intense mechanised clothing manufacture, employing hundreds of women. Wallis & Steevens opened its first ironworks near the railway station, and grew to a world-leading manufacturer of steam traction engines, road rollers and the like, employing skilled men and boy apprentices; run by Quakers, it looked after its workers. And, of course, there were all the associated services and trades. The town was transformed – in 1851 the population was 4,263; in 1871 it was 5,574 and by the time of the 1901 census it was 9,793 – more than doubling in fifty years.

The population of the whole union, 15,400 in 1831, increased by 1900 to 20,619, nearly 34 per cent. About half now lived in the town, whereas it had been less than one quarter in 1831. The rural population had actually fallen by about 1,000.

William Bear's national Agricultural Report of 1892 describes the working lives of agricultural workers (who always provided the largest group in the workhouse); there was enough work throughout the year for men, while women worked in the fields 'picking stones of the fields for road-mending, weeding, and doing work in the hayfield with their male relatives … at piece-work'. By this time, boys did not work for pay before the age of 12 or 13 and young girls only helped at harvest time.

In 1871 there were big changes in the way the country was governed at local level. Several government bodies were combined together for the purpose of 'the supervision of the laws relating to public health, the relief of the poor, and local government', forming the new LGB. Functions were transferred from the Home Office, the Privy Council and the PLB; many of these duties were already being performed by unions (registration of births, deaths and marriages under the Home Office, vaccination under the Privy Council, and more) so it 'tidied up' the situation. It was a powerful, top-level government department, and staff were transferred to their new sections automatically. In fact, very little changed on the ground in the administration of workhouses and poor relief.

How do our records change? The format of the minutes remains essentially the same, very dry and tedious: attending officers, examination of the books, invoices, out relief and payments to relieving officers (in summary only), the master's balances, the treasurer's balance and accounts, cheques issued, the appointment of the three guardians on the visiting committee for the next two weeks. The examination of accounts became so time-consuming that from 1893 separate meetings were often called in the clerk's office. At the end of each meeting 'other business' is included briefly, which is the most interesting part of the minutes.

At every meeting during this period there appear a number of individual decisions relating to the system of cross-charging between unions, or 'non-resident relief'. It happened when paupers from other unions moved to Basingstoke, or vice versa, and if the reasons were good – family support, possibility of work – then the person's home union would pay their union of residence for their relief. This had been going on for years, but with a greater movement of people, it had become a formal regular administrative task, now appearing in the minutes in detail. Nationally it involved thousands of people. Where the reasons for residence were not adequate, the pauper was 'removed' back home, and it is easy to imagine the amount of correspondence all this generated. Unfortunately, it is almost the only time we see names now, and too fragmented to be of any use.

A few examples from the 1880s: Eliza Cowdrey and children, settled in Hartley Wintney, were given 2*s* and eight loaves weekly; George Rabbits, from Hartley Wintney, and Sarah Frankham and children, were given relief including school fees; school fees paid for various children in Kingsclere Union; Elizabeth Adger was 'removed' from St George's Union, Middlesex; and Hannah Martin was accepted for relief by Kingsclere Union.[HRO]

All over the country, huge amounts of money were changing hands by cheque along with all the associated forms and returns – a truly Victorian exercise! There were always complications, split families, relatives taken into local asylums elsewhere … the variations were endless.

Another regular subject in the minutes was the chasing of relatives, particularly of people in the workhouse or the asylum, for money towards their support. This was rigorously enforced, and people who refused were prosecuted. And when inmates or paupers died leaving small amounts of money or goods, or if they received bequests, an appropriate amount was taken. Any unclaimed residue was paid to local charities.

On the other hand, turning to the MH 12 correspondence archive at TNA, the impression from 1872 is diversity. General local government matters are included, rather than just the affairs of the Poor Law union, and we lose focus. There is now information about the town of Basingstoke itself, separate from the rest of the union; two distinct authorities were formed under the 1875 Public Health Act, the Urban Sanitary Authority (USA) and the Rural Sanitary Authority (RSA, effectively the Board of Guardians), which were later to become separate District Councils. For a historian of the town, there is a gold mine here for someone willing to dig: increasing urbanisation, everything from building regulations to byelaws, land use to hackney carriages, reservoirs, gas, electricity and street lighting to new school boards, all creating a great deal of paperwork. In the last few years, we begin to see typewritten reports, carbon copies and rubber-stamped signatures. Sadly, it ends for us at 1900, the rest of it destroyed in the Second World War – all that wonderful detail has gone.

A Retrospective

Before moving on with our history of Basingstoke to the end of the century, this is a good point at which to pause and look back.

The system, now firmly entrenched in English social structure, was utterly standardised and uniform, complete with printed forms, and regular inspection and oversight kept everything relatively consistent. Looking at other unions and workhouses, it is almost as if we can substitute records, the only differences being places and names. It is all quite depressingly the same, the only differences being locality and attitude. Workhouses in industrial and urban areas experienced different stresses and biases; in a big inner-city workhouse, with many hundreds of inmates, useful work was not available for all of them, and more make-work tasks were employed. With more people, anonymous paupers drifting in and out, stricter discipline at mealtimes and in yards and dormitories was necessary – hence the iconic pictures of identically-dressed men or women sitting in silent rows at mealtimes, or picking oakum. Workhouses in industrial areas would ebb and flow with the vagaries of their local factories or mines. Some unions spent more or less money on staff, on additions to the basic diet or environment; some unions did not educate children at all until it became compulsory for them to do so.

In some areas there exist plenty of accounts from recipients of the system, but we have nothing like this in Basingstoke – the records are all about how it was done, rather than how it was experienced, which makes any kind of real comparison impossible.

Cruelty

The dominant perception today of the workhouse system is one of cruelty. It occupies a dark place in the national psyche. Celebrities on television burst into tears when finding that an ancestor had been in the workhouse, even though a large proportion of the population at the time had a brush with the union system at some point in their lives.

In fact, much of the really horrible degradation and cruelty happened in the first decade or so – before the Andover Scandal – after which, under the new PLB, there was more control and inspection, and episodes of overt mistreatment were less evident. This early time is where the shudder of horror mostly originates. The press was full of harrowing stories, the iconic *Oliver Twist* was published in 1838 at the height of the clamour, illustrations in pamphlets showed conditions frankly evocative of modern descriptions of Nazi concentration camps, there were shocking posters. And there was a popular belief that Andover was typical, which it was not. But much of this was not true, a lot of it was exaggerated and sensationalised. Little was seriously investigated or disproved – it was certainly never retracted, because, after all, people needed to be made afraid. It is a fact that people killed themselves, or allowed themselves to die, rather than enter the workhouse. Crowther points out that allegations of workhouse cruelty should be taken in the context of the times. It was a cruel age – hangings and floggings were common, casual cruelty to animals, children and women was almost an accepted norm, and the movement to improve the working conditions of children in factories and mines had barely begun.[1] And it was about attitude; the non-deserving poor had made a 'lifestyle choice' and were worthy of contempt – the same sentiment can commonly be found today.

But bad things did happen. From 1835 a great deal of power was put into the hands of local inexperienced, unsophisticated and sometimes barely educated men – farmers, tradesmen, clergymen – who were, in the early years, without much control or guidance. The concept of human rights was far in the future. With all the 'poor bashing' in the press in the previous few years, along with the novelty of the new 1834 Poor Law Amendment Act, it was too easy to put exactly the wrong people in charge at a local level.

Of course, people complained. Paul Carter, in his National Archives webinar (an online seminar), describes many letters of complaint in the MH 12 archive from paupers, and petitions from unions all over the country, particularly during this period, detailing denial of relief and medical assistance, beatings, imprisonment. These are 'relatively regular in some of the unions' correspondence', and this, of course, would be spread by word of mouth outside in the community and add to the fear. However, this was by no means universal and, conversely, he shows many guardians genuinely trying to ease the suffering of the system's victims.[2]

What about Basingstoke? There are just two letters of complaint in the MH 12 archive. Henry Phillips, whom we met in Part 2; and also Clara Elliott who in 1874 maintained – it was disputed – that she had been denied permission to leave the workhouse and her family to look for work.

Can we assume that there were actually no complaints of sufficient seriousness? Or were local people too illiterate, or living in communities too remote to get a letter written? This will remain unknown, and thus we must draw our own conclusions.

Discipline and Punishment

Life was difficult for those who could not settle into the workhouse regime. Many people were resentful and rebellious; some were mentally damaged and socially challenged; some were just plain bad. The early minute books are littered with individual acts of defiance, theft, fighting and violence. But the most common offence was leaving the workhouse without permission and wearing workhouse clothes – which was construed as theft, in spite of the fact that the culprits invariably returned, having nowhere else to go. Offenders were punished in accordance with the seriousness of their offence, ranging from being put on basic rations for a couple of days and/or confined for a few hours, to periods in Winchester prison on hard labour. There are regular newspaper court reports of inmates from Basingstoke being sent to prison in this way for violence, threatened arson or simply stealing.

Sometimes people just lost it:

> Philommon Dagon, a coloured woman, said to be of North America, was charged with damaging some windows and bed ticking at the … Workhouse. Master Atkins: 'I heard a great smashing of glass in the women's tramp ward', she was the only person in the room. 'Three bed ticks had been maliciously cut and the straw strewn about.'
> Chairman: '[She] used language of a most horrible description, too detestable to use in a court. She is the most foul-mouthed woman I ever heard in my life.'

She was sentenced to two months with hard labour.[3]

From the early 1840s the PLC finally decided that some workhouse punishments were excessive, and sought to curb casual incidents by requiring entry of each event into formal, monitored Punishment Books, kept in individual workhouses. A few survive in county archives. We do not have a Punishment Book for Basingstoke. Although there are a few photocopies of punishment book pages, on their own among notes of general workhouse conditions, in the Willis Museum, Basingstoke, they cannot be firmly identified as belonging to our union. But it is interesting to look at those for Alton and Kingsclere, neighbouring Hampshire unions, in the hope it might tell us something about what might have been going on next door in Basingstoke.

Alton Union was slightly smaller than Basingstoke (a population of 10,342 in the 1881 census), and Kingsclere about half the size (7,885). The misbehaviour of inmates was similar: fighting and assault; threatening, obscene or profane language; refusing to work; being noisy and disruptive or disobedient; absconding and occasional deliberate damage to property. But the two workhouses dealt with this quite differently.

Alton had about 290 entries between 1851 and 1910, an average of about five a year, more earlier and fewer later. The punishment meted out was always bread and water for up to two days, or confinement for a few hours, probably to allow a violent situation to settle down.[4]

Kingslere was very different. The number of entries, relative to the workhouse size, is about the same. However, they were much more inclined to take inmates before the magistrates, where they would be given short periods of hard labour in Winchester, and they regularly used corporal punishment. Several children were caned for stealing food or simply being disobedient, and one man was given '9 stripes with the Birch' for stealing in 1877. Several inmates received 'stripes on the back' for stealing, damaging flower and vegetable gardens and slitting beds. The regime was much harsher.[5]

The regime in Basingstoke feels different, and the Punishment Book is never mentioned in the minutes. The first chairman, Sclater, was very disinclined towards punishment of people he saw as victims – when 'four little boys' were brought before him as the magistrate in 1842 for habitually running away, he refused to convict them and ordered they be sent back without punishment.[HRO] This mindset seemed to prevail.

We have just two records of physical punishment in Basingstoke. In 1842 one Abraham Everard received '4 stripes on the naked back' for refusing to work, using bad language and throwing his shoes into the privy. Interestingly, the master that year, James Ellis, was only in post for one year, moving on to become a relieving officer – maybe his style did not fit in? (We met him in Part 2, when he had his windows broken by vagrants.) The other episode was much later, in 1899, and described in an inspection report; a boy on his way to school had set fire to a reed rick, causing 11s worth of damage, and was birched.[TNA]

In between, there are no minutes of punishment at all after 1871, although refusal to work and other misdemeanours are very occasionally mentioned. Inspector Fleming reported in 1878 that 'there have been very few punishments'. But there are fairly regular and graphic reports in the local newspaper of particularly violent, disruptive and foul-mouthed inmates being consigned to gaol.

Formal restraint of the out-of-control was used in the later years. In one letter to the LGB in 1897 the master reported a case 'where it was necessary to have 4 persons in charge of a woman for 2 nights and 1 day who was admitted to the House when verging on *delirium tremens*, and he states that cases of a similar nature are not infrequent'.

He asked for a padded restraint jacket 'for use when absolutely necessary'. This was initially voted down but later acquired after further problems. A lunacy inspector's report in 1900 stated that it had been used just twice, and not on resident 'lunatics'.

Basingstoke Workhouse

Some Demographics

By 1900 nearly a third of people over the age of 70 in England were in a workhouse. When they became unable to care for themselves, nobody was willing or able to take them in. These were the elderly who were not respectable enough for almshouses, which were longstanding private dwellings, often run by church or charity, specifically for those of a higher class who had 'fallen on hard times'.[6]

The population of the Basingstoke workhouse was constantly changing, but, as before, we are able to piece together some idea of what was happening. Inmate numbers varied between 150 and 190, with a reduction of about a quarter in the summer months, but the official number of beds was greater, now about 260. We find that most of this overcapacity after 1880 was somewhat theoretical and was supposedly accommodation for children, the able-bodied and the infectious sick, although the numbers became quite chaotic in the late 1890s with the guardians frantically moving groups of sick and elderly around between classifications and wards to cope with crises, as we will see later.

When the names from all eight census returns from 1841 to 1911 are run together, we begin to pick up some of the stories of inmates. From 1891 people begin to appear who were actually born in the workhouse, and this is the first time this is noted specifically, although a birthplace of Basing may have been previously used. Many of them, of course, were infants, but there were older children and young adults. Harriett Ballard, a laundress aged 29, gave her place of birth as the workhouse, along with her two sons, aged 7 and 3. Altogether in 1891 there were eighteen people who had been born there. Many elderly people appear in more than one census return, and this carries over into the twentieth century. We also see disabled people who were now living there permanently and appear in more than one census. For example, Anne Bohey, an 'idiot', George David, a blind farm labourer from Cliddesden, and Sophia Harding, an 'idiot', all appear in 1861, 1871 and 1881. John Harfield, a blind railway porter, is recorded for thirty years, from 1881 to 1911.

There was now a core of inmates who had become completely institutionalised, and it is evident that some people were regular residents, perhaps using the system, coming and going, to get by when times were difficult. Very obvious this late in the century is the fact that the majority of inmates, with very few exceptions, were agricultural or general labourers, or domestic workers of some kind, the people who were left out of local economic prosperity. And now nearly all of them were local people.

There are two ways to view the numbers in the workhouse. Census information shows the over 60s slightly increasing with the proportion of children falling, with a similar proportion of able-bodied adults, which is as would be expected with people drifting in and out all the time – remember that this is a ten-year, one-night snapshot where the sick and disabled are not identified (Appendix III). But, much more accurately, we also have yearly returns between 1880 and 1900, presented with the inspectors' reports in MH 12, which show the sick and elderly now more than half, numbers of children slightly falling and the average of able-bodied adults remaining fairly constant. These numbers are confirmed by odd figures that crop up throughout the records.

Men outnumbered women by about two to one, and this is the pattern throughout the country; old women were simply much more domestically useful as they could watch children or help with cooking and mending, so they were more likely to be taken in by family.

The reality of all this is that, by the 1880s and within an average inmate group of about 170, there were roughly a hundred or more sick and elderly, about thirty or forty children and about twenty or thirty adults, some of whom could perform useful work. In a report of 1890, it was actually mentioned that little painting or repair work was now done by inmates, and by 1900 private pallbearers were being

Fig.14 Workhouse returns by age and capacity, 1880-1899.

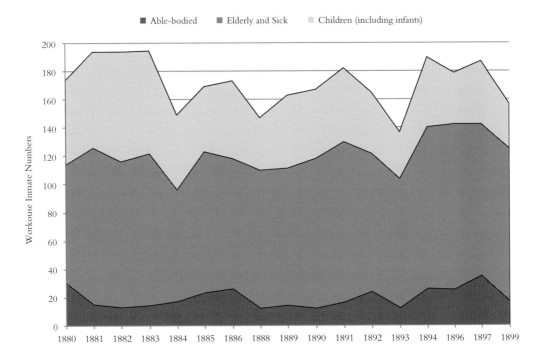

hired in.[HRO] Obviously these figures are approximate and move around – there was a brief period of too many able-bodied in the winter of 1885/86 – but we get the general idea.

This predominance of elderly and sick was reflected in improvements made in inmate conditions: comfortable chairs with backs, more stoves and coal, more bedding, more sensitivity around difficulties with food. Carrying chairs and wheelchairs were acquired. There was always pressure on space to provide elderly couples' rooms. By the end of the century, care of the old was far from conventional workhouse fare. In a 'Report on Aged & Deserving Poor' to the LGB, the author writes that:

> There is a special class of deserving Inmates of each sex, aged over 60, who have separate sitting rooms apart from the rest of the Inmates. The Master has been in the habit of allowing them to visit one another, and they have their breakfast and tea served in their own sitting rooms. The old women have dry tea and sugar served out to them, and … the Master to allow the men … the same privilege.

They were allowed increased liberty with flexibility in rising and bedtimes, and friends from outside could visit freely.[TNA]

Bear in mind that the building, now over fifty years old and past its original tenure, was designed as a form of relatively temporary incarceration for the reluctant poor, deliberately designed to be forbidding and difficult, with no plumbing or drainage and dozens of stairs. Never in anyone's wildest imagination was it intended to provide care on this level. In one report in 1898 it is noted that there were fifty bedridden people on the inspection day. It is this dichotomy, its dominance in the records, which forms the basis of our history of the later years of this period.

Inmate Life Generally

The daily round of work, food, prayers and sleep continued, mostly unchanged, but we have very little detail apart from bits and pieces, just an impression. In the absence of figures, it is impossible to work out exactly how much was spent per inmate, but it was a few pence per day.

Conditions remained primitive until the end of the nineteenth century, when improvement works were incorporated into the building of the new infirmary. In 1889 Inspector Fleming reported that bathing took place in the vagrant ward, where there were only two fitted baths, the water supply was from a well, pumped into a roof tank for distribution, lighting was entirely by lamps and candles, and all the toilets were earth closets, difficult to maintain and therefore often not done properly – all materials had to be carried through rooms and up and down flights of stairs to the outside. They were always a problem. Waste water ran into a field tank, the contents of which were used on the garden.[TNA]

Officially, the diet remained just enough, bland and boring. Between 1853 and 1896 the basic diet had improved slightly, not much more in quantity, but a little more varied with the addition of more soup and scouse (Irish stew), meat pudding and bacon on various days of the week. But breakfast still consisted of bread and gruel, and for supper bread, butter and tea. There were small additions of sugar for the elderly and a little jam for the children, and of course the medical officer could, and did, often prescribe extra rations, which meant that most people were actually doing better.

A very sparse diet for an able-bodied person in the workhouse for a short time was adequate, but not for the long-term residents, and adjustments were necessary. An inspector of lunacy in 1876 remarked that:

> Two of the men and three of the women have full diet, but the remainder are merely upon the able bodied diet which includes fresh meat on only one day in the week; bacon being given for dinner on two days, soup on two days and bread and cheese on two days. This diet is not in my opinion adequate as regards the quantity of animal food for persons of unsound mind, and unless a special and more sustaining dietary be approved by the Guardians and sanctioned by the Local Government Board, I would suggest to the Medical Officer the expediency of placing all in this class on extra meat dinners.[TNA]

This was done.

On a more positive note, during this period, the ingredients of basic foods were regulated – meaning there was less likelihood of skimping to save money – and food was made more palatable. A little allspice was to be added to the gruel 'occasionally', the soup was to include split peas, oatmeal, meat liquor, herbs and seasoning. It is likely that there were additions to this, with detailed official preparation instructions, 'Forms for the Preparation of Foods', being prescribed for meals such as broth, suet pudding, rice pudding, currant cake, dry fruit pudding, cocoa; the ingredients for many of these were being purchased in Basingstoke.

> 1 gallon Soup, to contain 24 oz meat, 16 oz peas or barley, 2 oz of oatmeal, 8 oz of fresh vegetables.
> 1 gallon Gruel, to contain 16 oz oatmeal and 4 oz treacle.
> 1 gallon Potato Hash to contain 24 oz meat, 96 oz potato, 12 oz onions. (1871)[TNA]

We know from elsewhere in the records that there was always plenty of pork and bacon, the pig farm being a thriving business in its own right, and the vegetable garden always did well – according to one minute entry in 1890 there were now about 9 acres next to the workhouse under cultivation. By 1899 fish was being regularly bought, evidenced by a problem with prices.[HRO] The employment of cooks in the last

decade boded well for the quality of the food, and better serving facilities were introduced, steam-heated closets and lidded trays for carrying food upstairs. Complaints by
inmates were taken on board on several occasions, for example the substitution of new
potatoes in the summer, the old ones being fed to the pigs. Occasionally, questionable
food (once, diluted brandy) was tasted for quality at a board meeting.

Beer continued for the sick and workers with difficult jobs – as medical officer
Johnson put it, work of 'a repugnant and dirty nature, viz Laundry and Closet
Work'; up to 100 pints a week were consumed. When an increase in the consumption of port and brandy was noticed in 1892, he stated: 'I am no advocate
for the indiscriminate use of stimulants, but in certain cases of illness, and in the
decrepitude of old age, I am satisfied that their judicious employment is of very
great service'. This was an ongoing problem, often cropping up in the minutes –
evidently alcohol was being given regularly to many people and there was concern
that it should not get out of hand!

As before, supplies were carefully watched. Traders had large and lucrative contracts with the union, and could no doubt be tempted to cut corners; competition
between them was fierce, with hinted accusations of underhand practices often
being made when contracts were awarded to competitors. There were continual
problems with the supply of bread throughout the union, with bad quality and
low weight. The situation needed to be persistently monitored. In 1886 this was a
sufficient problem to prompt an enquiry by Hampshire Police, who checked the
weight of bread supplied in several unions, and in 1897 Chairman Jervoise personally weighed bread supplied to the workhouse, and found it short.

Even coffins were sometimes substandard – in 1874 a pauper complained of the
poor quality of a coffin supplied. This was upheld by the board and the supplier
told, 'the coffins … must be substantial elm ones strongly made of ¾ inch board';
the board were particularly concerned that this quality was maintained. There was
huge inflation in the price of coffins between 1886 and 1900 in all three sizes, with
a large one rising from 10/6d to 22/6d.

Coal was another big consumable. Coal from Cannock Chase in Staffordshire
in 1875 cost £2 a ton, plus 1/6d to carry it from the railway station. Messrs G.H.E.
Stephens won the tender at £1 1s 6d a ton, delivered. Two years later, coke was
supplied by the Basingstoke Gas Company at 3/5d a bushel. The coal suppliers in
1893 (now Stephens, Phillips & Co.) evidently had difficulties with their cash flow
and differences in summer and winter prices, giving an indication of the size and
importance of the workhouse contract for a local supplier:

> Our object in taking your contract at the low rate we did was to give our horses
> and men employment during the slack summer months rather than discharge
> them … had we received your order on 30th June for 135 tons instead of 25 tons
> we could easily have arranged for the coal to be delivered.[TNA]

Work

As before, work for the maintenance of the workhouse and farm was the priority, but extra work tasks were often needed, particularly for casuals or vagrants, and this revolved around stone breaking and oakum. In 1873 a hand cart was purchased for conveying 'stones or other materials for use of the able bodied inmates of the Workhouse', together with loads of pebbles and flints.

But in 1892 the guardians wanted 'better employment' to be found for able-bodied men when the weather prevented them from working outside or in the 'garden'. Sack making and woodcutting were tried, with the former extended to women; Mr Carter agreed to pay 6*d* per dozen sacks, and to send someone to instruct the industrial trainer. It is not clear how this turned out, but stone breaking continued. In 1893 the practice was clarified: 'the Master do strictly enforce the Resolution … as to the employment of able-bodied male inmates of the Workhouse in stone pounding so far as may not prejudicially effect [*sic*] the proper carrying out of the absolutely necessary work in and about the Workhouse'.[HRO] Over the next several years, flints and stones in quantity were bought in, some of them specifically for the roads, under the supervision of the town surveyor.

This constant requirement to be doing something did not always go down well with inmates: a poster was printed and placed in wards in 1893 stressing that the master was entitled to ask them to perform any work required of them. He could set any adult male 'to work at his own proper trade, business or calling, or at wood chopping or sawing, labouring, digging or any other employment suited to his age, strength and capacity'.[HRO] Women, meanwhile, were 'to do nine hours work in Washing, Scrubbing and Cleaning or Needlework'. This was later amended to include, 'to pick 2lb of Unbeaten Oakum', when useful work was exhausted.[HRO] They were to be allowed adequate rest and could be medically excused.

The situation in the 1890s as regards the making of boots, shoes and clothing is confused but appears to have continued. The only hints we get are improvement works to the shoemaker's shop, minuted in 1897. Freeman, Hardy & Willis in Basingstoke wrote to the Board asking why they had received no orders for boots and shoes, but at the same time made-up clothing, along with drapery, was being bought in: 'grey cloth coats & vests' and 'brown cord trousers'. This suggests that there were not enough able-bodied inmates to make a significant contribution to inmate clothing.

The lower level of available workers extended to other areas, too, since casual paid local staff were frequently brought in to help in the laundry and kitchen. This included George Thomas, of whom it was noted that: 'when this man is employed for tailoring he be paid 3/- a day for 10 hours'. His status is not clear, but it is likely from the context that he is one of these workers.[HRO] It is also worth noting that the tailor's workshop was moved and expanded into space liberated by the building of the new infirmary in 1900.

THE BRABAZON SCHEME

Started in 1882 by Lady Brabazon to provide useful work for the non-able-bodied. Although slow to start, craft work soon became a mainstay in workhouses as guardians realised they could sell the results to make the scheme self-sufficient. By 1900, 177 Poor Law Unions were taking part.[7]

In 1893 the Brabazon Scheme arrived in the workhouse, to be carried out with the help and involvement of several of the ladies (see the 'Visitors and Inspections' section on p. 130) and the matron, 'the object of such scheme being the employment of the aged and infirm both men and women in Knitting, Crochet, Netting and various kinds of fancy work'.[HRO] By 1896 there were thirteen workers.

This was very successful in Basingstoke, with an annual bazaar held in the boardroom, starting in 1898. Goods made by the workers were presented at a home arts exhibition in the town, with inmates attending, and two certificates were awarded. When the local representative, Miss Neat, retired she wished to purchase 'something for the benefit of the inmates generally' – we have no more details.

Entertainment and Extras

The idea that inmates should be entertained and amused was relatively new, and is an indication of the different population, along with a growing desire on the part of local people to help in some way.

Music formally arrived. In 1873, 'the Rector and Churchwardens of the parish of Hartley Westpall having very kindly placed at the disposal of the Guardians a barrel organ for use within the Workhouse Chapel, Resolved unanimously that the same be accepted, and that the best thanks … be offered'. Three years later the chaplain provided a harmonium. In 1884 the master requested that regular arrangements for the playing of the harmonium should be made – sometimes volunteers did this, but £1 10s a quarter was granted to employ someone to play occasionally during the week and at Sunday service. By 1900 the harmonium had evidently broken down, and, following investigation by a group of guardians, an American stand-alone Estey pump organ was bought for £16.

In 1892, official sanction was given to the issuing of snuff and tobacco by the master in designated areas, usually the sick wards and the day rooms. These had been valued possessions and currency among inmates for some time, but their use was now official.

Local 'worthies' organised celebratory entertainments, often dinners to celebrate their marriages – although the line was drawn at fireworks. In 1887 a dinner was organised (at a cost not exceeding £15) to celebrate Queen Victoria's Jubilee – at the same time the Prince of Wales asked for public donations for the setting up of a Colonial Institute, the 'Jubilee Fund', and £84 8s 9d was raised by the Basingstoke Union. In 1895 we see the first of many entertainments by the temperance organisation, the Basingstoke District Band of Hope, and in 1897 the celebration of the Diamond Jubilee, with children being invited to tea by the Basingstoke Celebration Committee. There was a concert, a 'Treat', organised by the ladies during January each year, where gifts were given to each inmate, songs were sung and instruments played; these were reported in detail in the *Hants & Berks Gazette* (see the 'Visitors and Inspections' section on p. 130).

Inmates were often given small gifts, particularly on religious holidays – here are just two typical examples from the *Gazette* in 1897:

> Mr A. Julian, Church Street, informs us that he is willing to receive and forward to the Workhouse newspapers or periodicals illustrated or otherwise for the perusal of the inmates which kind friends may leave with him for that purpose. (23 January)

> Received by the master for Good Friday, 1897: Buns for the whole of the inmates from Mr Wadmore; buns for the children, Messrs. Glanville & Co.; sweets for the children, Mr Arthur Julian; jam and marmalade, Miss Leek (Basing). (4 April)

There was always a good Christmas dinner and gifts (disallowed for able-bodied men admitted within a week of Christmas Day). Descriptions of the festivities appeared in the *Gazette* every year. Master Thomas Arter gives a detailed picture of Christmas in 1896. At the board meeting beforehand:

> The Guardians found the entrance hall and their room profusely decorated in their honour. Such mottoes as 'Welcome to our Guardians', 'Health and Prosperity to the Chairman of the Board', 'A Merry Christmas', 'A Happy New Year' were conspicuous upon the walls, while festoons of vari-coloured paper hung across the room, and evergreen and paper roses gave a semblance of gaiety to a place which is ordinarily dull and cheerless.

Lunch on the day was:

> Prime roast beef, two kinds of vegetables and plum pudding. One pint of beer was given to those who preferred it, and ginger beer, Kope ale and stout was provided for the others … each man, and some of the women received an ounce of tobacco, and the women and children oranges, sweets, nuts, biscuits, etc.

There were carols, readings, recitations by staff and inmates.[8]

As for the poor outside the workhouse, out relief was always increased – sometimes doubled – at Christmas.

Workhouse Children

A substantial part of the workhouse population at this time remained children, many of them orphaned or abandoned, but details are scarce; Negrine remarks that this paucity of information about workhouse children is universal across England.[9] In the last twenty years of the nineteenth century it was recognised that a workhouse was not the best place for children to grown up; the LGB ruled that no places for children were to be provided in new workhouses (later in 1913 it altogether banned keeping children over 3 in any adult institution).[10]

Most of the records we have about children in Basingstoke Workhouse relate, not surprisingly, to their education. But we do have occasional scattered comments about their other welfare: in 1878, girls were still sleeping two in a bed, but by 1883 they all had separate beds.[TNA] There were often outbreaks of skin infections, and bad teeth were endemic, which was not consistently addressed until the 1890s when a dentist guardian, Mr Story, stepped in, providing his services for free. [HRO] Some of them had squints, but there is no record of how this was dealt with. We should bear in mind that their treatment was undoubtedly better than they would have received outside the workhouse.

The children were now in a single school with one schoolmistress, Matilda Smith (see the 'Staff' section on p. 131). There is no doubt that the consistent approach of one teacher had a positive effect on the children, and she was very successful. The curriculum became more formal: 'Religious Knowledge, Reading, Spelling, Penmanship, Arithmetic, English Grammar, English History, Geography, Industrial Skills',[TNA] the latter being performed by Mary Anne Tigwell for 'sewing & general industrial work' and various male trainers for the boys. The 1876 Elementary Education Act, under which the workhouse school was later certified, required each child over 5 to have a return on their progress. As time went on, everything was rigorously assessed and monitored by the education authorities, the reports being in MH 12.

There were three separate inspections for children now: the diocesan inspector, the education inspector and the workhouse inspector. The 1870s inspection found the school to be crowded, with over fifty children being taught. This was relieved a little when they had their industrial training, but there were problems with the younger children when the older ones, who helped out, left for service. And if the troublesome ones returned, things could get difficult, as one inspector reported in 1875: 'the tone of the school is not good and I am sorry to hear that several of the girls have come back from service with bad characters'. Around the same time a drill master was employed for the boys – Mr Todd, on £5 5s a year – and all schoolchildren were exercised outside at least twice a week.

In spite of occasional problems, inspectors' reports were positive: 'I believe that the children are as carefully educated as is possible in a W.H.' (1880); 'the children are brought up under as favourable circumstances as can be had in a W.H.' (1881);

'they seem very happy and contented … [cannot] imagine them better cared for or placed than they are' (1882). There were consistent favourable comments about their discipline, the success of their industrial training and their general demeanour, and even their singing, often led by the incumbent matron. As workhouse schools went, this was undoubtedly one of the better ones, so much so that neighbouring Whitchurch Union, in 1883, asked to send some of their children here – this was denied.

In 1897 Matilda Smith retired, to be replaced by Louisa Weekly. But the following year it was proposed that workhouse children would be better educated and socialised in the parish school in Basing. The immediate response of that school was that 'a majority of the Managers were strongly opposed to the plan … they were unable voluntarily to acquiesce in an arrangement which they considered wholly undesirable'. The Education Department stepped in, and firmly responded that a payment of 3*d* per child per week, between ages 3 and 15, should be made by the union. Basing school replied that they did not have room and 'that the introduction of the children from the Union was highly inexpedient'.[TNA] Arguments persisted, but the workhouse children started at Basing school that September; they fitted in well, were well-behaved, passed exams and obtained certificates; they also attended Sunday schools outside.

Miss Weekly's services were dispensed with, and Alice Palmer was appointed initially as 'female attendant for the children', to take them to and from school and care for their needs out of school hours. Palmer moved over to nursing – a sign of the times – and was replaced by Martha Ellis. Another sign of the times came in 1900: 'the boys' caretaker, Mr Sergeant, has gone to the front in S. Africa' (the Second Anglo-Boer War) and his job was kept open.[TNA] He did not return.

Children Sent Out

In many ways, it is more interesting to look at the youngsters who were sent away from the workhouse. It is not absolutely clear in most cases why some were sent away, but it is likely that they were proving difficult to manage or would benefit from professional training. In this age of Victorian philanthropy, many more schools and 'industrial homes' became available and these were certified by the LGB before workhouse children could be sent to them. There were huge efforts made to find places. Several girls were sent to Connaught House in Winchester, a home for elderly ladies, whom the girls learned to care for, earning prizes for good work. The home operated until 1930 and is now a community health centre.

Other homes for girls were the Hampshire Female Orphanage; the Globe Road Girls' Home and the Royal Female Philanthropic Social Home (which was specifically set up to care for and train girls from criminal and anti-social environments), both in London; and the Sandown Home on the Isle of Wight. In addition to rail fare and regular maintenance charges, outfits were provided for a few shillings, sometimes supported by local donations, and the girls were usually provided with a Bible and a prayer book. Indeed, by 1900, the provision of outfits for children moving on had become so common that the LGB issued an order that individual sanction for each amount was no longer required.

Boys presented a slightly different problem, and the union often inclined to a military solution. In 1881, four boys were sent to be trained as tailors in the Rifle Brigade in Winchester, with a view to entering the navy. Three years later, a boy was sent to HMS *Warspite*, a Royal Navy training ship – this was an expensive option, since the outfits cost £4 4s. Training ships were very popular at this time, providing discipline and a potential future for destitute boys – the *Warspite* trained 200 boys a year and turned out many thousands of future seamen.

A few apprenticeships were arranged, but this was not a common option in this rural part of England, where many poor boys ended up employed in agricultural or general labouring. We have minutes of an apprentice chimney-sweep and a shoemaker, Charles Laney, apprenticed to Charles Bristow in Hartley Wintney for four years. And one boy, Frederick Mayers, who was found unsuitable by one tradesman in 1900 and offered a trial by another; the outcome is not noted. But we get far more records of girls.

Of course, things sometimes did not work out, and as usual this is where we get a little more detail:

- Ann Curtis was removed from the Industrial Home for Girls in London in 1877 by her mother, and a letter from the school stated that 'she was not at all likely to do well in service owing to her strong self-will and temper, and Miss Twining is therefore inclined to think this is the best arrangement for her'.
- Sarah Wells, put into service in 1878, was found guilty of theft and 'general misbehaviour' and returned to the workhouse, following which she was sent to the Colchester Industrial School.
- Elizabeth and Rose Fuller went to The Orphanage of Mercy in Kilburn in 1883, but Rose was sent back. She was still an inmate in 1891, having failed in service with an 'unsatisfactory character'. One of the lady visitors, Mrs Hoare, took her on as a laundrymaid, a final chance to 'earn a good character', but this failed too. Rose continued to be a problem, 'her faults are … want of obedience & self-discipline', and the following year, now aged 16, she was sent to the Royal Female Philanthropic Society.[TNA]

Children with disabilities or special needs were also sent to appropriate schools and homes, and very considerable care went into finding them places; local donations often helped. These unfortunate youngsters were sent to, among others, the Bristol School of Industry for the Blind, the Brighton Institute for Deaf & Dumb Children, and the National Industrial Home for Crippled Boys. Ernest McGrath, a blind boy, was refused entrance into the Hampshire School for the Blind in 1897, because there was a question about his condition. Mrs Hoare (lady visitor) procured him a letter of referral to Kings College Hospital, but he was again rejected for admission – Mrs Raynbird (lady guardian) continued to search for accommodation for him, and we will meet him again in Part 4.

F.C. Goodall, a deaf and dumb boy with a cleft palate, was refused entrance to the Bristol School, and the guardians wrote to the Starcross Asylum in Exeter, asking the 'Boys' Trainer' to visit when he was nearby to assess him (the Starcross Asylum was still operating as a residential home at the end of the twentieth century).

Occasionally, girls were sent to Canada. Three girls received an encouraging report from Miss Rye in 1876: 'your two last little girls, Louisa May & Emily Goodman are … both doing well, they have both been adopted and are both living in the same village so that they should not feel lonely, but Emily Goodman is the best child of the two'. She sends addresses in Ontario and offers to send photographs of them. 'I see you ask also for Rosa Brown, she is a capital girl & you will be indeed surprised at her photograph when you see it. I wish these silly girls would write their friends oftener … Maria S Rye'.[HRO] The LGB had denied sanction to fund these children's emigration, but the board persisted and sent them anyway, at a cost of £12 each.

However, as time went on this became less common, and when attempts were made to send girls to Canada sanction was usually refused, particularly when agencies other than Miss Rye's were used. The LGB insisted that these girls should be personally escorted and put into recognised and monitored accommodation at the other end. Annie Burton was denied sanction in 1883, and was sent instead to Alton Home, in spite of the comments from the lady visitors:

> Burton has not been quite satisfactory in service, and had become so utterly depressed, and out of heart, that we felt the best chance of preventing her degenerating into a 'regular Workhouse Girl' was to emigrate her. She has not been guilty of any serious fault, is strong, and will, I believe, do thoroughly well when separated from old associations; she is most anxious to go and brightens up wonderfully when one talks to her about it.[TNA]

However, Annie Burton appears in the 1891 workhouse census, now 23, together with a 2-year-old son, Bernard.

MARIA SUSAN RYE

Maria Susan Rye, founder of the Female Middle Class Emigration Society, set up a system in 1869 whereby pauper girls between the ages of 3 and 16 could emigrate for work and a new life. She set up reception facilities in Niagara, Ontario, and found homes and work with respectable families for thousands of children. She personally accompanied them on the journey and constantly monitored them. The work of her organisation continued after her death in 1903.[11]

The records indicate great interest and personal involvement beyond the call of duty by individual guardians and lady visitors, with valiant and persistent efforts to improve the lives of these unfortunate youngsters. They visited, interviewed, cajoled, wrote copious letters and followed up at the various institutions, to make sure things were going well. On one occasion, in 1888, the chairman and the ladies were so keen to get two girls, Elizabeth and Annie Evans, off to Ontario, and away from the pernicious influence of their mother, that two guardians actually visited the offices of the LGB to reassure them of arrangements.[TNA] The lady visitors paid much of the pre-journey care and emigration of one girl, Alice Bone, with their own funds in 1890.[TNA]

Visitors and Inspections

Who were these people who kept an eye on the workhouse and its inhabitants?

There was now a successful system of rotation of guardians for the visiting committee; three of them were assigned fortnightly. In addition, there was the Ladies Visiting Committee – not less than thirteen in number, who became more and more influential in basic conditions and outcomes, particularly for women and children. These worthy ladies, of whom we have few details, seem to have been relatives of the guardians, many belonging to the local wealthy and aristocracy, the Chutes, the Portals, the Sclater-Booths, all the local big names – they had to be proposed by their committee and approved by the board. Basingstoke's first lady guardian appeared in 1899, when Mrs Raynbird was delegated to visit the Hampshire Asylum along with Revd Atty. There was no specific minute and she first showed up as one of the three visiting committee members; she was heavily involved in the care and placing of children. Shortly thereafter she attended a conference in Winchester on the 'Feeble Minded and Epileptic', and continued to be the board's representative at such functions over the years. We do not get her married initials until much later, which identify her as being part of the prosperous side of the Raynbird family, associated with land agency (often acting for Lord Bolton) and agricultural trading.

And, of course, there was the yearly inspection by the LGB inspector. In 1876 we see the first inspection of Baldwyn Fleming, who was to become involved in the new infirmary project more than twenty years later. He had moved from inspecting unions further north, including Nottinghamshire with its now famous Southwell Workhouse, and settled in Godalming, Surrey (from his private letterhead). He was responsible for fifty-four workhouses in Dorset, Surrey, Wiltshire and the Isle of Wight, including twenty-five in Hampshire.[12] The documents in MH 12 are full of his efforts – he was a sensible, humane and thorough man. The writer was immensely impressed with his tireless work and involvement and there is so much detailed information in his reports. He retired in 1910. It is quite noticeable that his reports, generally favourable, became more and more critical in the last few years of the century, but most of his negative comments were related to buildings or environment, things that could not be easily changed. We will look at this in more detail later.

Generally, though, the living environment of the workhouse was considered good. His summary comments over the years included 'everything in a clean and orderly condition'; 'no complaints received'; 'I am well satisfied with the condition of the establishment'; 'generally remarkably clean & well-kept'; 'the inmates appear to be comfortable and well cared for'; 'the premises are in good order'. There were occasional exceptions – in 1876, following the resignation of the Humbys as master and matron after problems and disputes, and before the Atkins had been in office long, there were some negative comments, which seemed to involve problems with general administration, not enough clothing or bedding made available, the wrong people in the wrong place, and the perennial problem of insufficient maintenance of the earth closets. A return visit by Fleming shortly afterwards found things mostly put right: 'the general appearance of the house is greatly improved & it will I trust soon be as smart & orderly as need be wished'.

In addition to the LGB inspector and the schools inspector, the chaplain continued to concern himself with the children, as did a diocesan inspector from Winchester. These reports continue to give us great insight into general conditions and what was going on day to day.

These people were all, of course, the main mechanism for the LGB to maintain control.

Staff

The staff, the mainstay of the workhouse, continued to provide a saga, the minutes riddled with adverts, applications, interviews and petty squabbles. But there was a small group of people who fitted in well, settled down and stayed for the rest of their working lives. We have already mentioned Anna Newell, inmate-nurse, who stayed for ten years and returned to be cared for in her old age. Another nurse, Hannah Brown, completely contrary to the trend of enormous problems in hiring and keeping nursing staff, stayed for nineteen years and resigned in 1889, an old lady.

Our three steady people, whose lives interweave throughout this period, are Mary Ann Tigwell, employed initially in 1871 as an industrial trainer for girls; George Ilsley, industrial trainer for boys from 1874; and Matilda Augusta Smith, the young Liverpool schoolmistress we met in Part 2, who arrived in 1860 and performed outstandingly throughout her career.

Mary Tigwell, a Basing girl, appears in the workhouse in the 1861 census as a child, and again in 1871 aged 20. She performed so many duties at various times that it is difficult to follow. In addition to training girls in needlework and general domestic work, she assisted in the classroom, acted as assistant nurse, and was often mentioned in reports as generally helping around the house. She applied for, and received, an increase in salary in 1892; in the words of the guardians seeking sanction, her duties were 'assisting generally in the work of the house, admitting and discharging Women, attending to female vagrants, etc.'[TNA] A year later she was working in the kitchen and laundry, having become 'physically unfit' for nursing duties. Matilda Smith offered to pay a small salary herself if Tigwell could help with industrial training again, which she was finding too much, since her own health was beginning to decline.

George Ilsley, industrial trainer in gardening (and tailoring is mentioned), also filled in as porter and even master on a couple of occasions, and, like Tigwell, often just helped out as needed. As his role diminished over the years, with training in gardening disappearing from his records for the first time in 1897, he was asked to turn his hand to cooking. The guardians proposed to send him for kitchen training at Portsea Island Workhouse, but this did not work out and was not sanctioned by the LGB.

In the last years of the century, all three of them finally left service. Matilda Smith retired through ill health, on a pension of over £54 a year. George Ilsley, also now ill with varicose veins and a leg tumour, also received a pension of over £34. The LGB at first objected to this, but were told that 'he was injured in the leg in 1880 when extinguishing a paraffin lamp which had exploded … that he has been kicked on the same leg by refractory inmates on 3 occasions'.[TNA] His now limited duties were taken over by the porter. Since Mary Ann Tigwell was not considered to be particularly infirm, there was an argument over her pension entitlement, and it is not clear what she received in the end.

As for the rest of the staff, the turnover was still considerable. Few people stayed long. The most important officers in the general running and ambience of the workhouse, as we have seen before, were the master and matron, and it is worth looking more closely at the post-holders during this period.

John and Jane Humby had been in post since 1868 and were blessed with a series of unsatisfactory porters: Thomas Moore accused the matron of 'uncivil & unkind treatment' of him and was accused of '[making] himself too familiar with the women'; George Giles was fired for swearing at her; David Hole became too ill to work; George Foster lasted two months; John Long only six. Mrs Humby had problems with both inmates and staff, and when Matilda Smith complained about constant disagreements there was a full investigation in 1875. There was bickering among the staff, overheard slights and arguments, accusations of 'forged testimonies' and improper conduct – Smith being 'under the hedge' with the porter. She was accused of consorting with the male staff, although this amounted to no more than conversations on the stairs or in the garden.[TNA] Smith received, fortunately for her, a glowing reference from the lady visitors, particularly for her continued and ongoing interest in girls sent out to service. Interestingly, the whole tone of Baldwyn Fleming's investigation report indicates that he was completely underwhelmed and unimpressed with the whole thing: 'the charges themselves were proved to be frivolous and magnified by animus which I would submit was greatly shown through the whole of the evidence both of Master and Matron'. Mrs Humby was exonerated of the charges, but the atmosphere was so toxic by now that the Humbys felt they had to resign.

The guardians themselves were exasperated, and asked permission to hire and fire senior officers without the tedious process of involving the LGB, to save time and effort – this was denied.

George and Elizabeth Atkins were appointed in 1876, from among no fewer than forty-two joint applicants, and their tenure of fifteen years appears to have been very successful, until an assault on an inmate in 1891 caused Atkins to be forced into resignation, with some reluctance on the part of the guardians. Atkins sometimes went beyond the call of duty, for example in 1885 when he missed an inspector's visit because he was in London trying to trace the family of an abandoned boy left by the police in the workhouse. This was criticised by Inspector Fleming, but the guardians defended his action. There was also an accusation by an inmate working as his clerk, that he was not keeping ration books correctly, but these charges were found to be without foundation and made by a man who was quite obviously resentful.

Atkins' terminal assault was strange and out of character and is worth describing because it is one of those precious rare incidents which gives us a peek through all the documents of a full inquiry. In October 1891, inmate William Moth (he had been in and out of the workhouse for thirty years, according to census returns) was hanging around in the road at the front of the workhouse, singing and begging from passers-by – he had received 3*d* from one woman. Moth was described in later statements as being dirty, disruptive and violent, 'a very spiteful old man and would do any one an injury when he is in his temper'.[TNA] He had been involved in several incidents, taking down his trousers in front of women, throwing a brick at another man. When Atkins and porter Legrove went out to bring him in, he picked up a stick and waved it at them. The porter took the stick from him, but Moth then picked up a piece of flint from a nearby pile and appeared to be throwing it. Atkins, having received a serious injury a year earlier in the workhouse in a similar incident, completely lost control of himself, seized the stick and struck Moth over the head with it three times. Moth was then grabbed 'by the collar', taken into the house, his dirty clothes were stripped from him and he was taken to be bathed and cleaned up. His bleeding scalp wound was treated by the nurse.

There were inconsistencies in the story, so Inspector Fleming called an inquiry, which makes fascinating reading – there were many witnesses and expenses were paid to those travelling in. The most interesting statements came from two labourers, watercressing over the road in the meadow, who saw the incident and actually heard the blows. Also it emerges that Moth was bathed, very unwillingly, once a month, and this time it was used as a kind of punishment, not only to wash away his blood. He complained that his 3*d* and his two 'baccy boxes' were taken from him. A telling picture of regular anti-social behaviour, fights and eruptions of endemic violence on the part of various individual inmates emerged from statements – porter Legrove had also been hit several times by inmates. The workhouse could be a violent place.

George Ilsley and Melissa Smith acted as master and matron for several weeks after the departure of the Atkins, and were paid £4 2s 1d and £2 4s 3d respectively.

Henry and Mary Fenton then held the positions for four years, paying 2/6d a week for the maintenance of their son. There is little in the record about their time in office, except for an incident where Fenton failed to follow up on a report of a male inmate hiding in the women's laundry, and was reprimanded. They left in 1896, 'to obtain better appointments elsewhere'.[TNA] Ilsley again stepped in to perform as temporary master.

The new master and matron from 1896 were Thomas and Alice Arter, also with a child aged 4 to support. Thomas Arter is of particular interest because his papers are the only surviving personal records for Basingstoke Union. His papers are in the HRO and consist of two bundles of cuttings, programmes, letters, and incomplete diaries. Much has been torn out, and the whole thing is fragmented, but there are fascinating glimpses. He had a particular interest in writing the histories of various inmates. It is sometimes difficult to tell whether these were people in his previous workhouse in Bromyard (where he had started his workhouse career as porter) or in Basingstoke, but a feeling of empathy and sympathy comes across in his accounts. He wrote a detailed history of porter Robert Legrove, a great example of how people became destitute: Legrove had spent ten years in the Grenadier Guards, worked as a sergeant in the East & West India Docks police in London, but was then unable to work when his wife became ill. She subsequently died and he became ill himself, ending up in a workhouse for a time.[13]

Shortly after starting, Arter was violently attacked by John Castle (who was still there in the 1901 census, listed as a shoemaker aged 74), who struck him over the head with a spade. Arter remained out of action for many weeks – paid help was brought in to keep his books and records, and George Ilsley again stepped in. Arter never fully recovered, suffering illness as a direct result of his injuries. He resigned in 1922, still suffering from severe headaches and memory loss which he attributed to this attack.[14] Castle was sentenced to a year's hard labour in Winchester. This incident was so severe that it was reported in newspapers as far away as Huddersfield.

There was another unfortunate episode, which involved Matilda Smith. In 1891 she approached the clerk for his advice:

> She was induced by false representations made to her by the Revd Dr James Caspar Clutterbuck, late one of Her Majesty's Inspectors of Workhouse Schools, and influenced by his position as a clergyman and Inspector, to pay to him, for investment … the case appears to be an extremely cruel one, as the money obtained from Miss Smith represented the whole of her savings.[TNA]

She had seen reports in the press of similar frauds which drove her to investigate, and she lost £150, having been completely taken in by requests for confidentiality and silence, and the issue of bogus receipts. Clerk Lear approached the LGB, but the outcome is not clear.

By 1897, superannuation was being deducted from the salaries of most of the staff, and when they left there are records of the pensions paid to them in MH 12. That same year, officers' rations were reviewed: they were receiving 7lb bread, 6lb meat, 7 pints of milk, 1lb flour, 7lb vegetables, [unclear] fish per week, and 4/6*d* worth of groceries, to be supplied by an approved trader and entered in a book.

Nurses

The employment of nurses became a continual and serious problem, probably exacerbated by the board's unwillingness to employ enough of them, given the considerable change in workhouse demographics.

Between 1873 and 1900 thirty-two qualified nurses were appointed at various times in the workhouse, some of them only staying for a couple of weeks. The minutes indicate that the finding and appointing of nurses seemed to be a prominent and persistent issue for the board, who were constantly advertising, interviewing (providing candidates' train fare), corresponding with the Workhouse Infirmary Nursing Association (WINA), or obtaining LGB sanction. On a couple of occasions, the whole laborious process was completed only for the applicant not to turn up. In 1898 the board refused to pay travelling expenses to successful candidates until they had been in service for six months. The one shining exception was Hannah Brown, previously mentioned.

It is not difficult to imagine the working lives of nurses in Basingstoke Workhouse, from various comments and reports. The regime of work was grindingly demanding, in what one candidate described as 'distasteful surroundings' – perhaps a couple of women, only one qualified, along with a handful of inmates, dealing with dozens of elderly, sick, bedridden and sometimes difficult or dirty people, scattered over three or four floors. Not to mention the awful plumbing and sanitation. Simply the act of bathing patients was difficult, and nurses were worn down by weeks on end of night duty, cobbled-together living rooms and sleeping areas, where they were constantly woken by noise all day and night. And, until 1897, there was the requirement to supervise new female intakes and their subsequent regular personal hygiene. There were 'Rules for Nurses', rigid and restricted as to eating,

> ### WORKHOUSE INFIRMARY NURSING ASSOCIATION
>
> The main point of contact for acquiring trained nurses was the Workhouse Infirmary Nursing Association, which had been founded in 1879 by Louisa Twining to promote the specialised training of workhouse nurses. By 1890 the Association had trained almost 100 probationers and appointed almost 300 staff. Even so, demand for its nurses outstripped supply. Each year it received requests for 200 or more nurses but could only supply 70 or 80.[15]

sleeping and resting, as well as nursing duties, almost mirroring the lives of the inmates. In 1899 a new 'Statement of Duties' was drawn up, not by doctors and nurses, but by two 'Reverend gentlemen' and Mrs Mitchell, a lady visitor.

In addition, there was a perpetual murmur of accusations of interference and lack of respect for their work and profession, together with indifferent control and restriction of essential supplies. This was evidenced in a major enquiry in 1895, where the master and matron accused Nurse Quaintrell of neglect, but the report ended up giving her more autonomy: 'the Committee are unanimously of opinion that with respect to the differences between the Master and the Nurses they have arisen through the Master being rather too exacting in minor details in carrying out the duties imposed upon him'.[TNA] Nurse Quaintrell resigned in 1896.

There was little social support: in 1898 Nurse Lear asked for Thursday evenings to attend a class at her church – she was to take that day as her fortnightly day off, and the other evenings were to be taken from her daily exercise hours. No flexibility here.

All these were not local problems, but general ones. There were dozens of national meetings and reports, describing exactly the conditions experienced in Basingstoke and deploring the lack of authority, the living conditions, the inevitable effect on inmates: '[If] she will pass through her duties in a hard, dreary manner, she will fail to bring the kindly, cheerful spirit essential in the monotonous life of workhouse wards, where the patients often remain for years, too frequently forgotten by their relatives, and with few outside visitors'.[16]

By 1900 a superintendent nurse in Basingstoke was paid £35 a year, and an assistant nurse £25. They also received a £2 allowance for uniform, along with the usual food, accommodation and laundry facilities.

A New Infirmary

The inmate population, the inadequacies of the building and the nursing problems all bring us to the most radical investment in the life of Basingstoke Workhouse, the new infirmary. Many workhouses, particularly those in cities, had found it necessary to provide separate buildings to care for the sick from the 1860s, but small rural workhouses lagged behind. Basingstoke's convoluted, difficult approach is interesting, and the records reveal much about conditions in the workhouse itself and the complex mechanics of getting things done.

From the mid-1890s, inspection reports were becoming more and more critical of care for the elderly, sick and infirm, and there is an overall impression that things were generally slipping. In 1895 there was a particularly long, detailed and negative inspector's report. In summary, with the large number of these unfortunates, many bedridden, there was overcrowding and bad sanitary conditions, and efficient nursing was impossible. Inspector Fleming expressed great sympathy for the nurses themselves.

There was pervasive damp and a leaking roof, inadequate and regularly blocked drains, occasional sightings of rats, and facilities for providing proper hot food for the bedridden were failing:

> The Dietary in use here may be sufficient, but it is not a good one. The Sunday dinner is bread and cheese. I am anxious that the inmates of Workhouses in this District should have a good hot meat dinner on Sundays. Several of the old men told me they considered the Sunday dinner the worst of the week. Before they came into the Workhouse they always tried to have a good dinner on Sunday, and generally managed to have a bit of hot meat and some kind of pudding.[TNA]

Caring sensitively for sick children was impossible:

> At the time of my visit a little girl, Rhoda Rogers, aged five, was in the Girls School. She had been constantly crying and begging to be allowed to go to bed, and had disturbed the other girls for hours. I was informed that she had cried during a great part of the night. The child was evidently unwell and altogether unfit to be in the School. She had been sent down from the Sick Ward because she had made so much noise moaning and crying that the other patients could not rest, and there was no other sick room where she could be placed. I requested that some temporary arrangement might be made for the child away from the school children. She would have been even more unhappy if her bigger sister had not been with her.

Rhoda was one of the unlucky children who became institutionalised, appearing often in the records, and we will meet her briefly again in Part 4. Infants (nine of them at the time of Inspector Fleming's visit) were cared for in a sort of *ad hoc* moving nursery, wherever it could be fitted in, by two old women whom he stated were unsuitable, and the floor was 'soiled by the infants'.

The Fentons, master and matron, did their best, providing warmer clothing for the old, more underwear, dressing gowns and bed capes, all this from re-using clothing – but it was the building that was the problem.

The guardians took this devastating report very seriously and there was a flurry of activity, much of it attempting, cheaply and ineffectively, to ameliorate the situation. The events leading up to the building of the new infirmary are tortuous and immensely revealing. Particularly interesting is that most of the following is taken from MH 12, and almost none of it appears in the minutes, in spite of meetings being reported in the local paper, suggesting that perhaps it was all too politically sensitive.

- *March 1895*: Guardian John Bird (proprietor of the *Hants & Berks Gazette*) proposed the building of a new infirmary, to provide 'most improved accommodation with modern appliances for the efficient treatment of the inmates and the comfort of the Nursing Staff'. Inspector Fleming attended the meeting. A group of guardians, led by Chairman Jervoise, visited the LGB in London to inspect possible plans, and an architect was to be appointed to design an infirmary 'on the lines of the one erected at Woodstock Union'. Woodstock Union in Oxfordshire was a union of similar size and character, and a good example to choose. An image of an 1898 OS map on the workhouses.org.uk website shows the size and footprint of their infirmary very similar to that eventually built in Basingstoke.

- *May 1895*: The full board agreed to proceed, but wanted a delay of six months. They were becoming less keen on the idea – it was far too expensive. Proposals for internal alterations were explored. Nevertheless, the question of a suitable site was raised. The LGB and Inspector Fleming expressed their 'sadness and disappointment'.

- *August 1895*: Arguments for and against a new building became very heated, as reported in a newspaper cutting from the *Hants & Berks Gazette*. John Bird wrote that 'this sort of tinkering and cobbling with a workhouse of the old-fashioned type was not worth the while; that in point of fact it would be money thrown away … very little time will elapse before the whole thing would be condemned'. Other comments included the fact that the building was 'more like a prison than anything else', and that 'these people who come into this House are not treated as Englishmen should treat a brother'. Chairman Jervoise pointed out that the board was exactly split on the question and there could be constant postponements. The guardians in favour took to writing personally and directly to Inspector Fleming and the LGB to appeal for more pressure.

- *September to December 1895*: The resolution to build an infirmary was officially rescinded, and detailed proposals were brought forward to make internal workhouse rearrangements. Even today, it is fairly obvious that this would not work in the long term. The chapel was to be used as a sick ward, installing the ubiquitous earth closets, and female sick and maternity cases were to be put in the old, now disused hospital building at the rear of the workhouse. Both accommodation and working conditions for nurses would deteriorate, with beds spread through the building, and there was no facility at all to isolate anyone. Many elderly sick would be on top floors, away from fresh air and outside access. It would cost £50.

An article in the *British Medical Journal* (BMJ), affixed in MH 12, was seriously critical. Apart from the 'forbidding aspect' of the building:

> The sick, aged and infirm are to be found all over the workhouse ... it was easy to picture ... ourselves the conditions of these wards in the winter when crowded with patients, the windows being shut to husband ... heat ... with the emanations from the various vessels, unemptied until the morning, and from the bodies of the old people, the conditions for the treatment of the sick cannot be considered favourable.

The article remarked upon the primitive sanitary conditions, bleak nursery, distribution of food getting cold, complete lack of privacy and care for women in labour, no isolation for 'troublesome or difficult' patients ... the list goes on.

In spite of all this, there is an impression not of neglect, but of the staff trying their best to do a good job. But recruitment was getting much harder. And proceedings for the purchase of land continued behind the scenes – as if the guardians knew this could not go on. Meetings became vociferous and strident and ran on late. As the BMJ pointed out in a later column:

> The argument that seemed to turn the scale was that ... there may be a prospect ... of some revolution in the condition of and provision for the aged and infirm; therefore let us do as little as we can ... Basingstoke is going to patch and make the rent worse.

There is so much argument here in MH 12, between different factions of the guardians, the LGB and Fleming, letters to the press, responses to the BMJ ('the sense of the country will be in favour of the department putting considerable pressure on the guardians') – literally inches of paper. And, of course, by November it was too late in the year to start anything new, anyway. There were now so many old and sick in the workhouse that it was difficult to know where to put them.

By 1896 the divisions among the guardians were getting personal – in one meeting there were hoots of derision: 'Twaddle!' and 'Nonsense!'. The disagreements were stoked by the receipt of tenders for the internal works. There was even a plot to introduce more guardians, somehow, to swing the vote in favour of a new building. We know this because John Bird, a passionate supporter of the infirmary, was sending newspaper cuttings of reports of the meetings, which were pasted into MH 12.

What could the LGB actually do, in the event of the guardians ignoring a refusal to sanction the internal works? This is the first time since 1834 that this question was asked in Basingstoke. The pro-infirmary guardians pointed out that the board needed to 'become alive to the fact that under a velvet glove there is an iron hand'. Inspector Fleming answered one letter diplomatically: 'compulsory powers were only exercised with the greatest reluctance, & would be very unlikely to be put in force against so good a Bd. as Basingstoke has been'. And Basingstoke was not the only union experiencing these problems – some of them are mentioned in MH 12, particularly Carlisle and Coventry. At Mildenhall, the LGB had insisted on limiting intake entirely to sick and elderly, making the situation untenable and forcing the issue.

During the course of the year, the internal reworking continued, with the chairman being asked, very politely, to attend the LGB in London to explain. The games continued, with the LGB asking for detailed plans, and the board responding that 'these alterations … are of a trifling character and do not necessitate plans'. Chairman Jervoise was again summoned to London to explain. A set of plans was eventually submitted, split into several small jobs, attempting to get around the need for sanction – for example, the covered walkway to the hospital building only costing £14. The auditor objected. Almost every item of correspondence at this time, on most subjects, was replied to with a remark of some kind by the LGB regretting the lack of an infirmary – they were very expert at persistent nagging.

That year there was a serious outbreak of whooping cough and measles in the workhouse and, predictably, it was difficult to control – there were three deaths, and nurses had to be hired in. Guardian A.L. White wrote to Inspector Fleming, complaining about the situation, and that separation between men and women was breaking down under the present arrangements; other guardians wrote adding their voices. Fleming wanted to do a full review visit along with the LGB medical inspector, Dr Fuller, but this had to be initially postponed due to the 'murderous attack' on the master (Thomas Arter; see p. 134). His report that December was amazingly practical, diplomatic and restrained under the circumstances, and he details some of the sad cases among the elderly. He and Dr Fuller wrote in the visitors' book:

> We much regret to find that the arrangts. made for the care of the sick are still extremely inadequate as we feared they would be. So far as present possibilities extend the officers deserve credit for the general state of the establishment. In the body of the House much cleaning & painting have been done with excellent results.

In 1897 the purchase of a piece of land to the north of the workhouse from Lord Bolton for £550 was proceeding, almost in the background; the money was borrowed from the Ecclesiastical Commission for England, to be repaid over thirty years. And Fleming's routine report in April (it was twelve pages long, typed and then printed) was so damning and critical as to provoke another special meeting of the guardians and they finally gave in. It had taken two years.

A new infirmary, on the style of the one at Woodstock, was to be built, to accommodate fifty-six patients. There were still arguments for another postponement, but the motion was carried. All the major pro-infirmary players were appointed to a new committee to oversee the project: the chairman and vice-chairman, Revd A.L. White, J. Tigwell, R. Wallis, J. Bird, J. Morris, G. Ames and R. Portsmouth, all powerful men in the area. Fleming commented that 'I am heartily thankful for this decision!' Richard Sterry Wallis was appointed as architect, and resigned as a guardian for Basingstoke.

That October, full plans and specifications were available. These are held at TNA, but they are unfortunately disintegrating and cannot even be unfolded for examination. The infirmary was to be built a couple of hundred yards up the hill from the workhouse, near the railway line. There is a huge amount of information over the next three years relating to this project, far too much to include here. There are many descriptions and it is clear that it was to be a very modern, state-of-the-art facility, two storeys in height with a third central floor for the nurses; there were waiting rooms, bathrooms, lying-in wards, a dedicated labour room and a surgery. There was a kitchen with stores and larder. The infirmary is clear in subsequent OS maps, and one external photograph survives.

Fig. 15 (left) Basingstoke Infirmary, *c.*1900. (Basingstoke Heritage Society)

Fig. 16 (below) 1930 OS map image of the infirmary.[17]

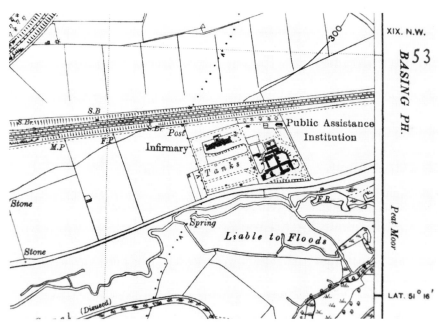

The opportunity was taken to include new services, gas, water mains and sewage, and £10,000 was borrowed from the Public Works Loans Board.

A memorial stone was laid on 27 May 1898 by the chairman, and the chaplain said a prayer. It was of Portland stone, 2ft 6in high, 4ft long, with an inscription showing the names of the chairman, vice-chairman, clerk, architect and builder. The names of the guardians were written on parchment and placed in a bottle within the stone.

More Building

In 1897, around the time the new infirmary was finally being agreed, a new board-room was proposed. This did not go unremarked by various guardians and the LGB, since it was at the same time that all the difficult and protracted arguments about the expense of the new infirmary building were coming to a head. The LGB reluctantly sanctioned it, 'although they express their regret that plans for an infirmary with proper accommodation for the nurses have not also been submitted'. But even Fleming stated that the atmosphere in the old one was 'insufferable'. The successful tender was that of Henry John Goodall, at a cost of £600, and a loan was required. This was a very fancy area, with its twenty-two panes of glass separately insured, its anaglypta wallpaper (there were major difficulties with applying and painting this, with the walls being wet most of the time), its modern and expensive tables, 'smokers' chairs', mats and stylish hat pegs.

It seems as if, once the guardians had decided to spend money upgrading their facilities, and once they had access to utilities, their ideas expanded. There was more progressive thinking; perhaps the personnel had changed. Gas lighting was noted in the workhouse in an 1899 report, but the board drew the line at installing a telephone between the main building and the hospital building at the rear, and hung on to the speaking tube for the time being. There was at least one telephone in the workhouse in 1900, later extended to the kitchen and the master's quarters. These were internal, not connected to an exchange outside until 1911.

There was extensive research on cooking by steam. In spite of some argument within the board, Barford & Perkins of Peterborough won the contract to install modern gas cookers for £183 15s. They also supplied four boilers for £65 10s and Basingstoke's Mussellwhite & Son built a new boiler house for £35 12s. Hot water pipes were extended around parts of the building for heating and to the laundry. The boilers were insured with the National Boiler & General Insurance Co.

The laundry also needed serious improvement. In 1889 six heated drying horses had been purchased from Thomas Bradford & Co. of Manchester at a cost of about £42 – these were large cast-iron frames affixed to a wall. Large copper vats were also bought, and in 1898 a Barford & Perkins washing machine. This was not sufficient, however, and in 1899 a new project was started to build a new state-of-the-art laundry in the north-west segment of the workhouse, quite extensive works including an underground water tank, water movement systems, a roof cistern and coal store – the cost, including new fixtures and fittings, was just over £1,000. We have some rather attractive architectural drawings for this in MH 14.

There are also drawings for a new £100 mortuary building – with space for four coffins and post-mortem facilities, a hearse house and viewing window – and an engine house and tanks for the new sewage system. Twenty-five water closets were installed in the workhouse to replace the old earth closets (at last!), at a cost of £396. We also know that new detached receiving wards were built, but it is not clear where these were situated, probably to the west of the workhouse. The new boardroom at the front of the building, the tanks for sewage disposal, the laundry and the mortuary can all just be seen on the map in Fig. 16.

The Infirmary is Opened

Finally, in 1900, the infirmary was finished. We have records of the whole complicated process: insurance, fire precautions and hydrants, a new modern kitchen range, an internal telephone. An engineer was appointed (not living in) to maintain the building and plant. There are detailed lists of fixtures and fittings for the wards and nurses' quarters, blinds, carpets and rugs, couches and chairs, mirrors, incandescent gas lighting, picture rails throughout where appropriate. Two wheelchairs and a carrying chair were purchased. Surrounding roads and fences were upgraded, plants and trees planted, some at the personal expense of the guardians.

Additional staff were advertised for, including a general servant, although there was some difficulty obtaining them; there was another frenetic period of adverts, applications, interviews, people not turning up. The master and matron were paid a bonus of £2 10s each for extra work in building and setting up the infirmary – Baldwyn Fleming noted that 'I wish the Gdns. had been somewhat more generous.'[TNA]

The opening ceremony took place at 3 p.m. on Thursday, 3 May 1900, reported in great detail in the *Hants & Berks Gazette* the following Saturday, along with a delightful drawing of the building. There was a large gathering of people – residents

Fig. 17 Drawing of the new infirmary in the *Hants & Berks Gazette*, 5 May 1900.

and officials from the parishes, the ladies visiting committee, the mayor and corporation of Basingstoke, together with all the workhouse staff. It was a showery day, and people assembled in the boardroom to be led up to the new building by the chairman, the path lined with flags. Two large Union Jacks flew over the infirmary.

A key was presented to the chairman with the inscription: 'Presented to F.M. Jervoise, Esq., D.L., J.P., Chairman of the Guardians of Basingstoke Union, by R.S. Wallis and Charles Smith and Son, Architects, on the occasion of the opening of the New Infirmary, May 3rd, 1900.' Over the door, the word 'Welcome' was framed in flowers; the company entered a large ward, and there was a service with prayers, performed by the chaplain with assistance from children from the workhouse. Speeches were made by Portal and Jervoise – transcribed in the newspaper – visitors were shown around the building, and 'an excellent tea was served at buffets on three sides of one of the largest wards', catered by C.H. Owen of Basingstoke.

From Thomas Arter's notes, patients were moved up to the infirmary later that month, and at the time there were five nurses and one general servant – the first servant was dismissed because she was pregnant. Fleming noted that 'the new building is quite one of the best medium sized infirmaries in my Dist.'[TNA]

The Union

The men who ran the union continued to be drawn from the same group of gentlemen farmers, businessmen, professionals, traders and clergy. We no longer have names in our records, apart from the three selected to be visiting committee at each meeting, and lists of names appear in local trade directories. But we get hints: in August 1879, 'during the next few weeks, the majority of the Guardians will, in all probability, be fully engaged in harvest operations and consequently unable, without considerable inconvenience, to attend a Meeting of the Board'.[TNA] Chaloner William Chute of the local stately home, The Vyne, and married into the influential Portal family, took over as chairman from Rycroft in 1885, and in turn he was replaced by Francis Michael Ellis Jervoise in 1890. Notably, Wyndham Spencer Portal, whom we have met before, continued to be a major player in the affairs of the union, sometimes deputising as chairman and in other capacities. Even when these men retired, they remained interested and involved, serving on various committees.

We have no portrait of C.W. Chute, but the Jervoise family kindly provided the writer with the delightful picture of F.M.E. Jervoise, opposite.

As usual every year all the committees were reappointed. For the workhouse these included the general purpose committee, the farm committee and various *ad hoc* committees. Outside the workhouse, several committees reflected the range of responsibilities; among others, the school attendance committee (after the 1876 Education Act) which supervised the work of the new attendance officers and enquiry officers – these were often the relieving officers in the early years, who knew the territory and families.

And the general work of out relief continued. At nearly every meeting there were decisions brought before the board. Claimants, as before, were given relief in the form of a couple of shillings, bread, meat, outfits for children, and help with funeral expenses. We have some numbers from 1872 to 1881, and it is clear that the recipients of out relief fell by about 400, over 50 per cent, during this period. This reduction would have been caused by a combination of factors, among them the availability of more work, and the more efficient control of out relief itself. Also significant, and often mentioned in the minutes, was the growth of friendly societies, where a few pence a week could be put away regularly to provide sick pay and a basic pension. After 1875 these were nationally controlled and audited and became very popular – by the late 1880s there were about 27,000 friendly societies all over the country.[18] Charities were now better organised and more effective as another means of community support.

After 1881 the numbers flattened out, with about 450 to 500 people a year being relieved; this number is so consistent that one can perhaps assume that we were down, more or less, to a hardcore of permanent cases.

Fig. 18 Francis Michael Ellis Jervoise (1844–1903).

Local Government Arrives

The poor law union had become the effective instrument of government control, and we see huge changes in the administrative responsibilities of the board of guardians. Under the 1876 Divided Parishes Act, small pieces of outlying parishes, fragmented since they related to old estate ownership, were to be combined and joined for greater administrative efficiency – a tidying up. Beech Hill in Berkshire was finally annexed to Bradfield Union to the north in 1878, and at the same time Mortimer West End was brought into Basingstoke Union. This action continued for years, with public meetings and enquiries, correspondence and reports relating to the process itself,[TNA] with copious minutes relating to arrangements for poor relief, vaccinations, bread supply moving into and out of different areas.

The union, now also the Rural Sanitary Authority (RSA), was responsible for the registration of voters and control of polling stations; in 1888 three electoral divisions were set up for the rural areas, with a total population of 12,600, with new polling stations – we know this because of the papers in TNA relating to grants received for funding. The union/RSA was also responsible for the administration behind the establishment of new civil parishes.

In 1894 the new Local Government Act established elected rural and urban district councils. We first see the Rural District Council (RDC) mentioned in the records; this was essentially the same group of people with the same chairman, with board and RDC meetings held in the workhouse, one after the other 'with a short interval for bread and cheese'.[19] This system remained until the end of the union. Growing Basingstoke town appointed extra guardians to the union, now ten in total; the workhouse boardroom was running out of space to accommodate them all so future meetings in the town hall were proposed, but this was felt to be politically undesirable. This problem continued until the building of the new boardroom in 1897, previously described. The authorities for the town itself (the Urban Sanitary Authority) became the Urban District Council (UDC).

That year George Lear, the clerk, was given an increase in salary, having held the office for more than twenty-five years with a considerable increase in the scope of work, as we can see. A month later he died, to be replaced by Arthur Lear, a relative in the same firm – the handwriting in the minute books remains the same. The salary was now £175 per annum, comprising working for the union, the RSA/RDC and the school attendance committee. Lear resigned in 1896 and was replaced by Hugh Wills Chandler – we have his rather attractive letterhead used as a bookmark in a minute book.

The sale of the few remaining parish properties continued. In 1878 the parish of Bramley wished to sell a tenement and garden that was in such bad repair that they could not afford to keep it. Weston Patrick property, in 1881, was sold to Lord Bolton for £55, which was a relief to some of the guardians who did not want 'objectionable premises' erected on the site by an 'outsider'. The proceeds of a sale in Preston Candover, to Lt FitzGerald of North Hall, were so small (£8) that they were placed in a Post Office account for the benefit of the parish. In 1884, at the request of the vicar of Preston Candover, the remaining amount was spent improving the cricket ground, adding to a donation by the Purefoy Jervoise family and the Fitzgeralds. The LGB was happy to sanction this.

Various Poor Law Conferences, locally and nationally, were subscribed to, and delegates sent. The *Hants & Berks Gazette* asked to attend board meetings in 1882 and were initially refused. Later they were allowed access to the minutes, and finally allowed inside in 1895, since the board was now essentially the RDC, but matters of relief were to be private. We now have a glimpse of what was actually going on in board meetings, and some cuttings were pasted into MH 12.

The separate annual medical reports for town and country were regular and detailed, and provide a comprehensive insight into conditions in rural north Hampshire, and the thriving town at the end of the nineteenth century.[TNA] The main causes of death were heart and lung disease and tuberculosis, but the death rate among children was high: half to one third up to the early 1880s, after which we lose the detail. As would be expected, the biggest problems, particularly for children, were the ubiquitous ebb and flow of infectious diseases: measles, whooping cough, scarlet fever and enteric diseases.

There was enormous success, year on year, by both authorities in 'nuisance' abatement, works often proudly listed in the medical reports: cottages were repaired or condemned, drains laid or repaired, cesspools cleaned, refuse heaps removed and earth closets installed in place of old privies. And noticeably, as living conditions very gradually improved towards 1900, there were occasional years when epidemics were few and far between. But doctors noted that controlling infection in children was always very difficult. In 1885 one rural doctor reported that the high death rate among poor children was mostly due to bad food and conditions, and milk being difficult to get in remote villages. They were often eating 'bread sop', bread soaked in water and sweetened. It was a regular thing for schools to be closed for weeks on end to try and limit outbreaks, and it was noted that there was no way for clothes and bedding to be cleaned.[TNA] Naturally, it was the occasional outbreak of smallpox, usually brought in from London or the south coast, which caused the most trouble.

At the same time, there were difficulties regarding the requirement for emergency medical treatment in the area outside the town – there was simply nowhere to take severely sick or injured people and they were often sent to the workhouse, where there was perceived to be something resembling a hospital. When the town's cottage hospital was opened in 1879, injured workmen were still occasionally being sent to the workhouse. But we know from doctors' expense claims in 1898 that surgery was now being performed in the cottage hospital, with extra payments for the use of chloroform – Henry Hoare, an inmate, had specifically been taken there for a leg amputation. And there were many minutes relating to payments to the town cottage hospital for treatment of the poor rural population.

Points of Contention: Town and Country

The relationship between the new town and country authorities was an extremely uncomfortable one. The town dominated the union economically, and they were perfectly aware of it. But the union was still functioning within the town. It was still responsible for the town's poor, it was completing the town's ownership of land return and was still administrating rating valuations (often with protracted arguments); in 1880 it was necessary to appoint valuers for assessing not only areas relating to the railways, telegraph, gas and waterworks, but new kinds of property within the town, such as Wallis & Steevens Iron Foundry, and May & Co.'s large brewery and malt house. It was the town's increasing influence which led to extra Basingstoke guardians being appointed, mentioned earlier. Some matters were split, such as separate inspectors for the Basingstoke canal within the two authorities, and separate medical officers of health, although these men were drawn from the same group of poor law union doctors. School attendance and vaccination remained under the remit of the union/RSA/RDC. It was the subjects of health and environmental conditions which ultimately became the biggest sources of contention.

The first major problems between the USA and the RSA emerged in 1872 with the state of the Basingstoke Canal. Under the provisions of the Public Health Act, the union, wearing its RSA hat, complained about the 'offensive and dangerous state of the Basingstoke Canal' to the LGB with the request that it be inspected and remedial steps taken. It was no longer navigable, a tunnel having caved in:

> It is in a most miserable neglected condition, the water low, the mud high and rank vegetation completely filling up the channel … the sewage of a considerable part of the Town of Basingstoke is discharged into the canal, this sewage I found to be of a most offensive description, and the canal, especially the head of it forming a basin within the Town.

It was therefore the town's problem. This was still going on in 1874, when the rector of Basing wrote to the LGB:

> As year after year passes away one finds us no nearer the removal or abatement of a most dangerous and intolerable nuisance. We live in fear and trembling for the consequences of longer delay … should there be a dangerous outbreak of fever no approach should be at my door as having failed to bring before the constituted authorities the real state of the case.[TNA]

A related argument was the proposed disposal of the town's sewage, logically and geographically to the lower east of the town, away from the high chalk downs and near the river – and the workhouse. It was proposed to distribute it:

> To a meadow close to the much frequented highway leading from Basingstoke to Basing and within 80 yards of the South West of the Union Workhouse, and from thence into a stream passing within a few yards of such Workhouse and also parallel to and adjoining the said Highway from Basingstoke to Basing is likely, under certain circumstances to prove injurious to the health of Inmates of the said Workhouse and to persons living near' (1874).[TNA]

The town (USA) now had the RSA, the LGB and Lord Bolton against their scheme – they had to rethink, going through various options, and they eventually came up with an alternative, but this was again rejected. In 1877 there was a full inquiry involving everyone, including landowners, farmers and the proprietors of the canal. There is an enormous amount of correspondence and other material in MH 12 on this subject, but eventually a satisfactory plan was agreed, at a cost of £18,000, borrowed on loan by the town.

None of this helped, of course, when the requirement for an isolation and infection hospital for the area emerged in 1878 with a serious outbreak of smallpox, together with an 'awful' epidemic of measles. The LGB came to the conclusion that a single isolation hospital for the whole area would be the best course of action – it made perfect sense; a joint committee would be appointed, costs, services and staff allocated, and the running costs shared between the USA, the RSA and the Poor Law Union.

The town did not agree. They wanted their own hospital. In the words of Fleming: 'the USA are, as I learn, jealous of interference from the other local authorities & are anxious to have the management of the infectious hosp. entirely in their own hands'. A conference was called in the town hall in May that year, where Nelson Rycroft and Wyndham Portal expressed their wishes, but the mayor:

> Did not show much disposition to meet the views of the Gds. & the RSA ... I think it is better to let this matter rest for a while, as I have reason to hope from what I heard when I was last at Basingstoke, that the USA will in the end make sufficient provision for all the infectious cases likely to occur within the Union.[TNA]

In 1884, under great pressure, the board decided to renovate and adapt the old separate workhouse hospital as an infectious facility for the rural areas, but the LGB pointed out that this could not be used for non-paupers, the general public. An outbreak of smallpox in 1885, carried by a traction engine driver living in Basing, illustrated all the difficulties of the situation. He was sent to the workhouse isolation wards, and there was then another case within the main building – not only was he a non-pauper, but there was a risk of spread to the inmates. Medical officers were admitting patients as there was nowhere else to send them. Fleming was unhappy:

> The upper wards of the Inf. Hosp are about on a level with the old men's ward in the main building … the distance between the end of the old men's ward & the wall of the inf. hosp. would probably be about 20 yards … all the cases among inmates occurred among the occupants of the old men's ward.

He even made a drawing showing the hillside site. There follows a huge report relating to smallpox and scarlet fever in the district and in the workhouse, including non-paupers, mostly illegible, fixed in the gutter of the folio, but he makes his point.[TNA]

However, nothing came of it, except that the workhouse stopped taking infectious cases altogether in November that year. Medical officers found themselves having to hire in nurses and continually complained about the situation. The argument grumbled on for years, with much difficulty every time there was a major epidemic and with the LGB continually 'poking' the guardians to build something. Eventually, after public complaint, an arrangement was set up in 1892 to admit infectious rural paupers to the town's own new infectious hospital, 15s for adults and 12/6d for children; of course there were arguments over who was or was not a pauper, and it all became very distasteful.

While all this was going on, the question of the town's growing sewage problem again caused controversy, and in 1887 another scheme was planned by the town for upgrading sewage disposal, which the RSA again vetoed on the same basis as before: the outfall and tanks were too near the workhouse, and would pollute the stream across the road. There was another huge enquiry, more disagreements and arguments, the scheme this time condemned by the medical officers. All this makes fascinating reading, and offers an insight into the way things were done.[TNA]

The bad feeling even extended to parish boundary alterations. When there was a town proposal in 1890 to incorporate Eastrop and Basing into the urban authority, there was a telling comment from the RSA: 'without wishing, in any way, to put themselves in an antagonistic position towards the Town Council of Basingstoke, they cannot see favour of the transfer', the sections in question not being 'sufficiently urban in their character'[TNA] There were similar comments relating to other adjoining parishes, Cliddesden and Monk Sherborne.

The End of the Century

So we arrive at 1900, and Poor Law authorities were effectively now providing a national system for the care of the sick, elderly and infirm poor, with the continual conflict – so familiar today – of doing the best they could with as little money as possible.

Interesting signs of the times appear in the minutes. Among them, the purchase in 1897 of supplies of an antitoxin for treating diphtheria, recently developed, from Borroughs Willliams & Co. in Basingstoke. And in 1900 a proposal to the LGB that cyclists and owners of motor cars should pay tax to contribute to the maintenance of local roads.

And regarding the workhouse and infirmary, the last report we have from Baldwyn Fleming in April 1900, just before the infirmary was completed, tells us that:

> The old part of the House is quite the old type of W.H. with small windows, high in the walls, rough stone stairs, dull wards & unattractive buildings generally. A good deal has gradually been done in the way of improvement, & the beautiful Infirmary which will soon be ready will afford excellent & modern provision for the sick & their nurses, as well as for maternity cases. In the old house there is cleanliness & good order as far as is practicable, but it would be difficult to make it smart or up to the more recent standards of W.H. accomm'n. A new laundry & receiving ward block is about to be built, also a mortuary. So far as they go these will constitute valuable improvements.[TNA]

Part 4

1901 to The End

Our union moved into the new century going about its work as usual, but from now on we have, year by year, continual change imposed from outside.

Attitudes and ideas about the nature of poverty were radically changing. There was a move towards a fresh start, to remove the repression of the old localised system and bring in a new one of properly controlled assistance, a duty to provide the environment for work and aspiration, and this lead ultimately to national relief measures which are still fundamentally in place today.

In 1905 a Royal Commission on the Poor Law and the Unemployed began a review, and this is reflected in our union with all the requests for information and returns. The members of this commission were far more qualified than the 1830s equivalent, including academics, civil servants, charity representatives and people experienced in the field. It took three years to produce forty-seven volumes of information, but they could not agree on a plan,[1] with a rather philosophical split into majority and minority reports published in 1909. In Basingstoke full charts, memoranda and synopses were printed, distributed and displayed in the town hall and the Mechanics Institute; they are unfortunately no longer extant.

However, some important recommendations did emerge. In 1908 universal old age pensions for the over-70s were introduced. This reduced out relief claims, but did not help with inmate numbers, since many could not look after themselves and were still desperately poor, the pension being no better than out relief. The 1911 National Insurance Act operated from 1913, bringing unemployment support to workers, although it was not yet universal and did not extend to agricultural workers until the mid-1930s. Interestingly it was considered by Prime Minister Lloyd George to be a temporary measure.[2]

In 1913 the Poor Law Institutions Order replaced previous orders from the LGB, allowing more autonomy for guardians, stricter nursing enforcement, efficient and standardised paperwork for medical and other relief (the case paper system). A major overhaul of the workhouse diet, more variety and choice, had already taken place in 1900. Perhaps more significantly, no healthy child was to live in a workhouse for more than six weeks, and terminology changed: 'workhouse' became 'poor law institution', 'pauper' became 'poor person', and infirmary inmates were now 'patients'.

But a monumental line is drawn under the social history of Britain in August 1914, the start of the First World War – everything changed. And serious reform was effectively put on the back burner for years. This is also where we will draw our own line in this century, since 31 December 1914 is the point at which the minute books are now restricted until the 2030s, and we will need other sources to continue our story.

The Union and Workhouse to 1914

The minutes continue in their dry form into the twentieth century, but the change in language and syntax is noticeable – it has become more economical and modern. In a mirror of the early days we now get weekly notes on individual named cases, every possible manifestation of the effects of poverty.

But over the years there is a very strong impression that problems of direct relief were slightly less prominent with the introduction of national relief, and much more was being done in the way of social care: neglected and abused children, abandonment of families, disabilities and illnesses, elderly support. Sick and disabled people were regularly being sent to specialist hospitals or homes, as we will see later.

Poverty in the area was not severe in those early years. In October 1904, Fleming wrote a circular letter regarding potential 'Distress, Winter 1904–1905'.[3] In response the guardians did not anticipate unusual problems: 'the number in the workhouse is decidedly below the average. The number on the out relief list but a shade above that of last year'. In rural areas, 'in two or three villages, however, there are several young men out of work, they are of unsettled disposition, have received little or no training and are said to be of no practical use when employed'.[HRO]

There was an increased representation of lady guardians, now with four or five at any time, and a formalisation of the ladies visiting committee to the womens committee, defining their role as befriending and helping girls and women to gain employment and independence, and to be active in helping the development and placement of orphaned and destitute children. Lady guardians, Miss S.J. Wallis (Wallis & Steevens Ltd, traction engine manufacturers) and Mrs Kingdon (J.M. Kingdon & Co., hardware traders) stayed for many years. Mrs Raynbird was still appearing in the record in 1917 although naturally her activities diminished.

Protracted arguments with the UDC continued over water supplies and placement of town sewage facilities.

In 1912 it was decided – unfortunately for us – to dispose of much of the archive of old papers and returns. A clerk was appointed and a room in

Basingstoke set aside for the job, with a cart to move records. It was a huge task and went on for many weeks, with the delegated clerk itemising his hours and collecting his fee.

In the workhouse itself, accommodation pressure had now been removed by the new infirmary and many of the spaces reverted back to their original use. Married couples were now given back their own quarters with separate night wards, and a new tailor's workshop was set up together with a bigger clothing store. The nursery was much improved. The old boys' schoolroom was altered by Mussellwhite & Son of Basingstoke to house the cook and assistant matron, with new sitting rooms, costing around £40. The chapel was reclaimed, refurnished and re-equipped and old surplus furniture was sold off. There was painting and decorating throughout. But the old boilers were a constant problem, with Wallis & Steevens engineers frequently being called in to consult.

In 1904, following an inspection report recommending a telephone to communicate with the fire brigade, the guardians decided not to 'place the Workhouse on the telephone system as in their opinion communication with the Fire Brigade by means of a cyclist messenger would be more certain and less liable to interruption'. It was not until 1911 that a fully connected telephone system was installed; there were to be no more than 500 calls a year, per the tariff, and anyone could use it at a cost of 2*d* per call, 'the same to be placed in a box by the side of the telephone and the contents of the box to be paid to the Treasurer yearly at Michaelmas', and a record book was to be signed by each caller.[HRO]

Keeping staff remained difficult, with constant changes and all the usual arguments, misbehaviours and liaisons, but there is less detail now, and again nurses' comings and goings are particularly difficult to follow; the friction between nursing staff and others continued. For the first time, we see regular small increases in salary across all staff, often larger ones to attract candidates.

In 1905 Thomas Arter's wife, Alice, died; Louisa Weekley, the former schoolmistress, was appointed temporary matron. The LGB recommended that Arter be replaced by a couple, but the guardians wanted to keep him and he stayed, along with his daughter. Weekley was formally appointed matron, with her own quarters, and she and Thomas married in 1907 – they were given three weeks' leave. Arter's daughter (she is not named), now 15, was apprenticed to 'a drapery company in Basingstoke', and for a time lived in the workhouse for a payment of 2*s* a week, later getting her own lodgings.

An interesting local note is that when Dr James Walker retired in 1911, after thirty-three years of union service, his pension was made up to the maximum on the grounds of his average travel distance of 4½ miles, 'and that since the introduction of self propelled traffic (particularly traction engines) Mr Walker has been put to extra expense in additional wear and tear of horses and carriages and during the past six years in additional wear and tear of tyres of his motor car'.[HRO]

Very occasionally, we hear of how lives moved on after the workhouse experience: a report in the HBG in 1913[4] describes how two 'gentlemen' turned up to view the workhouse. The brothers had been inmates in the 1870s and were then taken to America by their father. One of them was university educated, became the coroner in an American city and later mayor. Names and places were withheld.

Children

It is in the lives of children that we see the greatest change in this period. In 1901 workhouse children were to have a 'holiday in the country' for four weeks, arranged by Mrs Raynbird and other guardians, at a cost of 5s per child per week. This proved so successful that it continued every year. The attendance at Basing school worked well, with one or two inevitable discipline problems. But living in the workhouse was unacceptable.

The boarding out of children had been around since the beginning of the new Poor Law, formalised with the Boarding Out Order of 1870. By 1900 half of the unions in England were doing this successfully[5] but Basingstoke had always resisted. Under the provisions of the 1899 Poor Law Act, a sad list of thirty-two children, deserted, orphaned or illegitimate, was made in 1902 by the union, and thirteen of these were to be formally adopted by the guardians and boarded out. This updated list is to be found every year in the minute books. Occasionally children were sent to local 'cottage homes', arranged by Mrs Raynbird, but we have no details.

Another Boarding Out Order in 1909 prompted the LGB to ask what was happening with the remaining children, but the guardians were still very resistant to the idea of a dedicated children's home, thinking it 'undesirable'. However, the LGB persisted, culminating in an inspector's letter in 1911: 'the Guardians should lose no time in giving serious consideration to the question of the most suitable means of removing all children of school age from the Workhouse'.[TNA] The children's committee, formed in 1910 to concentrate on children's development, both in the workhouse and in the parishes, was replaced by the boarding out committee in 1911, who then began the process, for the first time inviting people from the community to join in decision-making.

Later that year, we see the formal arrangements, books and forms ordered, provision for cash for care and clothing. Initially twelve children were placed on the boarding out list, at a cost of 3s each in a suitable home, with an additional amount annually for clothing. This expanded over the next few years, involving about sixteen children, and regular payments to homes and for expenses appear in the minutes – dentists' fees, transport, schooling costs, additional clothing and personal boxes for them to keep possessions. This also extended outside the workhouse system to find homes for union children who were neglected or abused. Most of the workhouse children not boarded out were sent to various children's homes, such as Milton in Portsmouth, but a few were still resident; some were 'ins and outs', some came from dysfunctional families, or had behaviour problems.

The LGB was still not happy with this residue, and continued to prompt the guardians into providing a local children's home. In late 1913 the guardians began to look at various options for the provision of a cottage home, either converted or newly built. A year later they were starting to negotiate the purchase of a plot of land from Lord Bolton and were preparing building plans. The First World War intervened.

Other Residents

Life for the inmates was now a little less austere than before. The diet was much improved and more varied, as indicated by the variety of foodstuffs bought, and there were better cooking facilities. Furniture and bedding were more comfortable and much effort was made by everyone, both inside and outside the workhouse, to make life a little more interesting. Men and women were now allowed to visit one another, and tea was served on these occasions.

Every opportunity, not only at Christmas, was taken to provide entertainments or 'treats' and a list of those allowed to do this was maintained, from temperance groups to local musicians, from the mayor of Basingstoke to chairman Sir Richard Rycroft himself at his own home. And there were national celebrations, such as the coronation of King Edward VII in 1902. Books and magazines were regularly donated, making up a small library. Organist E.A. Leavey was permanently appointed in 1904 and a piano was donated by Mrs Pechell of Newnham. Dr G.B. Gardiner, of the prestigious Folk Song Society, was allowed to carry out research in the workhouse in 1906 for his national folk song archive.

But the fundamental bleakness was still there. When a list was made by the master in 1903 of men under 60 considered fit to be pallbearers, two were suitable: 'one fit, slightly mental, one fit but a small man'.[HRO] Eventually pallbearers had to be hired under contract. The workhouse was asked to subscribe to the purchase of additional land for burials at St Mary's church in Basing.

At the other end of life, the Registrar General issued a circular restricting the use of 'the Union' on birth certificates for children born in a workhouse – in Basingstoke in 1904 this was changed to Cowderys [sic] Down House, the first mention of this address, which would eventually become the name of the site.

A handful of lunatics were still living in the workhouse; there were four in 1911. An inspection in 1913 asked that their dayrooms be cheered up, and insisted that they be bathed once a week instead of once a month. Those being sent to the asylum from around the union were not transported by motor car until 1910. Guardians regularly visited those who were in asylums and tried their best to ameliorate their conditions, noting, for example, that crusts were cut off their bread and tea was of a good quality; a letter was sent to the superintendent of Hampshire Asylum in 1913 'enquiring whether he would object to a supply of tobacco being sent out of private funds for the patients of this Union who could not work and had no friends'.[HRO]

Those inmates fit for work were still employed in maintaining the operation. Even women in the workhouse around their confinement were to perform a daily task, but not permitted contact with anyone of 'known bad character'.[HRO] Laundry had become a big problem, and outside labour in 1905–06 was costing over £230 a year. A suggestion was made to fit new gas-powered laundry equipment, but this was rejected on grounds of cost. A tailor and a shoemaker were regularly employed, but this seems to have been on an *ad hoc* basis for provision of clothing only. When a shoemaker became an inmate in 1905, the tradesman's services were dispensed with temporarily – he complained, which is how we know. Very occasionally, inmates were still employed in decorating and repairs. A stocking/knitting machine and a Singer treadle sewing machine (£7) were acquired for the use of inmates, and the Brabazon Society continued to provide an invaluable service.

Vagrants were employed breaking stone, and when one man, Thomas Turner, lost control in 1908 and caused considerable damage with his 'pounding bar', the use of machines was increased with three more being ordered at a cost of £3 3s each, 'to be fixed in the cells'. Turner was committed for trail at the Assizes.

For a time we can follow in the minutes a handful of people receiving care, two of whom we have already met.

Rhoda Rogers, the little girl who appeared prominently in Fleming's 1895 report, sick and constantly crying, was later sent to the Girls' Training Home in London and from 1901 was sent to the country or seaside every year, sometimes for three weeks, paid for by the guardians. She was in various residential care homes until 1907 and then we lose track.

Ernest McGrath ended up in the West of England Institution for the Blind in Exeter, and, reaching the age of 18 in 1905, was employed as an assistant piano tuner and basket maker. He remained in Exeter, his income supplemented by the guardians, until 1910 when we have no further reports.

Another blind girl, Kate Kimber, was sent to the Liverpool Blind School and learned various 'industries', including chair-making. In 1903 she was taught massaging, and in 1905, now an adult, she returned home to be employed in the workhouse on 'light work' for which she was paid, 'generally making herself useful' as a general servant. In 1908 she was caning and seating chairs in the workhouse during her free time. In 1912 she had a child fathered by the cook, Algernon Todd – the ladies arranged maintenance for the child and Todd was asked to resign.

War

We arrive at 1914 and war in August, which was not registered significantly in the minutes since it was considered to be a small affair and would soon be over – when the male attendant nurse enlisted, his job was kept open and his pay made up 'for the duration of the war not exceeding six calendar months.'[HRO] This was a feature of the next few months, male employees disappearing and replaced temporarily by men who had been rejected for enlistment. None of them returned. Increases in prices from suppliers were viewed negatively and initially denied but later allowed.

Gradually, the catastrophe built up. In October 1914, the first inmate, Harry Stratton, applied to leave the workhouse to enlist, leaving his family and five children, offering to contribute from his pay – probably the first of many, but we do not know. Two boarded out boys, William Basing and Jack White, went to the navy: 'they shall adopt HM Navy as their permanent vocation'.[HRO] The rules were amended to allow other such young men to enlist, but there are no details. The LGB issued a circular regarding out relief to relatives of soldiers and sailors; this was to be paid from a national fund and details were to be erased from union records – they were not considered to be 'the poor'.

Rooms over the chapel were offered to house Belgian refugees, but it is not clear whether this happened. When neighbouring smaller unions asked to send their surplus poor, this was rejected: 'nearly 5,000 troops quartered in Basingstoke Borough (11,540 inhabitants at last census)'[HRO] and there was concern about local utilities being sufficient.

There our access to the minute books ends, the pages taped off, not to be seen until the 2030s.

1915 to 1930

From now on, the only systematic documents we have are the reports of the meetings of the board in the *Hants & Berks Gazette*, Basingstoke's local newspaper, and most of our information now comes from there. Reporting had been allowed, without relief details, since 1895. Microfiches of the papers from 1878 are held at the Discovery Centre in the town; it is an archive which is difficult to search or read, and very fragmented, but it is better than nothing and we can get a good narrative and some useful numbers.

The wartime newspapers to 1918 had few pages and used a tiny font. Among the war news, battles, casualty lists and austerity recipes it was impossible to find all the meetings, even if they were actually reported. But we do get fragments. In 1916 there were often not enough attendees to form a quorum, and 'no important business' was discussed – the LGB had suggested that, nationally, monthly meetings were acceptable for the duration. That year, the vice-chairman, Major Walter, was re-elected in spite of being at the front. The following year supplies of coal became difficult, and the master reported that a number of the older boys had gone to fight: 'some have done well, some have met with misfortune'. Overall, there is a dreadful, stunned feeling about these wartime editions. It is as if all the solid Victorian and Edwardian confidence was leaching away with the men and horses.

In 1916 there was an adjustment in the workhouse diet, allowing 'less meat and more pudding'. Arrangements were made for Red Cross nurses, if necessary, to assist in the infirmary (providing their own rations), and donations of bedsteads and bedding were made to the Red Cross for local hospitals – the ambulance could be used for the wounded if required. Remember that Hampshire is a south coast county, containing Southampton and Portsmouth, and was one of the areas directly impacted by war in Europe.

In the years from 1917 to 1920 there were fewer than 100 residents in the establishment, and even during the depressed years of the 1920s the number remained below 120, although some of this reduction was because there were now very few children. This meant that there was now surplus accommodation, which caused cash problems: 'there are two buildings which are difficult to heat … the number of inmates is small in proportion to the size of the buildings'. The board began to increase their practice of taking in people from outside the union for whom a charge could be made. 'Boarders', usually infirmary patients, were received mostly from Reading, Whitchurch and Southampton unions for a fee of about £1 each a week – numbers are difficult, because people came and went, but there were usually about twenty or thirty at any one time.

In 1918 the County Council requested that 'mental defectives' from around the county be taken in, and, after initial resistance, the board decided to receive only women who were capable of working. From now on, there were about twenty or thirty of these women resident; their conditions were regularly inspected by the county and it appears that they were settled and well cared for ('the staff dealt with their cases with sympathy and understanding'), and they worked in the laundry and kitchens. From 1922, many of them were housed in the 'east wing', which had been rented out since 1920 to the RDC to house the homeless, another way of using the space. In 1927 dedicated craft classes were arranged for them, initially started by the Hampshire Voluntary Society, and included 'singing, simple dancing and drill'.

In 1919 the Ministry of Health assumed the responsibilities of the LGB; for poor law purposes inspections were now carried out by the county medical officer of health's departments, moving the process closer to a national health and social security model.

It is worth mentioning at this point that the union's seriously mentally ill were retrieved from all over the county back to Park Prewett Hospital, which opened as a large mental hospital to the north-east of the town in 1921. It had been used for war work – a story in itself – which undoubtedly prevented the workhouse infirmary from becoming directly involved; in 1928 there were sixty-four Basingstoke union patients there.

In October 1922 Master Thomas Arter resigned, too ill with his old head wound to continue. Between sixty and seventy couples applied – this was now a secure, respected career. The first couple chosen declined because the living conditions and the state of 'the institution' were inadequate, then the second choice backed out on the same grounds. Mr and Mrs Credland, the third choice, accepted. The rapid turnover in staff continued.

As for the buildings, electricity generation had arrived in Basingstoke in 1914, and in 1923 it was extended to Basing. With the institution being directly on the road between, electricity was installed that year, replacing 202 gas lights and enabling efficient laundry facilities for the 2,000 items now being processed each week. There was a perpetual battle with extensive dry rot in the old workhouse. There were various attempts to economise on the 1 ton per day of coal being consumed. Wireless (radio) was installed in 1927, 'very much appreciated' by residents, the £120 cost raised by local subscribers.

In fact, much more effort was now being made to make life happier for the unfortunate residents. There were regular trips and outings, coach tours and entertainments or 'treats', often provided by local businesses. We also begin to see the infirmary occasionally referred to as Cowdery Down in the newspaper (a name which became official by the 1940s). In 1929 eighty inmates attended Thornycroft's motor factory for a dress rehearsal of the works production of *HMS Pinafore*, refreshments and coach transport provided. Forty-four people were taken by train to Weymouth that August for a day trip, and each resident received 6*d* at Christmas, donated by the guardians. In February 1930 all the resident women who could manage it attended the Grand Theatre in the town every other week to see films.

Depression and Vagrancy

The first serious post-war recession of 1920–21 brought years of hardship, bitter class division, unemployment and poverty, culminating in the General Strike of 1926, and later the Great Depression of the 1930s.

Of course, Basingstoke did not escape, and the problems dominated the reported minutes for several years. In October 1921 'a large body of the unemployed' assembled at the workhouse and a deputation was received. The relief work provided by the town was not paying enough and state relief was either not available or delayed, and deductions were made from individuals when local relief was given. Even a local 'temporary scale' did not include single men. Councillor Pheby JP represented the men: 'I have about 500 men outside who are practically starving'. Following angry meetings in Market Square and concerned that civil unrest would follow, the board held additional sessions and did what they could. But the extra relief could not be maintained for long, and the following January the guardians were forced to borrow £5,500 over two years, just to pay the unemployed poor. Various schemes were brought in to employ the men: stone breaking, road widening, but these were generally underfunded.

This situation continued, and in 1924 an attempt was made to reduce relief – the logic being that agricultural wages, the marker for calculation, were now lower – and there was heated discussion, the guardians being very uncomfortable about 'the wretched state' of some of the poor. A petition from Cardiff Union in 1925 was supported, asking the government to provide more help, when benefit was taking a week to be paid – in Birmingham Union, 11,000 claimed relief on one day, just for this reason. In 1926 the national sum for poor relief was £1.5m, and Fowler suggests that the union system 'had been hijacked to become a replacement for the failed system of unemployment benefit'.[6]

Unsurprisingly, from 1920 onwards we see an enormous increase in the numbers of vagrants or 'casuals' moving through the workhouse. The number given shelter and food overnight, usually followed by work, rose steadily from about fifteen or twenty a week in 1920 to between eighty and 120 in subsequent years, occasionally peaking at around 150 when there was local work attracting them, such as pipe laying in London Road in 1928. There were often a few women and children. This caused great strain on the system; extra beds, heating and food were necessary; in 1928 the police stopped issuing tickets and the master had to take direct responsibility; the workhouse doctor was taking more time examining 'between 12 and 40 casuals a day', and asking for more payment – this constant ebb and flow of people tramping across the countryside sometimes brought with them diseases, including smallpox, typhoid, scabies, influenza. Finding them work to do was difficult, but in 1929 someone had the idea of buying in wood for them to chop and bundle for sale in the neighbourhood, and that November 2,100 bundles were sold, providing a small profit.

There was general sympathy for their plight; 'some of them would be decent fellows who were honestly looking for work', and sick, elderly vagrants were often asked to stay longer to get out of the weather, but only if room did not have to be made for another influx known to be coming down the road. In 1929 the master provided support for an unemployed march from Portsmouth to London, helping a man with damaged feet and providing ninety-six blankets, which were later returned. Food and lodging had also been donated in the town.

The Children's Home
Homeless children were lodged in various institutions when they could not be formally adopted and boarded out – this had become a problem. One of the main homes used was Milton Home in Portsmouth, charging about 17/6d per child per week, and others were the Church of England Waifs & Strays Society homes. Two boys had been rejected by the Lord Wandsworth Institution in Long Sutton in 1923 (now a prestigious boarding school), which was 'not for the pauper class',

and two others that year were sent to Canada, under the auspices of Dr Barnardo's, at a cost of £28 10s each. Anything to keep them out of the workhouse. In 1926 Milton Home stopped taking children so a decision had to be made, and the plan for a local home to house between twelve and fifteen children was resurrected. The building should be in the same parish, Basing, not too close to the workhouse – to prevent the stigma – but near enough for laundry, supplies and supervision, and to the local school. A site was found, on the corner of School Lane (now Milkingpen Lane) and Hatch Lane in Basing; tenders were invited, and work commenced. A mortgage was raised from the Royal Liver Society for £2,256.

In a parallel to the original workhouse building and the infirmary, we see all the references in the meetings to the minutiae of establishing the home, fences and gardens, fixtures and fittings, household goods, employment of a foster mother and her assistant. A 1927 report from guardian Miss Chute confirmed the ethos of the decision: Milton Home was now boarding 300 children in three dormitories, girls, boys and infants, and individual care was impossible.

The new children's home was opened in January 1928, and it provided a focus for donations from the community: books, toys, sweets and buns, a rocking-horse, a wireless, and this continued, particularly at Christmas. There were usually twelve to sixteen residents, at an average cost of 2/10d a day in 1929; this included a few children from neighbouring unions who were also taken in for a charge of 17/6d a week.

This is the only Basingstoke Union building remaining, still a county children's home and now called Crossways; at the time of writing it requires extensive refurbishment and is to be sold by Hampshire County Council to help fund new children's homes in the area.

The System Ends

The workhouse system legally ground to a halt in 1929. The Local Government Act transferred most of the powers and responsibilities of the Boards of Guardians from April 1930 to county and borough councils. Unions were combined into Area Guardians Committees, who remained in management of the renamed 'Poor Law Institutions', and Public Assistance Committees, who managed out relief and benefits. Hampshire now had ten districts of which Basingstoke continued as one, comprising the town borough and the rural district.

> No public ceremony marked the end of the workhouse. No bonfires blazed, no fireworks soared skywards, no processions marched in triumph along the roads down which wretched, ragged families had once stumbled into separation and near-captivity. The country was settling down into the miseries of another great depression and if any ghosts walked at midnight that Monday they went unobserved … The union system, born in bitterness and tumult, died not merely unlamented, but almost unremarked.[7]

In Basingstoke, we can follow the evolution of this process, from the conferences and circulars in the mid-1920s, up to the final days. The board, consisting of the usual 'movers and shakers' of the area (often maintaining their military ranks from the war), understandably appeared to be puzzled and concerned about the new proposals, particularly the details of how these sensitive things were to be carried forward. Who could have the local knowledge? But it happened. The 'Last Meeting of the Board of Guardians' on 30 March 1930 was a very routine, low-key affair, sealing contracts for ongoing supplies, transfer of funds to the county, tributes to departing members and so on. The first formal meeting of the new committee took place on 5 April, a sparse eight lines reported in the *Gazette*. Former guardian Major General D.E. Cayley was later appointed chairman, the group including members of the RDC and the town authorities, two members from the county council and nine 'other persons'; clerk Hugh Wills Chandler continued in post.

After 1930

As for the public assistance institution (no longer called a workhouse) and infirmary, very little changed for a while. The same residents and patients remained, the same staff, the same sad parade of casuals, vagrants and mentally challenged, but children were now the responsibility of the local councils. For a time, we see the same old reports of violence and misbehaviour ending up in court and reported. But most of the relief for the poor provided during the difficult 1930s was outside the institution. Professor Carr-Saunders of Liverpool University stated in an article of 1934 that 'it is likely that during last year at one time or another one person in every fourteen or so ... was relieved by the poor law authorities'.[8] The HRO holds a few of the books and relief documents for the district up to 1940, but these are restricted.[9]

This continued to be the place where unexpected babies were born and adopted, quietly and discreetly. The author was contacted by an elderly lady who had heard that the forgotten workhouse was being researched; she had recently discovered an older brother who had died – he was born in the workhouse in the late 1930s and then disappeared; her mother had never mentioned him throughout her life.

During the Second World War (1939–45), two large hut-type wards, named Bramley and Candover, were built behind the infirmary and these continued in use after the war, separated into male and female wards and each holding thirty or forty patients. A 1950s photograph shows rows of beds down each side of each hut. After this point it is difficult to pin down exactly what happened to the buildings, but the emphasis was now definitely on Cowdery Down Hospital. The old workhouse building was put to various uses and parts of it were demolished over time; nurses were accommodated from about 1946, when the infirmary became an official training school for assistant nurses, and this necessitated heating, bathing facilities and a new kitchen.[10] It was also used as offices, out-patient facilities and training rooms. The new National Health Service took over the site in 1948. Nurses were still lodged there in 1971, as evidenced by a HBG report of complaints of the conditions. Everything was as expected: tiny windows; dark, grim outlook; ancient and failing plumbing.

The elderly patients in the now old infirmary were often desperately unhappy; they really did not want to be there:

> People still regarded the hospital there as the workhouse, and so when they were being put into the elderly care wards … they were in an awful state because they felt their families and their doctor were casting them into the workhouse, which had always been a place of fear for them all their lives'.[11]

It was where you went to die. There is another story of an elderly man absolutely refusing to enter the ambulance which was to take him to Cowdery Down for a period of convalescence.[12]

Finally it was over, one Saturday in December 1974. In the words of Rita Phillips, a nurse:

> The night sister rang me to say, 'Rita, is there any chance that you could come in and help us tomorrow? … because we are going to have to transfer all of these patients and all of their belongings to the new hospital' … the very antiquated plumbing and heating system at Cowdery Down had given up.

The process of transfer to the new North Hampshire Hospital in Basingstoke – just opened and not really ready – took about four days; some of the patients had been in Cowdery Down for twenty-five or thirty years and were so unsettled that they died during the following months.[13]

All the buildings were abandoned, and the following year were occupied briefly by the homeless; the remaining gatehouse of the workhouse was taken over by the 'Basingstoke House the Homeless' campaign for a time in 1976. When they were eventually evicted the site was not secured and vandals took over. A column in the HGB in April 1977 entitled 'A place of healing that died in shame. Wreckers turn hospital into danger playground', describes the situation; every window broken, baths and basins smashed and thrown from windows, tiles removed from roofs and some depressing photographs.

The council did not have the money to protect it, and later that year demolished everything and cleared the site; a pre-demolition plan shows the mostly intact infirmary buildings and hut wards, and parts of the workhouse still standing like old teeth, labelled as 'outbuildings'. The site stood empty for several years, the council trying to decide between an industrial park or a green leisure area. A new thirty-six-bed private hospital, BMI The Hampshire Clinic, was granted permission to build on the site and was opened in 1984, the main building exactly on the footprint of the old workhouse.

The story of our workhouse followed that of other institutions throughout England. Nationally, over the years residents disappeared into old people's homes, mental hospitals or residential homes. Many surviving infirmaries and workhouse buildings were absorbed into new hospitals, often being used as administrative blocks, and some were in good enough condition to be renovated for residential use, as in Andover and Alton. Basingstoke was one of the unlucky ones.

Conclusion

How do we end this saga?

Basingstoke Workhouse was no worse and a lot better than most. It certainly saved lives and helped many people into a better future, particularly children and the disabled. What has emerged is a cast of interesting characters who really cared and tried to help, five of whom particularly stand out:

- William L. Sclater, our decent first chairman, who can be imagined in his top hat riding a fine horse to the workhouse from his beautiful home in Upton Grey. He hated the system and set the tone of the board, which lasted to the end.
- Baldwyn Fleming, the hard-working, sensible inspector, who conscientiously wrote everything down in detail, and gave us so much information.
- Melissa Smith, the young Liverpool teacher who bucked the trend and stayed, doing an exemplary job with problematic youngsters in often difficult conditions.
- Mrs H.E. Raynbird, our first lady guardian, routinely present in the records for twenty years, attending meetings and conferences, getting involved, sorting out women, children and the mentally ill who had fallen through the cracks in society.
- Thomas Arter, the compassionate master who left us real accounts, from pauper stories to Christmas entertainment programmes, suffering from a head injury inflicted by an inmate which ultimately killed him.

The poor are still and always will be with us – so many of the statements and policies of today are hauntingly similar to those of the early union years. Even though the majority are transitionally poor, simply struggling with low wages or no job, they are very much on the receiving end of some pretty depressing social discrimination. Polly Toynbee, in her *Guardian* article of 16 December 2014, describes the 1913 report on the struggle to eat by Maud Pember Reeves, 'Round About a Pound a Week', putting it in modern context – she entitles her article, 'The Tories plan for poor people: stop them breeding'. The report has been published as a book in 2016 (see Sources).

Also in the *Guardian*, Frances Ryan's piece 'Death has become a part of Britain's benefits system' appeared on 27 August 2015: 'today's mortality statistics do not simply point to the death of disabled, poor, and ill people but of the system that was meant to protect them. Before our eyes the principle of a benefit system is being reduced from opportunity, respect, and solidarity to destitution, degradation and isolation'. Politicians and the media have stopped using the term 'social security' and replaced it with 'welfare', as 'it sets expectations much lower'.

The author personally has had far too many conversations with people who want to bring back the workhouse. Nearly two centuries later, we are going backwards.

APPENDICES

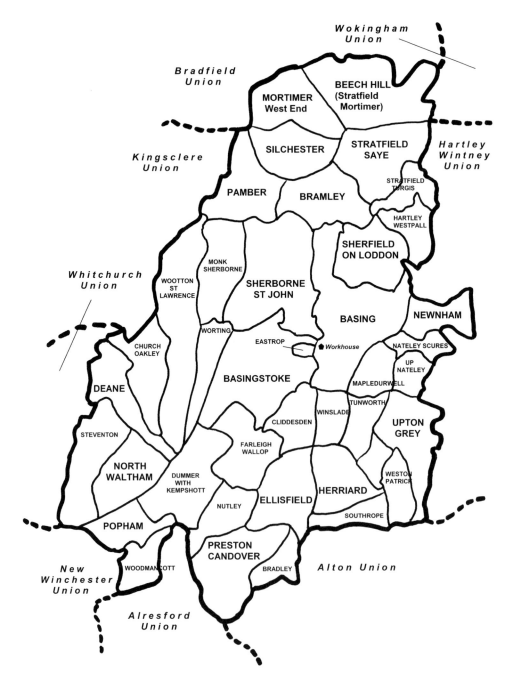

Wokingham
Union

Bradfield
Union

BEECH HILL
(Stratfield
Mortimer)

MORTIMER
West End

SILCHESTER

STRATFIELD
SAYE

Hartley
Wintney
Union

Kingsclere
Union

PAMBER

BRAMLEY

STRATFIELD
TURGIS

HARTLEY
WESTPALL

MONK
SHERBORNE

SHERFIELD
ON LODDON

Whitchurch
Union

WOOTTON
ST
LAWRENCE

SHERBORNE
ST JOHN

BASING

NEWNHAM

WORTING

CHURCH
OAKLEY

EASTROP

Workhouse

NATELEY SCURES

UP
NATELEY

BASINGSTOKE

MAPLEDURWELL

DEANE

TUNWORTH

STEVENTON

WINSLADE

UPTON
GREY

CLIDDESDEN

FARLEIGH
WALLOP

NORTH
WALTHAM

DUMMER
WITH
KEMPSHOTT

NUTLEY

ELLISFIELD

HERRIARD

WESTON
PATRICK

POPHAM

SOUTHROPE

New
Winchester
Union

WOODMANCOTT

PRESTON
CANDOVER

BRADLEY

Alton Union

Alresford
Union

APPENDIX I: PLAN OF BASINGSTOKE PARISHES.

This plan is compiled from a number of maps. Boundaries and parishes were repeatedly
changing from the 1870s; it is roughly the position in the last twenty years of the nineteenth
century as indicated in OS union boundary files in The National Archives.

APPENDIX II:
FLOOR DIAGRAMS of BASINGSTOKE WORKHOUSE.
KEY

Note: These are not intended to be strict plans and are for
impression only. They have been drawn from photographs
of large, inaccurate drawings made for drainage works
around 1899. In addition, they seem to be based on the
original design, possibly using the first building drawings,
and do not take account of various minor alterations which
happened in the intervening years. (TNA, MH 14/2)

1.	Entrance hall and porter
2.	Bread store and pantry
3.	Kitchen, knife store and scullery
4.	Dining area
5.	Women's wards (young women and girls)
6.	Men's wards (old and young men)
7.	Girls' school (play area walled to west)
8.	Boys' school (play area walled to east)
9, 10.	Female and male vagrant wards
11, 12.	Washing and drying rooms
13.	Lockups
14.	Wood, stone and oakum rooms
15.	Dead house
16.	Stable
17.	Coach house
18.	Cowshed
19.	Boardroom, offices and store
20.	Master's room
21.	Chapel
22, 23.	Female and male receiving wards
24.	Oakum store
25, 26.	Female and male accommodation
27.	Schoolmaster
28.	Boys' dormitory
29.	Schoolmistress
30.	Girls' dormitory
31.	Master's bedroom
32.	Men's accommodation
33.	Women's sick and lying-in rooms
34.	Children's sick room
35.	Men's sick rooms
36.	Female and male infectious wards
37.	Wash house / laundry

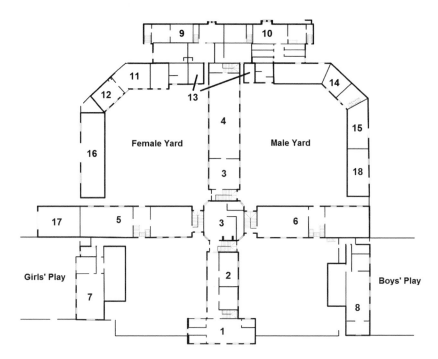

Ground floor

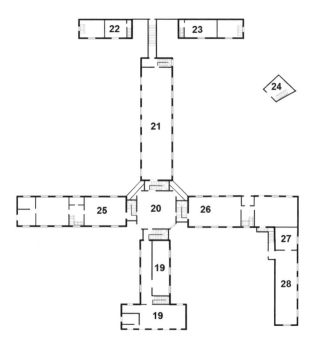

First floor

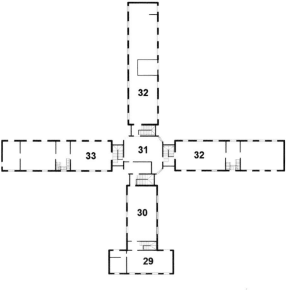

Second floor

Third floor

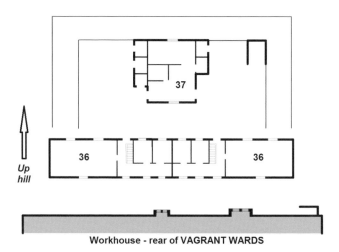

Rear buildings

APPENDIX III:
Basingstoke Workhouse, Ages from Census Returns, 1841 to 1911.

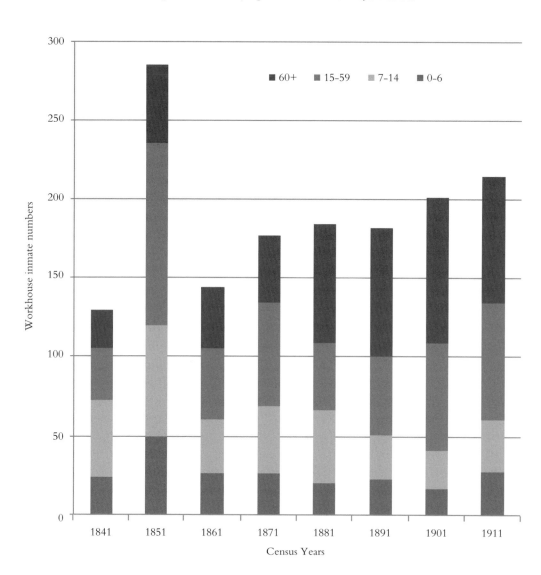

APPENDIX IV:
Extract from Amended Dietary, printed by the Basingstoke Union, September 1843.

		BREAKFAST		DINNER						SUPPER	
		Bread oz.	Gruel pints	Meat oz.	Veg. lbs.	Pudding oz.	Soup pints	Bread oz.	Cheese oz.	Bread oz.	Coffee pints
Sunday	Men	6	1½	–	–	–	–	8	2	6	1
	Women	5	1½	–	–	–	–	6	1½	5	1
Monday	Men	6	1½	–	1	8	–	–	–	6	1
	Women	5	1½	–	1	6	–	–	–	5	1
Tuesday	Men	6	1½	4	1	–	–	–	–	6	1
	Women	5	1½	4	1	–	–	–	–	5	1
Wednesday	Men	6	1½	–	–	–	1½	4	–	6	1
	Women	5	1½	–	–	–	1½	4	–	5	1
Thursday	Men	6	1½	–	1	8	–	–	–	6	1
	Women	5	1½	–	1	6	–	–	–	5	1
Friday	Men	6	1½	–	–	–	–	8	2	6	1
	Women	5	1½	–	–	–	–	6	1½	5	1
Saturday	Men	6	1½	3	1	–	–	–	–	6	1
	Women	5	1½	3	1	–	–	–	–	5	1

Adjustments, summary:

'Infirm' inmates, sweetened tea and ½oz. of butter in lieu of Gruel

Children under 9, 'as the Guardians direct'

Children between 9 and 13, the same diet as Women

Sick paupers to be 'fed, dieted and maintained in such manner as the Medical Officer…shall direct'

TNA, MH 12/10673

APPENDIX V:
Rare photographs of Basingstoke Workhouse in the 1960s. (Hampshire Archives and Local Studies)

Notes

Introduction

1. Englander, *Poverty and Poor Law Reform*, p. 1.
2. National Grid Ref: SU 654527.
3. Hampshire Archives and Local Studies, PL3/5/★★ series.
4. The National Archives, MH 12/106★★ series.
5. The National Archives, Podcast: 'we may live and die in a land of plenty'.

Part I: Early Years, 1835 to 1845

1. Hughes, *A Compendium of the Operations of the Poor Law Amendment Act …1836*.
2. Blaug, *The New Poor Law Re-examined*, pp. 230–43.
3. Crowther, *The Workhouse System*, p. 3.
4. The National Trust, *The Workhouse, Southwell, Nottinghamshire*.
5. Hawkings, *Pauper Ancestors: a guide to the records*, p. xvi.
6. Brundage, *The English Poor Laws*, p. 71.
7. May, *The Victorian Workhouse*, p. 12.
8. Dickens, *Architects and the Union Workhouse of the New Poor Law*, p. 9.
9. Longmate, *The Workhouse*, p. 76.
10. *First Annual Report of the Poor Law Commission, 1835*.
11. *Second Annual Report of the Poor Law Commission, 1836*.
12. Old Basing parish, Vestry minute book, 1819–35 (HRO, 3M70/126).
13. Letter from Christopher Edward Lefroy Esq. of West Ham in the Parish of Basingstoke (HRO, 10M57/PA24).
14. Notebook containing particulars of persons from parishes in Basingstoke Union applying for relief, Jul–Dec 1835 (HRO, 19M52/3).
15. The Victorian Web website: www.victorianweb.org/history/poorlaw/design1.html.
16. *Second Annual Report of the Poor Law Commission, 1836* (Appendix B, No. 7).
17. W. Sclater, *A Letter to the Poor Law Commissioners of England and Wales*, December 1836 (HRO, HP270).

18. Ibid. p. 11. (*'quaeque ipsa miserrima vidi, et quorum pars magna fui'*, *the Aeneid*, Virgil, 'and those terrible things I saw, and in which I played a great part'.)

19. C.E.L. Sclater, *Records of the Family of Sclater*, p. 65.

20. W. Sclater, p. 4.

21. Ibid.

22. Ibid., p. 5.

23. Longmate, p. 99.

24. W. Sclater, p. 5.

25. Ibid., p. 6.

26. Ibid., p. 7.

27. Ibid., p. 9.

28. Ibid., p. 8.

29. *First ed. OS map, 1:2500 covering Basingstoke, Chineham and Old Basing, XVIII.12, 1873, surveyed in 1872.*

30. Sale Notice, Wootton St Lawrence, (TNA, MH 12/10670).

31. W. Sclater, p. 10.

32. Ibid., p. 11.

33. Ibid., p. 12.

34. Ibid., p. 13.

35. Hansard: Mr John Walter MP, *Debate on The New Poor Law*, *23 February 1843*, vol. 66, cc1159–260.

36. Hansard: Sir Charles Napier MP, *Debate on The New Poor Law*, *23 February 1843*, vol. 66, cc1159–260.

37. Crowther, p. 41.

38. www.workhouses.org.uk, Alton Workhouse.

39. Hurren and King, *Begging for a Burial*, p. 325.

40. *Basing Parish Register of Burials*, Vol. VIII, 1813–75 (HRO, 3M70/6)

41. Englander, p. 37.

42. Crowther, p. 132.

43. Documents of Thomas Arter, 2nd volume (HRO, 15407/2).

44. Description of bone crushing from *Report from the Select Committee on Andover Union*, 1846 (HRO, TOP10/3/13).

45. Longmate, p. 121.

46. Hansard: Mr Ralph Etwall MP, *Debate on Andover Union, 5 March 1846*, vol. 84 cc625–76.

47. *Hampshire: the County Magazine*, July 1973, vol.13, No. 9, p. 34.

48. Hansard: *Debate on the Employment of Paupers, 4 February 1846*, vol. 83 cc454–8.

49. Longmate, p. 120.

50. Hansard: Sir James Graham MP, *Debate on The New Poor Law*, ibid.

51. Brundage, 'The English Poor Law of 1834', *Agricultural History*, p. 417.

Part 2: Consolidation, 1846 to 1871

1. Longmate, p. 122.
2. Longmate, p. 126.
3. Hansard: *Poor Law Administration Debate, 18 May 1847*, vol. 92 cc1064–92.
4. Ibid.
5. *Hampshire Chronicle, Southampton and Isle of Wight Courier,* 19 January 1867, p. 5.
6. *The Reading Mercury,* 30 July 1870.
7. Wyndham S. Portal, *The Poor and How to Help Them,* 1869 (HRO, 39M89/G7).
8. Photograph by Alexander Bassano, Library of Congress, USA (accessed June 2013).
9. *Hampshire Contemporary Biographies,* 1905.
10. Fowler, *Workhouse: The People, The Places, The Life Behind Doors,* p. 136.
11. Paxman, 'Out of the Way of Mischief', National Archives Podcast, January 2012.
12. www.workhouses.org.
13. *The Reading Mercury,* ibid.
14. Waller, *My Ancestor was an Agricultural Labourer,* p. 58.
15. Ibid., p. 31.
16. Ibid., p. 28.
17. Ibid., p. 27.
18. Union Accounts for Basingstoke, 1856–67 (HRO, 63M70/PO32).
19. http://en.wikipedia.org/wiki/Workhouse_Visiting_Society, May 2012.
20. Waller, p. 92.
21. Rose, *The Relief of Poverty 1834–1914,* p. 13.
22. Following the Elementary Education Act 1876, and we have their minute book to 1903 in HRO; they spent much of their time prosecuting parents for not taking their children to school.

Part 3: Challenges and Changes, 1872 to 1900

1. Crowther, p. 33.
2. Carter, TNA webinar: 'Why did people fear the Victorian workhouse?'
3. *Hants & Berks Gazette,* 'A Wicked Woman', 13 October 1883.
4. Alton Workhouse punishment book, 1851 to 1932 (HRO, 145A06/1/1).
5. Kingsclere Workhouse punishment book,1871 to 1907 (HRO, PL5/7/59).
6. Fowler, p. 171.
7. http://en.wikipedia.org/wiki/Brabazon_scheme, March 2014.
8. Thomas Arter, cuttings and notes (HRO, 154A07/1).
9. Negrine, 'The Treatment of Sick Children in the Workhouse by the Leicester Poor Law Union', *Family & Community History.*
10. Fowler, p. 148.
11. http://en.wikipedia.org/wiki/Maria_Rye, November 2014.
12. LGB Inspector's Statement of pauperism and expenditure (HRO, 38M49/C3/13).
13. Thomas Arter, ibid. (HRO, 154A07/1 and 2).
14. *Hants & Berks Gazette,* 21 October 1922.
15. Fowler, p. 161.

16. 'Nursing in Workhouses and Workhouse Infirmaries', a paper in *Printed reports and pamphlets relating to workhouse nursing*, p. 16 (HRO, 94M72/F608).
17. OS map: 1930 revision, *Hampshire Sheet XVIII, 6' to 1 mile*
18. www.friendlysocieties.co.uk/history.htm, February 2014.
19. *Hants & Berks Gazette*, many references, including 27 March 1897.

Part 4: 1901 to The End

1. Rose, *The Relief of Poverty 1834-1914,* p. 44.
2. Rose, p. 50.
3. In February 1910, Baldwyn Fleming retired and was replaced by John Walker Thompson.
4. *Hants & Berks Gazette,* 'From Workhouse Boy to Mayor', 12 July 1913.
5. www.workhouses.org.uk/boardingout/, June 2015.
6. Fowler, p. 216.
7. Longmate, p. 280.
8. *Hants & Berks Gazette,* 'A Century of Pauperism', 4 May 1934.
9. HRO, all restricted: books and ledgers for the Basingstoke Area Guardians Committee, PL4/3/★★ from 1930. There are also minutes of house and boarding out committees, 1935–38, various relief documents, 1933–40, and a few case papers and items of correspondence, 1933–34.
10. General Nursing Council for England and Wales, Cowdery Down Infirmary, Hospital Inspector's Report, August 1946 (TNA, DT33/1163).
11. Jo Kelly, DHSS Visiting Officer, 1970s.
12. Verbal report from Bob Applin.
13. Applin, *Taking the Pulse of Basingstoke,* p. 86.

Sources

Hampshire Archives & Local Studies (HRO)

PL3/5/1 to /29, Series, Basingstoke Union, Minute Books of the Board of Guardians, restricted after 31 December 1914.

PL3/5/34, Finance Committee Minute Book, 22 May 1923 – 18 March 1930.

PL3/5/38, General Ledger, 1923–30.

8M62/21, PLC, Order for the Keeping, Examining and Auditing the Accounts of the above Union, and of the several Parishes of which it is composed. Dated 19 August 1836.

19M52/3, Notebook containing particulars of persons from parishes in Basingstoke Union applying for relief, with notes of relief granted or refused, Jul–Dec 1835.

10M57/PA24, Letter from Christopher Edward Lefroy Esq. of West Ham in the Parish of Basingstoke to the guardians of the Poor of the same parish under the New Poor Laws.

HP270, Sclater, William Lutley, *A Letter to the Poor Law Commissioners of England and Wales on the Working of the New System*, Basingstoke, December 1836.

69A02/D2, First Edition Ordnance Survey map, 1:2500 covering Basingstoke, Chineham and Old Basing area, XVIII.12, surveyed in 1872, published at the Ordnance Survey Office, Southampton, 1873.

TOP10/3/13, Copy of bone crushing description from the Report from the Select Committee on Andover Union, 1846, in a bundle of pieces of non-ascribed information on the Andover Scandal.

154A07/1, Volume of cuttings and notes about Basingstoke Union Workhouse, kept by the Master, Mr Thomas Arter, c.1896–1905.

154A07/2, Various loose documents of Thomas Arter, the majority relating to Basingstoke Workhouse (2nd volume).

63M70/PO32, Union Accounts for Basingstoke Union, various dates 1856–67.

68M72/DU3, Bundle of papers and correspondence relating to the purchase or lease of land adjoining the Union Workhouse at Basingstoke.

10M57/Z76, Notice of Public Meeting for the Relief of the Poor, Basingstoke, 15 January 1867.

3M70/6, Basing Parish, register of burials, transcript, vol. VIII, 1813–75.

72A07/2, Printed report by William E. Bear to the Royal Commission on Labour concerning 'The Agricultural Labourer' in the Poor Law Union of Basingstoke.

145A06/1/1, Alton Workhouse punishment book, 1851 to 1932 (restricted from 1913).

PL5/7/59, Kingsclere Workhouse punishment book, 1871 to 1907.

94M72/F608, Printed reports and pamphlets relating to workhouse nursing.

30M96/13, *Poor Law in Hampshire Through the Centuries; A Guide to the Records,* Hampshire Archivists' Group, Pub. No. 1, 1970.

3M70/126, Old Basing parish, Vestry minute book, 1819–35.

39M89/G7, Printed pamphlet (inscribed from the author) entitled *'The Poor and How to Help Them',* a paper read before the Churchmen's Association for the Rural Deaneries of Andover, Basingstoke and Chibolton, by Wyndham S. Portal, 1869.

38M49/C3/13, LGB Inspector's Statement of pauperism and expenditure, 1891–92.

The National Archives (TNA)

MH 12/10669 to /10699, Series, Local Government Board and predecessors: Correspondence with Poor Law Unions and Other Local Authorities, Basingstoke 390, 1834 to 1900.

MH 14/2, Poor Law Union plans, 1872–1900 (various, Ashton-under-Lyne to Basingstoke).

MH 32/42, William Henry Toovey Hawley, correspondence and papers related to the South Western District (includes unions in Dorset, Southampton, Sussex and Wiltshire), 1853–57.

MH 32/43, William Henry Toovey Hawley, correspondence and papers related to the South Western District (includes unions in Hampshire and Southampton), 1858–74.

OS 24/195, OS Records of the Ordnance Survey of Great Britain, Basingstoke Poor Law Union (Hampshire): boundaries file, 1878–1902.

DT33/1163, Basingstoke: Cowdery Down Infirmary, General Nursing Council for England and Wales, Hospital Inspectors Report, August 1946.

Books

Anstruther, Ian, *The Scandal of the Andover Workhouse*, Geoffrey Bles, London, 1973.

Applin, B., *Taking the Pulse of Basingstoke: Memories from Before the National Health Service up to the Present Day*, BAHS, Basingstoke, 2005.

Brundage, Anthony, *The English Poor Laws, 1700–1930*, Social History in Perspective, Palgrave, Basingstoke, 2002.

Carter, Paul and Whistance, Natalie, *Living the Poor Life: A Guide to the Poor Law Union Correspondence, c.1834 to 1871, held at The National Archives*, The British Association for Local History, 2011.

Crowther, M.A., *The Workhouse System, 1834–1929: the History of an English Social Institution*, Methuen, London, 1983.

Digby, Anne, *The Poor Law in Nineteenth-Century England*, The Historical Association, London, 1989.

Englander, David, *Poverty and Poor Law Reform in 19th Century Britain, 1834–1914: from Chadwick to Booth*, Seminar Studies in History, Longman, London, 1998.

Floud, Roderick and McCloskey, Donald (eds), *The Economic History of Britain since 1700, Vol. 2: 1860–1939*, 2nd ed., Cambridge University Press, 1994.

Fowler, Simon, *Workhouse: The People, The Places, The Life Behind Doors*, The National Archives, Richmond, 2007.

Harvey, Christopher and Matthew, H.C.G., *Nineteenth Century Britain: a Very Short Introduction*, Oxford University Press, 2000.

Hawkings, David T., *Pauper Ancestors: A Guide to the Records Created by the Poor Laws in England and Wales*, The History Press, Stroud, 2011.

Higginbotham, Peter, *Life in the Victorian Workhouse, 1834 to 1930*, Pitkin Publishing, Andover, 2011.

Higginbotham, Peter, *Voices from the Workhouse*, The History Press, Stroud, 2012.

Higginbotham, Peter, *The Workhouse Encyclopedia*, The History Press, Stroud, 2012.

Higgs, Michelle, *Life in the Victorian & Edwardian Workhouse*, Tempus, Stroud, 2007.

Hughes, E. (Vice-Chairman of the East Ashford Union), *A Compendium of the Operations of the Poor Law Amendment Act, with some Practical Observations on its Present Results, and Future Apparent Usefulness*, Hatchard & Son, London, 1836.

Kitson Clark, G., *The Making of Victorian England*, Methuen, London, 1966.

Longmate, Norman, *The Workhouse*, Pimlico, London, 2003.

May, Trevor, *The Victorian Workhouse*, Shire Publications, Risborough, 2002.

Mitton, Lavinia, *The Victorian Hospital*, Shire Publications, Oxford, 2008.

Morrison, Kathryn, *The Workhouse: a Study of Poor-Law Buildings in England*, English Heritage at the National Monuments Record Centre, Swindon, 1999.

Pell, Albert (compiler), *Poor Law Conferences Held in the Year 1899-1900*, P.S. King & Son, London, 1900.

Pember Reeves, Maud, *Round About a Pound a Week*, Persephone Books, London, 2016

Pike, W.T. (ed.), *Contemporary Biographies, Hampshire at the Opening of the Twentieth Century*, W.T. Pike & Co., Brighton, 1905.

Rose, Michael E., *The Relief of Poverty 1834–1914*, Studies in Economic and Social History, The Economic History Society, London, 1982.

Sclater, C.E.L., *Records of the Family of Sclater: Formerly of Hoddington and Tangier Park in the County of Hampshire*, Yelf Brothers Ltd, Newport, Isle of Wight, 1966 (Private publication loaned to author by Trevor Hart).

Seabrook, Jeremy, *Pauperland: Poverty and the Poor in Britain,* Hurst & Co., London, 2013.

Shaw, Charles, *When I Was a Child*, Caliban Books, Firle, Sussex, 1903 (facsimile edition published 1977).

Stokes, E., *The Making of Basingstoke: From Prehistory to the Present Day*, eds Bob and Barbara Applin, Basingstoke Archaeological & Historical Society, 2008.

The Workhouse, Southwell, Nottinghamshire, guidebook, The National Trust, 2002.

Waller, Ian H., *My Ancestor was an Agricultural Labourer*, Society of Genealogists Enterprises Ltd, London, 2007.

Wilson, A.N., *The Victorians*, Arrow Books, London, 2003.

Newspapers and Academic Works

Bartlett, Peter, *The Poor Law of Lunacy; The Administration of Pauper Lunatics in Mid-Nineteenth Century England*, PhD thesis, London University, 1993.

Brundage, Anthony, 'The English Poor Law of 1834 and the Cohesion of Agricultural Society', *Agricultural History*, 48 (3), July 1974, pp. 405–17.

Blaug, Mark, 'The New Poor Law Re-examined', *The Journal of Economic History*, 24 (2), June 1964, pp. 229–45.

Dickens, Anna M. (AA.Diploma, A.R.I.B.A.), *Architects and the Union Workhouse of the New Poor Law*, Dissertation, Brighton Polytechnic, July 1982 (2 volumes).

Hampshire, the County Magazine, ed. Dennis Stevens. July 1976, Vol. 13, No. 9, p. 34.

Hants & Berks Gazette, on microfiche in the Basingstoke Discovery Centre, 1915 to 1931.

Henriques, U.R.Q., 'Bastardy and the New Poor Law', *Past & Present*, 37, July 1967, pp. 103–29.

Hurren, Elizabeth and King, Steve, 'Begging for a Burial: Form, Function and Conflict in Nineteenth-Century Pauper Burial', *Social History*, 30 (3), August 2005, pp. 321–41.

Negrine, Angela, 'The Treatment of Sick Children in the Workhouse by the Leicester Poor law Union, 1867–1914', *Family & Community History*, 13 (1), May 2010, pp. 34–44.

Roberts, David, 'How Cruel Was the Victorian Poor Law?', *The Historical Journal*, 6 (1), 1963, pp. 97–107.

Online Sources

A Web of English History: The Poor Law, Assistant Commissioners, www.historyhome.co.uk/peel/poorlaw/asscomm.htm

British Newspaper Archive online, www.britishnewspaperarchive.co.uk

Friendly Societies Online Reference and advertising directory for services, www.friendlysocieties.co.uk/history.htm

Genealogical survey of British and European peerage, www.thepeerage.com

Hansard online, http://hansard.millbanksystems.com/

Health and Hygiene in Victorian England, www.victorianweb.org/science/health/health10.html

Maria Rye, English social reformer and promoter of emigration, http://en.wikipedia.org/wiki/Maria_Rye

Marjie Bloy Ph.D., Senior Research Fellow, National University of Singapore, www.victorianweb.org/history/poorlaw/design1.html

Oxford Dictionary of National Biography online, www.oxforddnb.com/public/index.html

Parliamentary Papers online, http://parlipapers.chadwyck.co.uk/marketing/index.jsp

The Brabazon Scheme, http://en.wikipedia.org/wiki/Brabazon_scheme

The Development of the London Hospital System, 1823–2013, www.nhshistory.net/poor_law_infirmaries.htm

The National Archives podcast: 'Out of the Way of Mischief', Briony Paxman, 5 March 2012, http://media.nationalarchives.gov.uk/index.php/out-of-the-way-of-mischief/

The National Archives podcast: 'We may live and die in a land of plenty…:
the Victorian poor in their own words', Paul Carter, 1 April 2014,
http://media.nationalarchives.gov.uk/index.php/victorian-poor-words/
The National Archives webinar: 'Why did people fear the Victorian workhouse?',
Paul Carter, 3 September 2014, http://media.nationalarchives.gov.uk/index.php/
webinar-people-fear-victorian-workhouse/
The National Archives web calculator for equivalent money values from history,
www.nationalarchives.gov.uk/currency/results.asp#mid
The Victorian Web, The Price of Bread, www.victorianweb.org/history/work/nelson1.html
The Workhouse, www.workhouses.org.uk

Other Sources

First Annual Report of the Poor Law Commission, 1835, House of Parliament
Parliamentary Papers, online.
Second Annual Report of the Poor Law Commission, 1836, House of Parliament
Parliamentary Papers, online.
Twelfth Annual Report of the Poor Law Commission, 1846, House of Parliament
Parliamentary Papers, online.
Royal Commission on Agriculture, 1896, Vol. IV, Appendix C, p. 589.
Poor Law Unions: Return to … the House of Commons, 3 July 1862 … a return of the
area and population … p.16.
Poor Law Unions: Statement of names of Unions and Poor Law Parishes in England and
Wales … in 1881.
A Letter to Sir R Peel, Bart, M.P., on the practical operation of the Poor Law Amendment Act,
by 'A Guardian', Effingham Wilson, Royal Exchange, and Charles James Murphy,
New Brentford, London, 1838, (Price 2*d*.)
OS map: First ed. OS map, 1:2500 *covering Basingstoke, Chineham and Old Basing,*
XVIII.12, 1873, surveyed in 1872.
OS map: *Basingstoke area, Sheet XVII.12, 1' to 1 mile, c1838.*
OS map: *1930 revision, Hampshire Sheet XVIII, 6' to 1 mile.*
'Important Poor Law Conference at Basingstoke', *Reading Mercury, Oxford Gazette,*
Newbury Herald, and Berks County Paper, Saturday, August 6, 1870, p.2.
'*Basingstoke in the 19th Century*', a composite of articles by Arthur Saunders, editor of
Hants and Berks Gazette in the 1940s, prepared by members of the BAHS.
The Poor Law Guide and Union Advertiser, ed. Charles Mott, March to December 1843,
in the British Library.

Index

Also from the History Press

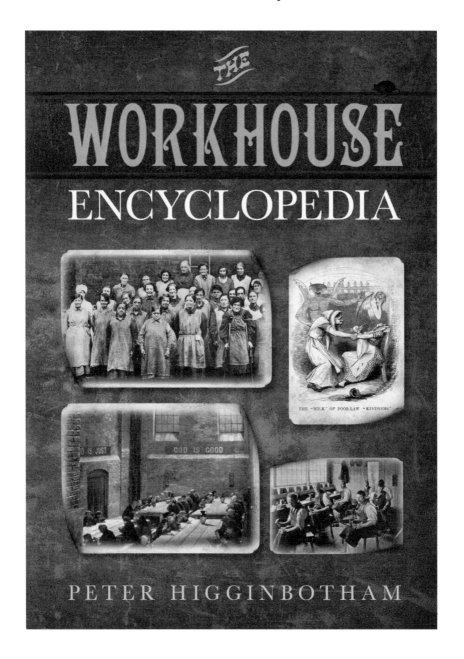